D0882896

INSIDE

☆☆☆☆ THE ☆☆☆

THIRD
HOUSE

BEN SARGENT

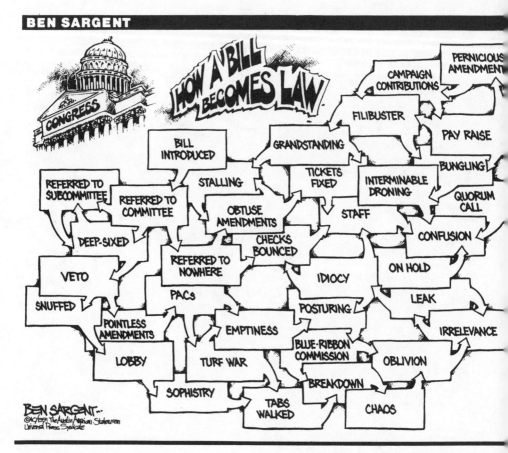

— Reprinted by permission of Ben Sargent

INSIDE

☆ ☆ ☆ ☆ THE ☆ ☆ ☆

THIRD HOUSE

A Veteran Lobbyist Takes A
50-Year Frolic Through Texas Politics

H.C. PITTMAN

EAKIN PRESS ⬧Ɛᴾ Austin, Texas

FIRST EDITION

Copyright © 1992
By H. C. Pittman

Published in the United States of America
By Eakin Press
An Imprint of Sunbelt Media, Inc.
P.O. Drawer 90159   ★   Austin, TX 78709-0159

ALL RIGHTS RESERVED. No part of this book may be reproduced in any
form without written permission from the publisher, except for brief passages
included in a review appearing in a newspaper or magazine.

ISBN 0-89015-879-7

1   2   3   4   5   6   7   8   9

Library of Congress Cataloging-in-Publication Data

Pittman, H. C.
    Inside the third house : a fifty-year frolic through Texas politics / by H. C. Pittman.
    p.   cm.
    Includes index.
    ISBN 0-89015-879-7 : $21.95
    1. Texas — Politics and government — 1865–1950. 2. Texas — Politics and government —
1951. 3. Politicians — Texas — History — 20th century. I. Title.
F391.P67
320.9764 — dc20   92-30776
                                                                                                  CIP

ii

Contents

Foreword

BY BILL HOBBY

For eighteen years I had the uncommon privilege of presiding over the Texas Senate. There are thirty-one members of the Texas Senate, some of them elected from districts larger than several states. Once every two years, for 140 days at a time, and as often after that as the governor chooses, they make decisions on the issues that affect our lives.

Senators and the 150 members of the House of Representatives decide how well our children will be educated, whether our parents will have state-paid nursing home care, how good our highways will be, and how much tax we will pay. They decide how much it will cost to get our auto licenses, how much teachers will be paid, what tests our children will take in school, and whether we do jail time for driving while intoxicated.

After sixteen years in the House of Representatives, eight of them as Speaker, Gib Lewis could recall many accomplishments. But the most popular thing he ever did, he said, was sponsor the bill allowing Texans to turn right on red.

Sometimes it seems like the labor is for naught. When I became lieutenant governor, there was a school finance crisis, an insurance scandal, and overcrowded prisons. When I left office, there was a school finance crisis, an insurance scandal, and overcrowded prisons.

Serving in the Texas legislature is exhilarating, frustrating, fatiguing, hard on your marriage, and bad for your health. One state representative from Comanche said recently (or words to this effect), "I've

v

been here nine years and it's time I went home before I'm as crazy as everyone else around here."

Watching the Texas legislature is either addictive or very lucrative, to judge from the numbers in the galleries every day. This is the "Third House" that H. C. Pittman describes. It has times of heartstopping drama, long periods of tedium, and some of the funniest moments in history. This is an appropriately rambling description of the humorous highpoints.

"I've been in the Senate forty years . . . seen many changes . . . and been against every damned one!"

Acknowledgments

Satchel Paige said, "Don't look back . . . something may be gaining on you!" When I look back, I see good luck for finding so many to help print this catalog of happenings around the "Dome." I would have to be faster than a cattle auctioneer on a hot Saturday afternoon.

To thank them at one sitting, I start with Punkin, Ann, Nancy, Chelsea and Nmmi, the girls in my house. Thanks to Dilley, who got me started with a dare. A special *gracias* to Betty King, a queen if ever there was one. Also to Connie Robinson, Stacey McAdoo, Kathleen Orillion, Christine Braunger, and so many others who gave more than enough of their time and talents in thinking and computering.

Thank you and "Amen" to Dr. Gerald Mann, who survived as a chaplain for the House and Senate. From maybe the bottom he has grown and is pastor of Riverbend Baptist Church in Austin, where membership is growing faster than Baptists can dip! He made it so easy for me to use his prayer "zingers." We are convinced that most of those got through.

Gracias to author John Knaggs, who has been of special "out of the way" help. His books are growing in popularity faster than johnson grass in our old hometown of Cotulla.

We thank Legislator/Judge Neil Caldwell for his great cartoons. They show it like it is.

To judges, lawmakers, officials, secretaries, barbers, and a whole herd of others, we give a "Hi-Five." I am lucky to have been around when each of you were around. To all, "thank you" from as deep down as I can go.

House in session, in the 1980s.

— Courtesy Austin History Center

OPENING THE FRONT DOOR

"An election is only funny in a democracy."
— Mark Russell

This book is about colorful characters under our Lone Star. We identify such from a flour salesman to a presidential candidate to Bicycle Annie. You can read "straight through" or "read-around," picking the characters, tricks, or words or quotes that interest you first. We write this disclaimer before Monsignor Fred Bowmar and Elizabeth Terry. Ninety-two percent of the time, we use real names and places; for the rest, "we didn't mean to."

People hanging around in the balconies and halls of the Capitol and other rooms of government are known as members of the "Third House." They watch, guide, defend or promote for us when we fail to pay attention.

It has been said many times that there are two things you never want to see being made: sausages and laws! The first time you look down from the legislative balconies to watch the scrambling below, you are probably like the Texan from Big Sandy who made his first trip to Washington City and was asked what he thought. He replied, "Reminded me of a log floating down the Trinity River covered with ants — and every damn ant thought he was steering."

Well, those scrambling below represent us! They have the "perks and powers" we give them. When we "no like" what's going on, we can believe Pogo's horrifying observation, "We have met the enemy and it is us!" *We* are all in the Third House!

Way back in the "pass the biscuits" age, Governor Pappy O'Daniel identified a "fourth house." He said that this group includes the independent bureau chiefs, commission members, and agency heads who play powerful roles in our "*guv*ment." Governor Ann Richards says she is also frustrated by the layer of 208 and more agencies who lay their own tracks.

"On the hill" is where it all happens. There is where the humor and "practical politics" chart the destiny of our system. The oft-times hilarious incidents, accidents, and "school type" tricks or treats sometimes can create the laws and regulations under which we live.

Walter Wainwright, past president of the Texas Society of Trade Associations, says that there are more than 300 trade, union, and professional organizations with headquarters in Austin, and about a hundred more in different parts of the state. There are 1,072 political

Governors Allan Shivers, Preston Smith, and Price Daniel with newsman Dan Rather, movie star Lee Meriwether, and Board Chairman H. C. Pittman at Headliners party in 1977.

action committees registered in the state (we will gossip about "to pac or not to pac" later in this book). With all the other media throwing papers on our porch and "sound biting us on the tube," there is not much use for those like the little old tennis-shoed lady who said, "You can't blame the mess on me . . . . I never voted a day in my life."

This book is a gathering of such matters. The faults and virtues of those operating in politics mirror ours, magnified by the pens and lens of a sometimes not-so-clean and frequently hungry press.

We are *all* inside "the Third House." We have our landlords (governors), legislators (heroes or zeros), and our judiciary *(alcaldes)*. We have our Texas-style colorful characters. They are what this book is all about.

One thing for sure is that the ratio of the different breeds in "our house" — be they Republican, Democratic, red, white, or blue — is becoming more and more equal. No telling what is going to come about when we get this mixture stirring full-time.

Not long ago, down in Houston, Henry Cisneros of San Antonio said, "Ahead for us is a future totally unlike what our fathers could have imagined." Right now, Anglo males make up forty-seven percent of our labor force. Within ten years, only fifteen percent of new workers will be young white men. Hispanics currently comprise twenty-eight percent of the Lone Star population; that percentage is growing by one hundred percent each decade.

We Texans are known for and proud of our "colorful characters." Dallas editorial writer Scott Bennett recently wrote about our Texas-style colorful characters, saying they had a quality that "old Texas" found endearing. "New Texas" seems to be trying to decide if our historic colorful style is a throwback in manner, a petty anachronism, or a spirit they will adopt, cherish, and continue. Wanna bet?

Some say they ain't making them like they used to. They are around but harder to color in this age of computers and sound bites. Lee Atwater was famous for his advice to would-be politicians: "Play dumb and keep moving!" That's what a lot of them seem to be doing these days.

Down in the Cotulla brush country from whence I came, there is a saying: "If you can't run with the big dawgs, better stay on the porch." Now, let us open the door. Get off the porch, go inside, and see what people are hollering and laughing about . . . You go first!

DER
THE HOUSTON POST ©

MRS. GOODWRENCH

— Courtesy the *Houston Post*

Members of the "Third House" giving rapt attention to the activities on the floor.
— Photo courtesy Austin History Center

LANDLORDS

THE GOVERNORS

The Governor's escort committee.
— Courtesy State Representative Neil Caldwell

JAMES E. AND
MIRIAM A. "MA" FERGUSON

Governors of Texas 1915–1917 (Jim);
1925–1928; 1933–1935 ("Ma")

☆   ☆   ☆

"Bless our politicians — it ain't easy to straddle a fence and keep both ears to the ground at the same time."

One-liner prayer by the Senate Chaplain, Dr. Gerald Mann

TEXAS LUSTER

· Jim passed the bar on a dollar and four bits, which bought a quart of "Four Roses" for his examiners!
· Jim Ferguson was the first impeached governor of a U.S. state.
· Ma was the first woman elected governor of a state!
· Jim said, "When the law gets in the way of practical business, it don't mean anything!"
· Ma said, "If the English language was good enough for Jesus Christ, then it's good enough for the children of Texas."
· Jim said, "Politics is like a game of billiards. When you put up your cue, the game is over."
· Miriam's campaign slogan: "Two governors for the price of one!"
· Official invitations to Ma's inaugural ball referred to her as "her excellence."
· Jim claimed he was "only carrying wood and water" for Governor Ma.
· Ma granted 2,000 pardons her first term!
· Jim refused to sign the University of Texas appropriations bill!
· Ma said, "Let's take the sheets and put them back on the bed where they belong!"

☆   ☆   ☆

Jim Ferguson

Jim Ferguson's initiation into the artful world of politics began when Judge X. B. Saunders urged his colleagues to admit young Jim to the State Bar of Texas without requiring him to answer a single law-related question. An old friend of Jim's late father, Saunders asked the young Ferguson how much money he had on him. When Jim replied, "A dollar and four bits," the examiners sent him out for a bottle of Four Roses whiskey. With that, they toasted his admission to the bar.

Jim Ferguson's political career officially commenced with his 1914 campaign for governor. Although Jim had left the farm at the age of sixteen, never to return, he aimed his gubernatorial campaign at the rural population of the state, earning for himself the nickname "Farmer Jim." His first administration was quite successful; he kept his campaign promise to the rural masses to limit tenants' rents and kept his vow to veto any legislation pertaining to the controversial prohibition issue.

Jim was easily reelected in 1916, but his second term proved more problematic. Many of his troubles arose from his dealings with the University of Texas. During his feud with the university, he demanded the resignations of the school's president and several members of the Board of Regents. He managed to have six faculty members fired and threatened to veto the university's entire appropriations bill. There were a number of possible explanations for Ferguson's undeclared war on UT. Reportedly, he had once tried unsuccessfully to get his brother a teaching position at the school. He allegedly was angered at what he perceived to be the academic community's snobbery toward his wife and daughters. He may have remembered his campaign promises to emphasize funding for rural schools and education for the masses, rather than higher education for the privileged. And he had a business-man's point of view and was convinced that the size of the university's budget was due to inefficient administration, easy workloads for professors, and the inclusion of dead men on the payroll! When Jim was asked for an explanation of the feud, he said, "I don't have to give any reasons. I am Governor of the State of Texas."

Jim's controversial dealings with the university resulted in a campaign to impeach him. Prohibitionists, women's suffragettes, and other groups opposed to his administration joined UT alumni, students, and faculty in a powerful coalition against him. Among the official charges brought against him were misuse of public funds and both civil and criminal violations of state banking laws. The charges were dismissed but resurfaced in a second investigation. The biggest

Miriam A. "Ma" Ferguson feeding her chickens.
— Courtesy Center for American History, University of Texas at Austin

charge involved a secret cash endowment of $150,000 that Jim alleg-
edly had received from the Texas brewers' lobby in return for his support of anti-prohibition laws. Jim denied it, but later added, "One half
of the legislature that sought to impeach me spent their time drinking
the brewers' product."

The investigation committee voted to impeach Jim. In the last
two days before his governorship ended, he issued twenty pardons,
bragging, "I am going to be governor as long as I want to be." But
when he heard rumblings that the Senate was attempting to pass a
judgment barring an impeached governor from future reelection, he
quickly resigned.

After his resignation, Jim returned to Temple, claiming, "Politics is like a game of billiards — when you put up your cue, the game
is over." So Jim temporarily put up his cue and turned his attention to
the publication of a newspaper he called *The Ferguson Forum*. Some political opponents ridiculed Jim's unrelenting stance against prohibition
and nicknamed the paper *The Ferguson For Rum*. Jim claimed that *The
Forum* would be devoted to agriculture and livestock, but one humorist
commented that the only livestock regularly covered was the herd of
"political jackasses" in the state.

Ma and Pa Ferguson voting in Bell County.
— Courtesy Center for American History, University of Texas at Austin

It was not in Jim's nature to totally renounce the world of politics, and he used *The Forum* to promote his renewed campaigns for governor. He ran again in 1918, but the legislature decried his campaign as unconstitutional and managed to keep his name off the ballot. He launched a presidential campaign on the American party ticket, and when that failed, made an unsuccessful bid for the U.S. Senate. Jim announced for governor again in 1924, but an injunction was filed and he was held ineligible. The next day, Miriam Ferguson, Jim's wife, filed for candidacy.

Miriam "Ma" Ferguson

The historical figure of "Ma" Ferguson is a composite of reality, propaganda, and myth. A closer look at the truth reveals an interesting, if at times ironic, picture. Even the name "Ma" Ferguson gives a false impression. Miriam A. Ferguson came from a wealthy family,

Ma Ferguson and her Shivers ribbon.
— Courtesy Center for American History, University of Texas at Austin

loved fancy cars, and always dressed well. She refused Jim's first two offers of marriage, standing firm until he could prove to her that he would make something of himself. The folksy, down-home image evoked by the name "Ma" was campaign propaganda created by Jim Ferguson and had nothing to do with the real woman. To attract the rural vote, Jim proclaimed her "Ma, Mother of the State of Texas." Her family shuddered.

Miriam's campaign slogan extolled the virtues of "Two Governors for the Price of One." One astute observer responded, "Yeah — Jim's price." Miriam openly challenged the Ku Klux Klan, which had gained quite a stronghold in Texas politics in the early 1920s. In her campaign, she appealed, "Let us take the sheets and put them back on the beds and put the pillowcases back on the pillows where they belong." A Ferguson supporter at an anti-KKK rally quipped, "All you owls hunt your holes. The eagle is here." Because she frequently wore a bonnet, Ma would proclaim, "Make a choice: the bonnet or the hood."

Voters chose the bonnet and Miriam Ferguson's inaugural invitations referred to the first elected woman governor in the United States as "Her Excellency." (Actually, they read "Her Excellence," but that was a misprint.) Miriam's election was in large part due to the votes of her fellow women, despite the fact that Jim had previously been extremely vocal in his opposition to women's suffrage. Luckily for the Fergusons, however, Jim's opinion regarding suffrage was in the minority, and thus could not prevent women voters from making his wife the first elected woman governor in the United States.

During Governor Miriam Ferguson's administrations, her husband served as de facto co-governor. Although Jim insisted that he was "only carrying in the wood and water" for the governor, he sat in on highway board meetings and conducted other gubernatorial business. Contrary to many accounts, however, Miriam Ferguson was not a mere figurehead. She could be tough with private as well as public policy: she wouldn't allow drinking or smoking in the Governor's Mansion. She appointed three women to sit as special justices on the Texas Supreme Court — the only all-woman supreme court in any state in the Union. True to her anti-Ku Klux Klan platform, she passed a law preventing the wearing of masks in public, and the Klan's power ebbed rapidly in Texas after her election.

Still, the joint governorship of Mr. and Mrs. Ferguson was a stormy one. Jim was accused of cronyism in awarding highway contracts and in other matters, a charge to which he may have answered with one of his favorite philosophies: "When the law gets in the way of practical business, it don't mean anything." Governor Miriam tried to pardon her husband for his transgressions during *his* official tenure as governor, but the legislature disallowed it. She did return to her husband's practice of liberal clemency for prisoners. Some 2,000 pardons were granted in twenty months during Ma's 1924–1927 administration. She defended her actions by saying, "No dying mother shall plead in vain for a chance to see again the wayward, unfortunate son before death shall claim her into eternity." When the issue of teaching foreign languages in public schools arose, Ma reportedly commented, "Stop learning our kids dirty rotten French and Spanish. If English was good enough for Jesus Christ, then it's good enough for the school children of Texas."

Miriam lost reelection campaigns in 1926 and 1930, but in 1932 she returned to the governor's chair, serving a rather uneventful second administration. Her reelection made her the only governor of Texas to serve two nonconsecutive terms until Bill Clements' reelection in 1986.

The Fergusons' three-decade reign over Texas politics ended in 1935. Although their campaigns and administrations were riddled with controversy, cronyism, and contradiction, their indelible mark on Texas politics has endured. Although nearly sixty years passed before another woman was back in the governor's office (see the chapter on Ann Richards), most agree that Governor Miriam and Governor Ann have done their gender proud!

☆   ☆   ☆   ☆   ☆

TEX-TAX

1927 population: 4.6 million . . . Legislative appropriation: $13.9 million

Per head tax: $2.80

1935 population: 6 million . . . Legislative appropriation: $27 million

Per head tax: $4.50

JAMES V. ALLRED

Attorney General 1931–1935
Governor of Texas 1935–1939

☆   ☆   ☆

"Remind us that anyone can be unbeaten, untied and unscored on, if he's never played the game."

One-liner prayer by the Senate Chaplain, Dr. Gerald Mann

TEXAS LUSTER

· Won five gallons of gas in a foot race at a Czech rally in 1924 campaign.
· Earned a pun from Mae West ("a gal a day").
· Won Pike's Peak on Rice's Cotton Bowl win over Colorado, but lost when Stanford beat SMU in the Rose Bowl (1936).
· Won the sawbones vote with printed handbills showing a chiropractor introducing his opponent at a political rally.

· Fumbled when he tried to push Coke Stevenson into retirement.
· Supported most of "New Deal" legislation to become first of liberal governors.
· Tried to create a "unicameral legislature"!
· Picked colorful Edward A. Clark to be his secretary of state.
· Took parimutuel betting out of Texas law books.
· Signed Texas Centennial Law.
· Rode a horse with $6 surcingle given to him by friends "to ride anything the legislature trots out!"

☆ ☆ ☆

When James Allred was elected governor of Texas in 1934, he was, at the age of thirty-five, the youngest governor in the United States at that time. Perhaps even more impressive, the Cumberland Law School graduate from Wichita Falls had already served four years as the state's attorney general. It was, in fact, during this second term as attorney general that his friends and supporters petitioned him, through a unique gift, to become a candidate for governor. They sent him a surcingle (used by rodeo performers in riding wild steer), accompanied by a letter suggesting that he "ride" into the governor's office: "Jimmie, your friends out here think that you can ride better bareback than these other fellows can with their cowboy outfits, but we are sending you a little old $6.50 surcingle, and with that you can ride anything they trot out and it will be a cinch to ride their legislative 'bull' right on into the Governor's Mansion."

Allred took up the invitation and entered the 1934 gubernatorial race. His opponent, Tom Hunter, opened his campaign in Hillsboro, where he invited the mayor to preside at a rally. Allred found out that the mayor was a chiropractor and he notified every medical doctor in the state. It had a tremendous impact at a time when the fight to legalize the chiropractic trade was intensely bitter. Another incident which helped Allred was a letter written by Tom Hunter during the prior legislative session, committing his support to a general sales tax. Allred duplicated and distributed the letter throughout Texas, making the general sales tax a major campaign issue.

Edward A. Clark, who became Allred's secretary of state (and later President Lyndon B. Johnson's ambassador to Australia), described Allred as the last candidate to make a statewide courthouse-calling campaign. Allred made a campaign appearance at a Czech rally in Bell County, where one of the events of the day was a foot race. The

Governor James Allred and entourage at his 1935 inauguration.
— Courtesy Center for American History, University of Texas at Austin

young Allred entered and won (one report suggests that he may have been the only completely sober contestant). First prize was five gallons of gas.

A man of tremendous charisma, Allred was described by one political observer as "a man of principle with strong convictions. He was absolutely fearless, politically and personally, in pursuit of any objective he deemed to be for the common good." Called the last of the "people's governors" (until Ann Richards), Allred initiated several social welfare programs, including old-age pensions, teachers' retirement, workmen's compensation, unemployment assistance, and child welfare. Most of the New Deal-inspired legislation now on the Texas statutes was introduced during Allred's administration. Allred was the only Texas governor fully committed to the programs of Franklin D. Roosevelt, and was identified as one of the few true "liberal" Texas governors.

Although Allred succeeded in setting up a number of assistance programs, the Texas legislature refused to fund them. In 1935 the state treasury was so short of funds that members of the Texas House of Representatives reportedly sat at their desks with umbrellas hoisted because there wasn't enough money to fix the leaking roof of the Texas Capitol. In fact, by 1938, the government was more than $19 million in debt. Notoriously anti-big business, Allred taxed chain stores, opposed the low-income regressive sales tax, and unsuccessfully tried to start a state income tax, raise the tax on crude oil, natural gas and sulfur, and reduce the rates of public utilities.

Allred did succeed in taking the parimutuel betting law off the statute books. He supported the effort to establish a unicameral legislature, but made more than a few enemies when he tried to push (future Governor) Coke Stevenson into retirement from his position as Speaker of the House. Allred also signed legislation that created the Texas Centennial celebration, which marked a century of independence from Mexico. It was hoped that the Centennial would generate jobs and money. Mae West even spun a pun for the Texas Centennial and the governor. Sending her picture to Allred, West wrote across the picture in red ink that she was sure the Texas Centennial would be a gala day, "and 'a gal a day' ought to be enough for anybody."

Allred was noted for enjoying a good joke. He once played a practical joke on reporter Richard Morehead, who later described the incident: "Once a middle-aged, pious, woman-chasing state representative from a small North Texas town confronted me irately at the capitol

Governor James Allred with his family after his 1935 inauguration.
— Courtesy Center for American History, University of Texas at Austin

with a demand that I mind my own business. As a young reporter for
United Press (International), I was astounded by his charge that I had
called the night before and asked who was the woman I saw him with
at an Austin hotel. I denied everything. During the day, I learned that
the call came from the Governor's Mansion and the caller was Governor
Allred, using my name. Allred disliked the legislator anyway."

Once Allred was the victim of a huge practical joke. On New
Year's Day 1936, he attended the Rose Bowl festivities in California,
where Southern Methodist University was playing Stanford University.
At halftime, a telegram delivered to Allred in his box seat advised him
that Lieutenant Governor Walter F. Woodul, with whom Allred had
differences, had called the Texas legislature into special session. (In the
governor's absence from the state, the lieutenant governor acts as governor.) Allred was horrified at the message. He raced back to his hotel,
caught the first plane home, and upon arrival, discovered the whole affair was a prank. Aides said the governor never found the source of the
telegram, although he had "several suspects around the statehouse."

In another football-related incident, Allred assumed "ownership" of Pike's Peak when Rice defeated Colorado University in the Cotton Bowl — the result of a wager with then-Governor Teller Amons of Colorado. After an address at the site, Allred jabbed a Texas flag into the snow and proceeded to engage Amons in a raucous snowball fight.

The year Allred's second term as governor ended, President Roosevelt appointed him as a U.S. district judge. While serving that post, Allred hosted a lunch at the Driskill Hotel, inviting one hundred old friends. Longtime acquaintance Richard Morehead recalled that, "The black-haired, fast-talking Allred was in rare form. He introduced every guest present and gave personal reminiscences of many of them. Some of the friendships dated back to his youth. Nearly all had been Allred's friends during his thirty years of public life." Three weeks after this unintentional "farewell party," Allred died unexpectedly in Corpus Christi.

☆   ☆   ☆   ☆   ☆

TEX-TAX

1939 population: est. 6.3 million . . . Legislative appropriation:
est. $28.5 million
Per head tax: est. $4.70

W. LEE O'DANIEL

Governor of Texas 1939–1941
U.S. Senate 1941–1949

☆   ☆   ☆

"Remind us that a nut is a man with a new idea until it succeeds."
One-liner prayer by the Senate Chaplain, Dr. Gerald Mann

TEXAS LUSTER

· Campaigned on platform "Ten Commandments" with motto "Golden Rule."
· Less johnson grass and more smokestacks!
· At each daily radio show, cast member hollered, "Please pass the biscuits, Pappy!"

- First to use radio in political campaign.
- Traveled in loudspeaker-equipped bus with papier-mâché dome of the Capitol.
- Said, "Honor thy father and thy mother: doesn't that mean old age pensions just as plain as day?"
- Didn't pay his poll tax!
- Raised funds by passing out miniature flour barrels inscribed "flour not pork" and gave excess money raised to Red Cross after elected.
- After the campaign, rival Bill McGraw said, "I have just received the most expensive fiddle lesson in history!"
- The more than 60,000 people in Memorial Stadium at his inauguration were so reverent they stood for the singing of his song "Beautiful Texas."
- Ran for U.S. Senate against LBJ in 1941 and won!
- Origin of constitutional limit on spending that became envy of debt-ridden governments everywhere.
- Recommended that water be imported from Rocky Mountain springs to solve West Texas drought.
- Preceded Ann Richards in his worry about the "Fourth Division of Government" centered in various boards and commissions in Austin.

☆   ☆   ☆

The administration of Governor W. Lee "Pass-the-Biscuits-Pappy" O'Daniel showed that electability is no proof of quality, nor does it shield against mediocrity. O'Daniel, in fact, was totally ignorant of government and had no political experience before his campaign for governor. His election campaign began as an advertising stunt to sell more "Hillbilly" flour. O'Daniel sang his own songs and delivered evangelical homilies on a daily radio program advertising his flour. On Palm Sunday in 1938, he asked his radio audience whether they thought he should run for governor. More than 50,000 messages came pouring in, cheering him on. (Only four told him not to.) At each daily radio show, a cast member would yell, "Please pass the biscuits, Pappy!" Eventually, they passed him the governor's chair.

O'Daniel's platform of the Ten Commandments and the Golden Rule was received enthusiastically by Texans tired of what Pappy O'Daniel referred to as "professional politicians." He promised funds for the elderly, saying, "Honor thy father and thy mother: doesn't that mean old age pensions just as plain as day?" He dubbed his crusade

W. Lee O'Daniel, governor of Texas (1939–1941) and U.S. senator (1941–1949) with his "Please Pass the Biscuits Band" as they became among the first to travel all of Texas in a sound truck.
— Courtesy Center for American History, University of Texas at Austin

O'Daniel family as they move into the Governor's Mansion.
— Courtesy Center for American History,
University of Texas at Austin

Governor "Pappy" at his desk.
— Courtesy Center for American History,
University of Texas at Austin

"the people's campaign" and traveled in a loudspeaker-equipped bus with a papier-mâché dome of the Capitol on top. During the campaign, Pappy proclaimed, "I don't know whether or not I'll get elected, but boy, it sure has been good for the flour business." He was a true showman, soliciting funds at rallies by passing miniature flour barrels inscribed "Flour, Not Pork." The response was so overwhelming that more money was raised than was spent, and after the election, the excess was donated to the Red Cross. When smart-aleck hecklers asked why he had not paid his poll tax, Pappy replied, "First, I don't believe in asking people to pay to vote, and second, I read names of those two-bit politicians who want to be governor and decided they weren't worth paying a dollar and a half to vote for!" He brought the house down. His opponent Bill McGraw, the early favorite, attended an O'Daniel rally and remarked, "The jig's up. I've had the most expensive fiddle lesson in history."

Indeed, the jig was up and Pappy won the election. O'Daniel was inaugurated at the University of Texas football stadium — no other venue was large enough to hold the crowds of farmers who came to see their hero, "a man of the people," sworn in to office. More than 60,000 reverent supporters actually stood with bowed heads for the singing of O'Daniel's song "Beautiful Texas." He originated the concept of a radio campaign, and was the first entertainer in the country to win such a high political office.

O'Daniel enjoyed being governor. In his office he had a speaker connected to the House and would listen to the deliberations of the legislature. Sometimes he would send an aide to cool things down if he thought they got too rough. He taped radio broadcasts from the Governor's Mansion, saying to his staff, "That'll make them bastards cry, won't it?"

Despite his populist platform, O'Daniel became the most avid business supporter the state had ever had. He was more salesman than politician, though, and having won the governorship, he didn't know what to do with it. Lieutenant Governor Coke Stevenson actually ran the government. O'Daniel's administration originated the constitutional limit on spending, but it was Stevenson and W. O. Reed who did all the mulework. O'Daniel, for his part, announced nifty slogans like "less johnson grass, more smokestacks." Some O'Daniel actions included his recommendation to import water from Rocky Mountain springs to solve the West Texas drought and his approval of a constitutional amendment limiting regular sessions to 140 days.

In his address to the legislature in 1941, Governor W. Lee O'Daniel decried "this giant, headless, irresponsible fourth division of government. These independent boards and commissions enjoy power without responsibility and leave the chief executive with responsibility without power." O'Daniel said he "must detour around powerful administrative agencies which are in no way subject to his authority." He didn't do much about this problem, however.

O'Daniel's lack of political ability did not keep him from being reelected with a record one million-plus votes. He didn't finish out his second term, however. In 1941, O'Daniel ran for the U.S. Senate against Lyndon Baines Johnson and defeated him by a 1,000 plurality. The brewers' lobby feared they would lose millions of dollars if prohibitionist O'Daniel was governor, so they saw to it that he became a senator instead.

☆　☆　☆　☆　☆

TEX-TAX

1941 population: est. 6.4 million . . . Legislative appropriation: est. $29 million

Per head tax: est. $4.80

COKE R. STEVENSON

Speaker of the House 1935–1939
Lieutenant Governor 1939–1941
Governor of Texas 1941–1947

☆　☆　☆

"Lord deliver us from ourselves and long-winded prayers."
One-liner prayer by the Senate Chaplain, Dr. Gerald Mann

TEXAS LUSTER

· For colorful landlord . . . "Calculatin' Coke!"
· Hated politics but loved government.
· Loved to live at his "no phone ranch." Said he was stuck in a
  mudhole for eleven days trying to return!
· Used his pipe as a gavel when presiding as Speaker.

- Usually got standing ovation after each session because of his fairness.
- Visited Texas prisons and slept in cell with convicts!
- Important visitor found him sitting in the mansion, barefoot, no shirt, shelling peas! . . . When the roof leaked, Coke just moved to another room!
- Secret of his success in politics, he said, "I have discovered what people want . . . They just want to be left alone!"
- Fathered a child when he was seventy-two!
- First to be asked to serve a second term as Speaker.
- Bitter about his 1948 Duval defeat by LBJ!
- As lieutenant governor, guided the historical constitutional "pay-as-you-go" plan.

☆   ☆   ☆

"Coke Stevenson is neither a sign nor a sound to hear. He castigates no element of the people for the enjoyment of others, sings no hymns of hate, makes no appeal to group prejudice. Indeed, he can keep quiet longer and use fewer words in breaking his silence than anyone who has loomed large in Southern politics in many years."

This description by a reporter of Stevenson's era aptly portrays the self-educated lawyer-banker-rancher from Junction whose rugged appearance and "strong, silent" manner once inspired a comparison to John Wayne. An unabashed conservative who reportedly considered political office to be a public trust not to be exploited for selfish or personal gain, Coke once asserted that he never deliberately intended to become a public official, but each time ran "for the purpose of getting a particular job done." He hated politics but loved government, and despite his lack of formal education, taught himself history, particularly the history of Texas, and reportedly took great pride in his heritage.

Stevenson entered state government in 1928 when he was elected to the House of Representatives. He served five terms in the House, including an unprecedented two consecutive terms as Speaker of the House. While he was Speaker, the legislature passed a bill making it mandatory for all Texas drivers to secure licenses, and Stevenson was issued license number "1," which he retained for the rest of his life. As Speaker, Stevenson often used his pipe as a gavel, but at the end of a typical day's session, his fellow legislators rose and applauded their leader for his unwavering sense of fairness. Highlights of Stevenson's tenure in the House of Representatives include his authorship of a bill

Coke R. Stevenson

which established the office of state auditor, and his hands-on approach to prison legislation (he reportedly not only visited Texas prisons but slept in cells with the convicts).

Stevenson was elected lieutenant governor in 1940 and was re-elected to a second term, but it was interrupted in 1941 when then-Governor W. Lee O'Daniel resigned to take a seat in the U.S. Senate. Stevenson completed O'Daniel's unexpired term as governor, and then was elected to full terms of his own in 1942 and 1944. As governor of Texas throughout World War II, Stevenson devoted his administration to the war effort, with state issues necessarily remaining secondary. One of the most significant achievements of his administration was the

adoption of a constitutional amendment which put the state government on a "pay-as-you-go" basis, prohibiting the legislature from
spending more money than the state comptroller certified would be on
hand when the bills came due. Also adopted during Stevenson's
administration was the so-called "Good Roads" amendment, which allowed the state to dedicate tax revenue to building and maintaining
one of the nation's best highway systems. Stevenson's administration
also witnessed the passage of a bill giving Mexican immigrants entitle-
ment to "full and equal accommodations in public places." Stevenson
won his second term against a dozen Democrats without a runoff, and
against a nominal Republican candidate.

Coke took refuge from the demands of public life at his much-be-
loved Hill Country ranch. Reportedly during his years with the legislature, his wife Fay would have the car waiting outside the Capitol at
adjournment to avoid any delay in getting to the country. Despite the
fact that the nearest town had only a telegraph machine, Coke refused
to install a telephone at the ranch. He once claimed to be "stuck so bad
in a mudhole [he] was there eleven days." And Stevenson brought his
down-home attitude to the Governor's Mansion as well. One important visitor found Coke sitting in a back room of the mansion, barefoot
and bare-chested, shelling peas. Another acquaintance observed, "If
the roof leaked in the mansion, Coke just moved over. If water got all
over, he just went to another room." A decidedly unpampered governor, Coke reportedly rose every morning at 5:00 A.M., brewed his own
coffee in a battered coffeepot, sipped it as he did his reading, and then
ate his breakfast in the kitchen of the Governor's Mansion on a metal
worktable.

Coke Stevenson was extremely accessible as governor. His relationship with the press was the closest of any Texas governor. He held
press conferences on an almost daily basis and discussed the state's
problems openly. Stevenson was moderate in all things, but believed
socializing was best done during the daytime and that nights should be
reserved for sleeping. Although Stevenson probably best fit the notion
of "cowboy," he frequently wore low shoes instead of cowboy boots.
One reporter stated, "[H]e is a ranchman, born and bred, but no man
has ever been able to get him to be picturesque for political purposes."

Stevenson didn't run for a third term but in 1948 vied for a seat
in the U.S. Senate. His opponent was Lyndon B. Johnson. Part of the
Stevenson campaign strategy was to buy only five gallons of gasoline at
a time so he could contact more people at service stations and ask them

to vote for him. But while he visited with service station attendants one or two at a time, Johnson drew crowds of hundreds and even thousands by campaigning with his helicopter, the "Johnson City Windmill." The official results showed Johnson a winner in the Democratic primary by a mere eighty-seven votes. The election remained controversial, however, as some observers accused Johnson's campaign of election fraud.

After this defeat, Coke Stevenson retired to his beloved ranch on the South Llano River, practicing law in Junction for another twenty-seven years with his son, Coke, Jr. He fathered a second child with his second wife at the ripe old age of seventy-two.

Coke was once asked to what qualities he attributed his lengthy and respected political career. He replied, "The secret of my success in politics is that I have discovered what people want. They just want to be left alone."

☆   ☆   ☆   ☆   ☆

TEX-TAX

1947 population: est. 6.8 million . . . Legislative appropriation: est. $743 million

Per head tax: est. $109

BEAUFORD H. JESTER

Governor of Texas 1947–1949

☆   ☆   ☆

"Lord, teach us to be mediators instead of gladiators."
One-liner prayer by the Senate Chaplain, Dr. Gerald Mann

TEXAS LUSTER

· Only Texas governor to die in office — died in a Pullman in Corsicana on July 11, 1949.
· Served as member of Texas Railroad Commission.
· Defeated ex-UT President Homer Rainey in classic no-holds-barred conservative/liberal swat fest in 1946.
· Branded by some as cheerful, outgoing playboy . . . He loved people and the rigors of campaigning.

- Pursued a "people's path" campaign through every nook and cranny of the state.
- Led to passage of historic "right-to-work" act blocking mandatory union membership in Texas.
- Led the state to organized public education under Gilmer-Aikin Act.
- Had charge of "our house" when horrible Texas City blast rocked that city on April 16, 1947.
- Headed longest biennial session of legislature, January 11 to July 6, 1949! A 140-day limit on such followed.

☆   ☆   ☆

A Corsicana attorney and member of the Texas Railroad Commission, Beauford Jester ran for governor in 1946 against former University of Texas President Dr. Homer Price Rainey and former Attorney General Grover Sellers. Dr. Rainey had been fired by the UT Board of Regents two years earlier (after publicly accusing them of overstepping their authority in the firing of three UT staff members over Rainey's protest), and liberal Democrats had urged Rainey to run for governor on a vindication platform. In what was described as a bitter campaign, Jester reportedly took the "high road" in discussions about the Rainey dispute, while Sellers, the third candidate, mercilessly lambasted the ousted educator. An outgoing individual who loved people and the rigors of political campaigning, Jester cheerfully pursued his "people's path" campaign, visiting places where statewide candidates seldom ventured. Since 1939, when Allred left the governor's office, the state's politics had become increasingly controlled by conservative Democrats, and Jester easily defeated the liberal Rainey in a runoff election.

Early in Jester's administration, the state experienced one of its greatest disasters when on April 16, 1947, a ship loaded with explosive nitrate blew up in the harbor at Texas City. It was reported that 550 persons were killed, hundreds more injured, and an estimated $35 million in property damage inflicted.

Despite this tragedy, Jester's administration managed to accomplish a great deal. Construction and expansion of most state programs had been postponed during World War II, and because of the reduction in expenditures and the recently adopted "pay-as-you-go" provision of the state constitution, the state treasury was in excellent condition. Jester's first term saw the passage of the state's right-to-work law, prohibiting mandatory union membership, and the establishment of Texas State University for Negroes in Houston. The same legislative

Governor Beauford Jester with President Harry Truman and Cactus Jack Garner.
— Courtesy Center for American History, University of Texas at Austin

Governor Beauford Jester at a state dedication ceremony.
— Courtesy Center for American History, University of Texas at Austin

session took steps to improve the state's public education system, creating the so called Gilmer-Aikin Committee that was composed of legislators and educators whose mission was to recommend educational improvements to the 1949 legislative session.

That phenomenal session, the longest in Texas history, lasting from January 11 to July 6, 1949, was certainly one of the most productive. Foremost of the session's accomplishments was passage of the Gilmer-Aikin bills which effected a complete reorganization of the Texas public school system, updating it from an outmoded program based on a rural economy to a system which was considered one of the best in the United States at the time. Other accomplishments of that legislative session included: creation of a Legislative Budget Board to plan and oversee spending of the state's finances; establishment of a legislative council to conduct research for the lawmaking branch, replacing individual special study committees; reorganization of the Texas prison system to such an extent that it went, within a few years, from being criticized as one of the worst in the United States to being one of the best; creation of a State Board of Hospitals and Special Schools to modernize treatment for mentally and physically ill citizens requiring public facilities; the repeal of a century-old poll tax as a requirement for voting; and the establishment of a Youth Development Council with a citizens' governing board to supervise the treatment of juvenile delinquents.

Implementation of these remarkable new programs was left to the following administration, however, because five days after the session ended, Governor Jester suffered a heart attack in his Pullman berth en route from Dallas to Houston and died. The only Texas governor to die in office, Jester was succeeded by then-Lieutenant Governor Allan Shivers.

Jester's political career was cut unexpectedly short, but despite its brevity, his administration left behind an astonishing record of progressive legislation. Although Jester's detractors complained that he sometimes failed to act when action was imperative for fear of offending his friends and supporters, and others criticized his "playboy" reputation, many historians credit him with being perhaps the most effective governor Texas ever had.

☆　☆　☆　☆　☆

TEX-TAX

1949 population: est. 7.2 million . . . Legislative appropriation:
est. $1.5 billion
Per head tax: est. $221

ALLAN SHIVERS

Senate 1935–1946
Lieutenant Governor 1947–1949
Governor of Texas 1949–1957

☆　☆　☆

"Remind us that the government which robs Peter to pay Paul eventually Peters out."

One-liner prayer by the Senate Chaplain, Dr. Gerald Mann

TEXAS LUSTER

- Only governor to hold a union card.
- Played part of governor of Texas in a movie.
- Shivers had a "stun file" and a "file 13" (stun is "nuts" spelled backward).
- Conservative who accomplished more liberal goals than any "liberal."
- A Democratic convention, led by Shivers, endorsed a Republican candidate for president!
- "Nobody is against me," Shivers would say on television, "except the CIA, PAC, ADA, NAACP, and PARR!"

Governor Allan Shivers
— Photo by Gittings

- Marked in the Bible for successor Price Daniel the 6th verse of the 4th chapter of Philippians.
- "There is more to timing in a political race than there is in a track meet," Shivers declared. "There are times when anyone could be elected — and there are times when the best man who ever ran couldn't win!"

"If I had to have a man lead me into battle, I'd be happy to have it be Allan Shivers." — LBJ.

☆ ☆ ☆

Shivers' tools of government and politics were forged in a legislative furnace. He was a state senator for twelve years and, as the saying goes, never quite got over it. Some say, however, that conservative Allan Shivers accomplished more liberal goals than any acknowledged liberal ever did in Texas. In 1946 Shivers won the lieutenant governorship and was subsequently reelected to a second term. A noted authority, Dr. J. William Davis, said that Shivers "helped shape the office of lieutenant governor. Shivers' ideas, practices, and techniques of leadership were significant in turning the office of lieutenant governor in the direction it has since taken." One of Shivers' views on the office was that it provided excellent training for the governorship, a post which Shivers assumed at the untimely death of Beauford Jester on July 11, 1949. Shivers served the balance of Jester's term, then was elected to three consecutive terms.

The Shivers administration, although controversial, was instrumental in shaping Texas politics. Early on, Jim Ferguson told Shivers, "I'm winding up a political career of a great many years, and you're just beginning one that may or may not last many years. But I want to give you one bit of advice. Don't let yourself get to hating so many people that you don't have time to like anyone." Shivers took that advice to heart!

His many years in the Senate may have accounted for the productive (though not always smooth) working relationship Shivers enjoyed with the legislative branch. But he could and did hit hard when he felt circumstances warranted. As lieutenant governor and as governor, he often had to handle radical or unruly elements in the legislature. During a particularly boisterous legislative session, a cohort, Speaker Senterfitt, was ready with a rules revision. The presence of many new members in the legislature and the careful organization of the conservatives made it possible to get this rule adopted and thereby hogtie the anti-administration forces in the House.

Shivers seemed to have had no fear. He once said, "There is nobody against me, except the CIA, PAC, ADA, NAACP, and PARR." In 1954 he called a special session to address the issues of budgeting for hospitals and schools. He summoned all the lobbyists to the Governor's Mansion and laid down the law: "We're gonna raise this much money and we think this is your fair share." He then told each one how much his particular industry should raise. "Now y'all can get together, do whatever you want to, but know that you will do this. If you're not going to do it voluntarily, we're going to do it to you." Some recalcitrant lobbyists resisted. Shivers convinced them — by threatening to call the bosses of the companies they lobbied for.

His East Texas birthright included a pleasant personality, with which he overcame any resentment the electorate might have felt toward a person of wealth with substantial business ties. Never a favorite of career labor or minority group leaders, definitely at arms-length with those Lyndon Johnson was to describe as "effete intellectual snobs," Shivers managed to keep animosity at a low level. An admirer termed him a typical East Texan who "never comes out of the same hole he went in."

In 1956 political thunder was rolling on both sides as LBJ gave Shivers his first and only political defeat in the party conventions. As the most powerful man in Texas, Shivers was expected to head the Texas delegation to the National Democratic Convention one last time, but Lyndon ran as "favorite son" and displaced Shivers as party leader. The enigmatic relationship between Shivers and Johnson, close personally, sometimes violent politically, drew the attention of many. As Johnson put it, "Allan and I understand each other. We cut each other with the same knife."

No other governor, except perhaps James Stephen Hogg, saw as many of his protégés move on to higher offices as Shivers. The difference between Hogg and Shivers is that Shivers helped his young men move up and thus extended his influence on state government.

Shivers had other unique political maneuvers under his hat. He led a Democratic convention to nominate a Republican candidate for president, and helped carry Texas for the Republican national ticket. Shivers felt that since the national Democratic party had failed to pay its just debts to Texas, he was justified in leading the voters to the Republican mountain.

Allan Shivers was the only governor ever to hold a union card — certainly the only governor to acquire one during an election campaign, in a year when he was battling union leadership. Shivers played a bit part in the 1954 movie *Lucy Gallant* — as the governor of Texas. He was a natural for the part, already having had years of practice. To get onto the set, however, he had to join the actors' union; when he got his paycheck ($87 for a day's work), he promptly endorsed it to the actors' equity fund. He didn't quit his day job.

At the end of his governorship, Shivers followed a tradition set in 1925 by Governor Pat Neff. He chose a Bible passage which he considered good advice for his successor. Shivers marked for Price Daniel the 6th verse of the 4th chapter of Philippians: "Be careful for nothing: but in everything by prayer and supplication with thanksgiving let your requests be made known to God." In other words, "Quit worryin', God will provide." This was good advice for Daniel, by nature a worrywart.

I worked with J. J. "Jake" Pickle in organizing thirteen central counties for the Shivers race in 1950. The Waco businessmen did not want McLennan County to be the only county in the state to fail to vote for Shivers in his race against Caso March, a Waco native. We organized, and a few days before election, I went to the great McLennan County city of West to place an ad in the Czech newspaper published, printed, and distributed there. (There were some 200,000 Czechs living in North Central Texas.) I gave the publisher, Joe Holacek, $100 and asked him to write and print the ad. In that race, Shivers' wife Marialice's Catholic religion was a hot topic with the Baptist folk. I did not know until later that the ad mostly bragged on what a devout Catholic Marialice was and had little to say about Shivers' candidacy. Had that ad been placed a week earlier, all hell and damnation would have broken out and I would have gone to hide from the Baptist folk!

After so many years in the political saddle, Shivers distilled his knowledge into a single observation. He said that the worst thing ever to befall a Texas governor was air conditioning. In the days before refrigeration, a governor merely had to summon the legislature to Austin for a midsummer's afternoon session to have lawmakers begging to pass whatever the governor desired, just so that they could get out of town. Maybe that was his secret.

☆   ☆   ☆   ☆   ☆

TEX-TAX

1957 population: 7.7 million . . . Legislative appropriation: est. $2.2 billion

Per head tax: $286

PRICE DANIEL, SR.

House of Representatives 1939–1944
Speaker of the House 1943–1944
Attorney General 1947–1953
U.S. Senate 1953–1957
Governor of Texas 1957–1963
Texas Supreme Court Justice 1971–1979

☆ ☆ ☆

"Teach us that sticks and stones may break our bones, but words can break our heart."

One-liner prayer by the Senate Chaplain, Dr. Gerald Mann

TEXAS LUSTER

- Time and tides rolled during the illustrious career of representative, speaker, attorney general, U.S. senator, governor, justice Price Daniel, 1939–1979.
- This short, nonsmoking, ex-WWII captain announced his candidacy for governor in 1927 while a student at Baylor!
- Only person in history to go through Washington to get to the governor's chair in Austin!
- Journalism was big in his early years . . . Carrier for *Beaumont Enterprise* and *Houston Post* . . . High school editor, cub reporter for Fort Worth's *Star Telegram*, editor of Baylor's *Daily Lariat* (published daily except Friday, Saturday, and Sunday).

Governor Price Daniel
— Photo by Fabian Bachrach

- Relentlessly fought Texas sales tax but got tagged "eight pennies for Price!"
- Refused to spend money on Governor's Mansion . . . His head was hit by a falling chunk of plaster!
- Man of tremendous persistence . . . Long battles for the tidelands and cheatings going on with dormant bank accounts!
- Created the "Immortal Fifty-six" to defeat sales tax proposed by O'Daniel.
- Deceptive sense of humor as he won Headliners' wit battles with such as St. John Garwood — Cactus Pryor as referee!
- Ran for U.S. Senate on both party tickets!
- Served only ice water in the mansion . . . But won loud applause when his 7-UP was slugged as he ad-libbed with other governors at Headliners' banquet!
- Watched the Jim Hogg room the night Marshall Matt Dillon (James Arness) spent night in the mansion!
- Price, Jr., was known as "PD2" . . . Became Speaker of the House in 1973.
- Brother "Hoot" served as governor of Guam!

☆   ☆   ☆

Through the course of Price Daniel's four-decade political career, he earned the distinction of serving in all three branches of government — executive, legislative, and judicial. From Liberty, Texas, Daniel earned journalism and law degrees from Baylor University, where as a freshman he first announced his intention to become governor of Texas, though modestly admitting that he first hoped to become president of his class (which he did). Daniel financed his college education by organizing and leading a dance band, despite the fact that he'd never read a note of music in his life.

First elected to office in 1938, Daniel served three consecutive terms in the House of Representatives. He, along with a group who came to be called "The Immortal Fifty-six," blocked a sales tax bill, launched by then-Governor "Pappy" O'Daniel, who had unsuccessfully attempted to disguise it as a "transactions" tax. Daniel was unanimously selected Speaker during his last term. In 1943, after the legislature adjourned, he enlisted as a private in the U.S. Army, and he was discharged three years later with the rank of captain.

That same year, Daniel successfully campaigned for state attorney general, pledging to return Texas' tidelands to state ownership. The

leasing rights to these offshore lands had become a controversial issue,
and Daniel fought tirelessly on behalf of the state to secure these sub-
merged lands. Daniel believed Texas was entitled to the potentially
enormous revenues to be had from oil drilling off its shores in the Gulf
of Mexico. Daniel was reelected as attorney general in 1948 and 1950
— the latter election significant as it was won by the largest margin in
the history of Texas politics; the Republicans didn't even bother to
mount a candidate against him in the general election.

Daniel's continued advocacy of the tidelands issue resulted in his
election in 1952 to the United States Senate. His popularity was so
overwhelming at that time that the Republican party, lacking anyone
willing to serve as a sacrificial lamb, threw him its support as well.
During the ongoing presidential race, Democratic nominee Adlai Stevenson announced that he concurred in the federal government's right
to the oil. Daniel took a bold step, declaring himself a "Texas Democrat, not a national Democrat," and publicly withdrew his support
from Stevenson, proclaiming that Texas Democrats could feel free to
vote for Dwight D. Eisenhower, the Republican presidential nominee,
without losing status as Democrats in good standing. In 1953 the tidelands bill was signed into law by Eisenhower, who had pledged to support Texas' position on the tidelands controversy and subsequently had
received the support of many Texans at the polls. As a result of the passage of the bill, Texas' territorial boundary was set at ten and a half
miles offshore, more than three times the customary three-mile limit.
Billions of dollars of revenues from future oil and gas finds were thus
guaranteed to the state. As a junior senator, Daniel had successfully
engineered the passage of what was perhaps the most important piece
of legislation ever passed on behalf of a single state.

Despite Daniel's successful tenure as senator, he had his eye on
the governorship. He went on statewide television in 1956, telling his
constituents that he'd rather serve as governor of Texas than hold any
other office in the country but wanted to leave the decision up to the
voters. After a tremendous outpouring of letters, postcards and telegrams endorsing his candidacy, Daniel announced his entry into the
gubernatorial race. He won the election and resigned from his post in
the Senate, effective the day he was to be inaugurated as governor (January 15, 1957), thus earning him the dubious honor of being the only
public official in history who went through Washington to get to the
governor's seat in Texas.

Daniel took on the political humorists at the Headliners' roast
with equal confidence. One observer recalled that after a lengthy

"preparation" at the bar, Daniel and St. John Garwood fought a witty duel of words before the Headliners Club, without a ghost writer in sight. One night, James Arness (Marshall Matt Dillon of *Gunsmoke*) made an appearance at the annual Headliners' banquet, and Daniel invited him to spend the night at the Governor's Mansion. Daniel later said that "Marshall Dillon" got to sleep in Jim Hogg's bed. But Daniel reportedly refused to spend "three dimes" on the Governor's Mansion and insisted on keeping threadbare, dreary furniture around. Gubernatorial aide Jacobsen recalled that Daniel's inattention to Mansion maintenance was so bad that once, when he was ascending the stairs of the mansion, plaster from the ceiling fell on the governor's head.

The first governor to use electronic systems in his office, Daniel was able to hear and record legislative proceedings, using the information to his political advantage or for his amusement. His biggest disappointment with the legislature was his failure to block the passage of the state's first retail sales tax bill. Daniel fought the sales tax relentlessly, incurring the wrath of business interests which insisted upon it. When the legislature finally passed it over Daniel's protests to solve the state's fiscal problems, the public blamed him for it. Cashiers in restaurants and service stations, for instance, were reported as saying, upon being confronted with a check for four dollars, "and eight pennies more for Price."

Although Daniel had easily won reelections in 1958 and 1960, the state tax amendment damaged his popularity and he lost his bid for a fourth term to John Connally. Despite the fact that Daniel was not adverse to the idea of having Connally succeed him, a public opinion poll conducted by Joe Belden Associates convinced him that he could easily win a fourth term, thus making him the longest serving governor in Texas history. Daniel later admitted, "With that [the Belden poll], with my mail and all, I thought I had the pulse of the people. I was mistaken."

Daniel served in several federal capacities following his tenure as governor, including those of assistant to the U.S. president for federal-state relations and director of the Office of Emergency Preparedness. He was appointed to the Texas Supreme Court in 1971, an office he held until his retirement in 1979. The Daniel family name in politics was also distinguished by Price Sr.'s brother Bill ("Hoot"), who served in the state legislature during the late 1940s and early 1950s and was appointed governor of Guam.

Born during the heady days of his father's second term in the Texas statehouse, Price Daniel, Jr., was, as one writer put it, "to the political manor born." A mere two years after passing the bar, the younger Price was seeking his father's old seat in the legislature. An enthusiastic electorate in Liberty County sent twenty-seven-year-old Price to Austin. Known by the legislature as "PD2," Price, Jr.'s personality was described by some as aloof and reserved, not a "player." These qualities served him well, however, in the aftermath of the Sharpstown scandal, when his detachment was perceived as virtuousness. In what some called a public relations move (backed by a behind-the-scenes lobbying effort from his father), Price, Jr. acceded to the position of Speaker of the House in 1973. He called a Constitutional Convention in 1974 with the objective of substantially expanding openness in government and ending the long-standing power of big business. Almost immediately, he encountered resistance. His legislative colleagues resented this grand gesture, and detractors nicknamed him "Half Price" in an unfavorable comparison to his father.

At the height of the convention furor, Price, Jr. publicly called labor leaders callous and selfish. He also called certain convention delegates "cockroaches" and refused to apologize. Price saw his new constitution fail by only three votes, and although a watered-down version of the constitution was adopted the following year, Price had, by that time, abdicated his Speaker's chair, claiming that limiting a Speaker to one term would result in a more democratic House. Putting the brakes on his own political career, he returned to Liberty, practiced law and taught law and government classes. In 1978 he was defeated in a bid for the Democratic nomination for state attorney general.

Price, Jr. was a perfectionist in everything he did. "He prepared for each day as if it were a space shot," recalled one old friend. He would take fifteen minutes to set his wristwatch so the second hand and the hour hand would tell the precise time. He was fastidious about his grooming. At Baylor he'd engaged the services of a maid to iron his shirts because he was unhappy with the way the laundry did them. He wanted the collars left ironed straight up, so that each day after he had selected his wardrobe, he could hand iron the collar down to match the lay of the jacket and the knot of the tie. Those who knew him well said, "His daddy's money was his daddy's money. Price always wanted to make it on his own, to establish his own identity." An investigation of his untimely death in 1981 resulted in the murder trial (and acquittal) of his widow, and a book and TV movie recently melodramatized the scandal. The "luster" of the Daniel name . . . Price, Price, Jr., Bill (Governor "Hoot"), probably more than any other klan, is indelibly spread across Lone Star history. Who else has shown more?

☆ ☆ ☆ ☆ ☆

TEX-TAX

1963 population: 9.5 million . . . Legislative appropriation:
est. $2.9 billion

Per head tax: est. $305

JOHN CONNALLY

Governor of Texas 1963–1969

☆ ☆ ☆

---

*"Remind us, Lord, that you don't need a wiretap to know what
we're up to."*

One-liner prayer by the Senate Chaplain, Dr. Gerald Mann

TEXAS LUSTER

- "Got out of the peanut patch and fell in love with easy living . . ."
- Was once a disc jockey.
- Only grand marshal of Texas rodeo ever to wear an authentic cowboy suit with a Christian Dior label!
- Had himself paged in every airport he visited (and some he didn't) while campaigning.
- "The man I would want on my side if ever I was in big trouble," said LBJ.
- Left Duval County in 1948 with 203 names voting for LBJ, all alphabetical in blue ink by the same hand!
- Connally said about LBJ: "You know what's wrong with LBJ — he is ashamed of being a Texan and I'm not!"

Governor John Connally
— Photo by Bill Malone

- Bob Bullock once said about Connally, "He ain't never done nothin' but get shot in Dallas. He got the silver bullet!"
- Got one delegate in his $12 million 1980 campaign for president!
- A "political transvestite" who at the battle of the Alamo would have organized "Texans for Santa Anna," according to Liz Carpenter.
- Ralph Yarborough comments on Connally's switch to the Republican Party: "It's the first time in recorded history that a rat swam toward a sinking ship!"
- At a Houston banquet, Connally looked at humorists Morris Frank on his left and Cactus Pryor on his right and quipped, "I feel like a piece of bread between two slices of ham."
- Molly Ivins says, "If you want to get something done in Texas, you get John Connally or H. Ross Perot!"

☆　☆　☆

Political journalist Richard Morehead once described John Connally as the man who "came closer to being a movie fan's idea of a leader than anybody I knew in public office: handsome, wavy-haired, tall, and articulate with a high sense of drama." A man with a "bigger than life" presence and style, Connally hired Texas Rangers as bodyguards, and insiders said only Rangers at least three inches shorter than the governor were hired, for that "John Wayne" look. In a survey conducted by the Custom Tailors Guild, Connally came in second (behind Ted Kennedy) as the best-dressed politician, and he was thought to have been the only grand marshal of a Texas rodeo ever to wear an authentic cowboy suit with a Christian Dior label! Never one to shy away from publicity, during one campaign Connally's staff reportedly telephoned airports in every city visited and asked to page him for an urgent message. He was never there at the time. He reportedly liked to leave his office with one or two aides and build the group to be more noticeable when he arrived at his destination. And he traveled often, collected art, owned an airplane and homes in four cities. As one unidentified Texas insider put it, "He got out of the peanut patch and fell in love with easy livin' as quick as any man I ever knew."

The "peanut patch" was in Floresville, where Connally was born in 1917, one of seven children of a tenant farmer. He attended the University of Texas, where he was elected president of the student body and where his future wife, Nellie, was voted the University of Texas Sweetheart.

His political career began with his association with Lyndon B.

Johnson, who in 1939 offered Connally a job on his Washington staff.
When LBJ decided to run for the Senate, Connally worked on the campaign. In the fall of 1941, Connally began a four-year tour of active
duty with the U.S. Navy. Upon his return to the States, he, along with
a number of friends of Johnson's, established an Austin radio station,
KVET (named in honor of war veterans). Connally served as disc
jockey as well as general manager of the station for three years.

In 1948 Connally served as campaign manager for LBJ's now-in-
famous run for the Senate against Coke Stevenson. As the vote was
counted, the lead bounced back and forth. When it appeared Stevenson had won by 114 votes, Connally reportedly disappeared only to
reappear in Alice, Texas, where it was suddenly reported that Duval
County had revised its count, giving LBJ the victory. When Stevenson's men checked it out, the last 203 names on the voters list were
all written in the same blue ink and with the same handwriting. At
least eighty of the names were in alphabetical order, and at least three
of those named were dead and two denied having voted. As Jimmy
Banks remarked in his book *Money, Marbles, and Chalk,* those eighty-
seven votes, in addition to putting a future president "on first base,"
produced some unforgettable stories, including one which tells of a little boy in Alice, whom a friend discovered one day sitting on his front
steps and crying.

"What is the matter?" asked his friend.

"My father," the youngster sobbed. "He was here last Saturday
and he didn't come to see me."

"But your father has been dead for five years."

"Yes," sobbed the little boy. "That is true. But he was here last
Saturday to vote for Lyndon Johnson — and he didn't come to see me."

After Johnson's election, Connally reportedly considered running
for public office himself but opted instead to establish some financial
independence. He practiced law, and in 1952, he became the attorney
for Richardson & Bass, the independent oil operators, eventually becoming chief administrator and lobbyist for Sid Richardson's numerous interests. He later served as President John F. Kennedy's secretary
of the Navy, but he left that post in 1961 to return to Texas to run for
governor.

Connally reportedly said at that time that he came home to Texas
to run for governor because when Republican John Tower was elected
to the Senate he felt Texas was going to "hell in a handbasket." Connally's detractors have always insisted that Johnson "put him" in the

1962 governor's race. Connally maintained that just the opposite was true — that Johnson had done his best to talk him out of running. And besides, insiders insisted, Connally was never Johnson's "protégé," but rather a manager and implementer of LBJ's success. Nevertheless, the accusation that Johnson was trying to install a personal puppet in the governor's office — that Connally was, in fact, "Lyndon's Boy John" — proved one of the biggest stumbling blocks in Connally's path. As Connally explained it, "[LBJ] thought if I wanted to stay in politics, I had every opportunity to do so at the Washington level instead of coming back to take on an incumbent governor and an incumbent attorney general — who, on the face of it, had every advantage over me . . . I didn't have any great desire to run against [incumbent governor] Price Daniel. As a matter of fact, I had been very friendly with him. But I never thought he'd run."

Daniel, in fact, only decided to run when a public opinion poll convinced him that Connally could not win but that he (Daniel) could win a fourth term. The poll proved wrong, however, and Connally led the ticket in the first Democratic primary, landing him in a runoff against liberal Don Yarborough. The old Johnson organization that had been built in LBJ's Senate races of 1941 and 1948 backed Connally, and Yarborough was ultimately outspent by what was described as the "high-octane financing of the Connally Campaign." It was a tough, bitter race, however, and Connally embarked on a three-day, 800-mile whistle-stop campaign tour by special train across the state, from Texarkana to El Paso, garnering large crowds, lots of publicity, and ultimately the election.

The high point of Connally's first legislative session was the merger of the state department that administered parks with the one regulating hunting and fishing (an agency holding authority over the multimillion-dollar dredging of shell from Texas bays). Connally appointed three close friends of Lyndon Johnson to the new State Parks and Wildlife Commission. Almost immediately, the new three-member commission became entangled in a dredging controversy. Soon after, the three Parks and Wildlife commissioners adopted an order designating the land immediately across the road from the LBJ Ranch as the Lyndon B. Johnson State Park. Six months later, the state agency established a "private" fund to solicit contributions for buying the land. The three commissioners appointed themselves as the "private" administrators of it and began actively soliciting contributions. Connally later admitted that the Park Fund was "the most mishandled affair" of his administration.

Although long-standing opposition to Johnson by many of the state's Democratic conservatives caused much resentment of Connally, his wounding in the 1963 assassination of John F. Kennedy in Dallas seemed to alleviate much of this antagonism. Oswald's shots came within a few inches of killing the governor, and he almost bled to death before reaching Parkland Hospital in Dallas. Political observers say this tragedy jumpstarted Connally's flagging career, and indeed he was reelected governor the next year with a record 1.88 million votes. Many Connally critics grumbled, of course, including Bob Bullock, who was quoted as saying of the governor, "He ain't never done nothin' but get shot in Dallas. He got the silver bullet. He needs to come back here and get hisself shot once every six months."

During Connally's six-year tenure as governor, some legislators complained that he was often unavailable at a moment's notice as they traditionally had been able to do with other governors. In 1965 Connally reportedly maneuvered the election of his protégé Ben Barnes as Speaker of the House. With Barnes handling things in the legislature, Connally was free to concentrate on the issues that interested him. Political observers noted that, unlike LBJ, Connally did not enjoy the "lapel-grabbing and the cajoling and the false flattery" common to the operation of a legislature. Connally himself even said, ". . . [Y]ou haven't seen anything until you've seen the combined arrogance and vanity of a legislature."

Like the disgruntled legislators, some reporters also complained about a lack of access to Connally. But it seems Connally had no problem delegating authority, and he was generally able to pacify reporters by letting his press secretary George Christian handle the media. While some Capitol reporters were less than Connally fans, humorist Cactus Pryor commended Connally for his good sportsmanship. As Cactus put it, "He [Connally] brought a lot of grist to the mill. He'd make fun of himself and would hurl a barb back at you like a chicken farmer chunking rocks at a skunk. Late humorist Morris Frank and I worked Governor John over pretty thoroughly at a Houston banquet. When the governor took the rostrum, he looked at Morris on his left and me on his right and quipped, 'I feel like a piece of bread between two slices of ham.' "

Despite Connally's somewhat aloof or at least casual approach to members of the legislature and the media, he ultimately proved to be a strong leader by improving programs and seeing them adopted. He went to bat for higher education more — and more enthusiastically —

than had any of his predecessors, and most observers agree that the greatest accomplishment of Connally's six years in office was his support for improving higher education and increasing salaries for teachers at all levels. The 1965 legislature not only appropriated substantially more money for higher education, but they also established a new coordinating board and proposed an $85 million loan fund, backed by the state, for students in public and private education. Connally's tenure has also been credited with initiating improvements in water planning, industrial growth, tourist development, the library system, and the creation of the Fine Arts Commission. Economically and politically, Connally is considered to be a true conservative. This did not, however, prevent him from advocating the sale of liquor even in those conservative communities that had voted to stay dry. He also added parimutuel betting and racetracks to his program in his last few months as governor.

By the end of Connally's reign as governor, he had proved himself to be a consummate leader. Some maintain that he was the most effective and powerful Texas governor in this century. Judge Bob Calvert claimed that Connally "was every bit as successful in achieving his goals as Shivers was, but he was suave where Shivers was openly ruthless; Connally didn't have to have a bloodletting to prove he was master of the ship, but he was nevertheless known to be the master." Connally enjoyed the luxury of being governor of Texas at a time when a Texan was in the White House. In his book *The Lone Star,* James Reston, Jr., writes of Connally:

> He represented the passage of Texas into the modern age, and he advanced that passage, so that his state was associated as much with its technological instruments and its space capsules and its glistening skyscrapers as with its roughnecks and oil derricks. He came of age in politics as television came of age. In his personal deportment and his elegant diction, in his concern for Texas brains as well as its brawn, in his moderate, if uninspired, stance on race when other Southern governors spewed racist venom, in the energy he brought to the ossified machinery of state government, in the international, cosmopolitan air that Hemisfair brought to his stewardship, and in his general good humor, he represented a better present and a better future for his state.

In the latter four years of his governorship, Connally often promoted President Johnson's programs, particularly support of the war in Vietnam, to skeptical governors of other states. In this, his main adversary was then-Governor of California Ronald Reagan, and the confrontations between these two charismatic and eloquent men at National Governors' Conferences were legendary. Still, Connally and Johnson's relationship was often stormy, which makes sense when you consider one observer's remark that "you could take either one of their egos, slice it up, and have healthy portions for any six ordinary men." LBJ's support of Ralph Yarborough in the 1964 Senate race provoked one of the most serious strains between Johnson and Connally. Connally was reportedly furious when LBJ threw his support over to longtime Connally and Johnson foe Yarborough rather than their old friend Joe Kilgore. "I think he did his best to talk Kilgore out of running. That irritated me, because I thought he owed Joe more than that. I thought that was where his basic loyalty was; it damned sure wasn't to Yarborough. And it irritated me because by keeping Kilgore out, Johnson was helping Yarborough and he was doing it deliberately," Connally said. Connally disliked Yarborough intensely, and the feeling was mutual. Yarborough was among those who contended that Connally never would have won even a second term had he not been shot while riding with President Kennedy. And likewise, Connally was convinced that Johnson had saved Yarborough's political hide in 1964. Because of his antagonistic relationship with Yarborough, and because the other U.S. senator from Texas, John Tower, was Republican, Connally later said, "I'm one of the few men who ever served three terms as Governor of Texas without having a U.S. Senator he could really talk to. That made it very difficult."

Connally served three terms as governor despite the fact that he had once made a campaign promise to abolish a third term. And he made it clear that he never entertained any doubt that he could win a fourth term as governor if he sought it. "Nearly everybody seemed to agree with this — but that was not the problem," said Connally. "The problem, the question, was did I owe that much more?" It seems Connally always viewed participation in politics as more a duty and obligation rather than the fulfillment of a personal ambition. While Connally mulled over running for a fourth term, potential candidates "pawed sand," waiting for the governor to announce his intentions. In 1967 Connally went to Africa on a six-week safari, during which he generally remained out of contact with the governor's office. He later remarked, "I wouldn't say that this experience is why I decided not to run for a fourth term or even that it was while I was over there that I decided not to run. I cannot pinpoint exactly when the decision was made. But, beyond question, this provided the longest period that I'd had during my adult life to pause and reflect. And those circumstances did not argue very eloquently for me to continue in public life."

Connally ultimately decided not to run, and after his departure from the governor's office many Democratic party leaders expressed hope that he would run for the presidency in 1968, succeeding LBJ in his voluntary retirement. He didn't. He was, however, a key player in Lloyd Bentsen's successful challenge to Yarborough in the Democratic primary of the 1970 U.S. Senate race, and also in Bentsen's strong win over George Bush in the general election. It was his high-profile support of Bentsen in that election which set the tone of the Connally-Bush relationship. To add insult to injury, after the election, Connally was drafted by then-President Richard Nixon to be his secretary of the treasury. When Nixon offered him the cabinet post, Connally declined to accept until Nixon offered Bush a position, which turned out to be ambassador to the United Nations. Insiders said it was "the sort of grand, Texas-sized gesture that stuck in Bush's craw."

Connally campaigned hard for Nixon's reelection in 1972. The Nixon camp wanted him to form a support group called "Democrats against McGovern," but Connally suggested a more positive name — "Democrats for Nixon." That effort prompted Liz Carpenter, author and former press secretary for Lady Bird Johnson, to remark that had Connally been at the Alamo, he would have formed "Texans for Santa Anna." Connally's appointment to Nixon's cabinet marked a turning point in his career, for soon afterwards he proclaimed himself to be a Republican, explaining that he'd lost faith in the Democrats' national leadership and goals.

A formal welcoming of Connally into the Texas GOP was held in Austin, and Senator John Tower, the long-standing leader of Texas Republicans, made the official induction speech. One member of the audience remarked on Tower's speech: "Tower's saying Connally is welcome to join the church, but don't start out trying to lead the choir." And George Christian remarked: "He's [Connally's] about as independent as a hog on ice. He's not totally in step with either political party and he never will be. He does his own thing." And longtime adversary Yarborough quipped, "It's the first time in recorded history that a rat swam towards a sinking ship."

Speculation was that Connally might become Nixon's running mate in 1972 or that he was being groomed to be Nixon's successor. In 1974, however, Connally was indicted by a federal grand jury in

the "Milk Fund" scandal in which he was accused of accepting a
$10,000 bribe from the dairy lobby. He was acquitted of the charges,
but only after a national headline-grabbing trial. Political observers
said the indictment further eroded his political power, which had
begun to wane when he switched parties and after Lyndon Johnson's
death in 1973.

Connally attempted to revive his political ambitions in 1980,
when he campaigned for the Republican nominations for the presidency. But Ronald Reagan defeated both Connally and George Bush.
Connally's campaign ultimately proved disastrous: he spent $12 mil-
lion and won only one delegate.

After the humiliation of his $12 million delegate, Connally
turned his back on politics and at the age of sixty-three, started an ambitious business venture with his old protégé Ben Barnes. As one
writer put it, Connally "looked around his beloved home state of
Texas, on the cusp of a fantastic boom in oil and real estate, and saw
the opportunity to convert his powerful connections, tall good looks
and silver tongue into a Texas-sized fortune." He and Barnes borrowed
with abandon, signing personal guarantees for loans, and built upscale
shopping malls, office buildings, housing subdivisions, beachfront
condominiums, and invested in oil and gas wells. As the Texas economy soured, however, so did their fortunes, and by 1986, the Barnes/
Connally partnership was hit with a multitude of million-dollar lawsuits. Connally declared personal bankruptcy, and in 1988, he and his
wife auctioned much of their personal properties and belongings.

Despite this misfortune, a recent article on the former governor
reported that he had in the past few years redefined the stigma of bankruptcy. He and Nellie, having recently celebrated their fiftieth wedding anniversary, live in a condominium in an exclusive high-rise on
the edge of Houston's River Oaks. And Connally is still widely sought
after for his business expertise and political counsel. In fact, shortly before the Gulf War, Connally was tapped by Houston oilman Oscar S.
Wyatt to accompany him to Iraq, where they met with Saddam Hus-
sein and helped secure the release of Americans held hostage there.
(The Bush administration made no comment on those efforts.)

Back at home, Connally makes a handsome living as an attorney
and consultant for several major corporations. His fund-raising abilities are legendary and his perennial candidate's instincts have proved
useful in his recent business and political activities. It was the force of
his personality, say insiders, that prompted Governor Ann Richards in

1991 to name Connally as chairman of the Governor's Task Force on Revenue. Columnist Molly Ivins concurred on Connally's sustained power in the state when she wrote, "If you are trying to get something done in Texas, you get H. Ross Perot or John Connally."

☆ ☆ ☆ ☆ ☆

TEX-TAX

1969 population: 9.7 million . . . Legislative appropriation: est. $3.6 billion

Per head tax: est. $380

PRESTON E. SMITH

House of Representatives 1945–1950
Senate 1957–1962
Lieutenant Governor 1963–1969
Governor of Texas 1969–1973

☆ ☆ ☆

"May we not develop wishbones where our backbones should be!"
One-liner prayer by the Senate Chaplain, Dr. Gerald Mann

TEXAS LUSTER

- Took Price Daniel's suggestion to be more colorful.
- "If you don't like political jokes, don't elect them!"
- Thought protesters were chanting *"frijoles"* when they were yelling for the release of marijuana smoker Lee Otis Johnson.
- Brought down the rafters when he started his rebuttal remarks at the Headliners' roast with "Let he who is without stock cast the first rock!"
- Senator Dorsey Hardeman said to him, "That Preston Smith is the dumbest governor we ever had!" . . . Preston said, "I am Preston Smith." Hardeman looked, thought, and then said, "Aw, hell, I still mean it."
- He and wife Ima held old-fashioned howdy parties for people from

each district as soon as they located in the mansion. They came in busloads!
- Signed ERA Amendment to Texas Constitution in 1971.
- Used the term "we" to discuss his thoughts.
- Photographer Bill Malone bought him a pair of rims to wear at proclamation signings. When he was through, Smith would take the rims off for kids standing around and poke his fingers through the empty glasses.

☆   ☆   ☆

One of thirteen children of a tenant farmer, Preston Smith was the first West Texan elected governor of the state. After earning a business degree from Texas Technological College in 1934, Smith opened a movie theater in Lubbock, a business venture which he expanded into a six-theater chain by 1944, the same year he entered state government. Smith was elected to the House of Representatives and served three consecutive terms, notoriously passing one bill that made it a misdemeanor to count the number of ticket-buyers for a movie. This made it impossible to prosecute movie house owners who failed to report accurate box office receipts (which determine the rental price of a film).

After Smith's tenure in the House, he won a seat in the Senate and spent six years there. This extensive experience in the legislature would serve him well later, for Smith, better than most governors, knew how to deal with lobbyists and understood the feelings of legislators. He successfully ran for lieutenant governor in 1962 and held that post for yet another six years until his election as governor in 1968. Smith's primary opponent in the gubernatorial race was liberal Don Yarborough, whom Smith branded as "a hypocritical, radical, liberal opportunist who doesn't know what he is."

Smith's victory in the election was largely credited to his personal, hands-on approach to campaigning. As lieutenant governor, Smith accepted as many speaking invitations as his schedule permitted, crisscrossing the state tirelessly. Smith felt strongly that there was no substitute — not even money — for hard work. And while he took great pride in the long hours and hard work which got him elected, he habitually referred to himself as "we." In a 1969 interview, he said, "I don't think there's any question but that the hard work that we did by taking ourselves into the smaller communities and meeting the people was the key to our success."

Governor Preston Smith and wife Ima on his inaugural day.
—American History Center

Governor Preston Smith with First Lady on inaugural day. Ben Barnes waiting for his day!
— American History Center

Smith launched an impressive mail campaign as well, sending 400,000 individually-typed letters to the voters. Forty-seven thousand of those went to families named Smith and asked, "Don't you think it is about time one of us was governor?" Smith's campaign advisors wisely kept him off TV as much as possible, recognizing that he projected poorly and made a much better impression in person. Described as both an anachronism and a paradox in his political technique, Smith clearly did things the old-fashioned way. "My campaign methods will always be people-to-people and person-to-person," he declared.

Smith's approachability continued during his governorship as well. He maintained correspondence with many of his political constituents and often personally answered telephone calls to his office, without asking who was calling first. He'd simply pick up the phone and say, "This is Preston Smith . . . I am your governor." His accessibility extended to the media as well — in fact, he held more press conferences during his first six months in office than his predecessor John Connally had during his entire six years in office. Still, Smith's relationship with the media was sometimes prickly, and he notoriously found fault with nearly everything written about him.

Smith's open-door policy at the governor's office was matched by the hospitality at the Governor's Mansion, supervised by his wife Ima. In one stroke of political genius, Smith held a series of receptions for each of the state's thirty-one senatorial districts at the Governor's Mansion shortly after he moved into it. He invited all the people from each district to come and visit the Mansion at specified times. Most Texans had never visited the gubernatorial residence and they came in busloads from throughout the state.

Smith's affinity for hard work and accessibility paid off. He was renominated for governor without an opponent in the Democratic primary and easily won reelection. But his openness with the press cooled somewhat after the so-called Sharpstown scandal brought a barrage of unfavorable publicity. In 1971 the Securities and Exchange Commission began an investigation of state officials who had received loans in 1969 from the Sharpstown State Bank in Houston in order to purchase stock in National Banker's Life Insurance Company, both businesses owned by Houston tycoon Frank Sharp. Fast profits were allegedly made in return for help in passing two bills beneficial to Sharp's interests, particularly legislation that would allow his bank to avoid federal scrutiny. Several officials and office-holders were implicated. Governor Smith, who had participated in stock purchases but had vetoed the bills, sustained adverse publicity but no legal problems. Smith managed to handle even this political hot potato with aplomb when facing certain uncomfortable ribbing about the incident at the Headliners' roast. Smith approached Cactus Pryor and asked, "You're going to roast my ass about this Sharpstown thing, aren't you?"

"Yes, Governor, I am," Cactus replied.

"Well, you've got to," Smith continued. "It's expected of you. But would you do me a favor? Would you write me a rebuttal?"

Cactus eagerly complied, and when Governor Smith walked to the microphone following his introduction, he began with these words, "Let he who is without stock cast the first rock." There was an uncomfortable moment of silence, then, as Cactus described it, an explosion of laughter erupted that was heard all the way to Amarillo.

Cactus once told Smith that he was one of the funniest governors Texas ever had, but a few incidents were reported where the joke was on him. In the late 1960s, soon after Lee Otis Johnson was sent to jail

Governor Preston Smith, TADA presidents Finley Ewing and Jack McKenzie with bill sponsor Dean Cobb, H. C. Pittman, and Senator Bill Moore as the governor signs a bill establishing the Texas Motor Vehicle Commission.

on what many felt was a trumped-up drug charge (possession of two marijuana cigarettes), Smith spoke to students at the University of Houston. Protesters began to yell, "Free Lee Otis." Smith finished the speech undaunted but later remarked to reporters that it seemed odd the students should yell *"frijoles"* (as in beans) while he spoke.

Smith caused another uproar when the University of Texas played Notre Dame for the first time, and he delivered a speech, mispronouncing coach Ara Parsegen's name, then went on to welcome the visitors from "Illinois." When Parsegen got up to the podium, he politely said, "Thank you very much, Governor Schmidt."

On yet another occasion, Preston went to see Senator Dorsey Hardeman. Dorsey said, "That Preston Smith was the dumbest governor we ever had." Preston said, "Well, Dorsey, you're talking to Preston. I'm Preston." Dorsey thought for a moment, then said, "Aw, hell, I still mean it."

Early in Preston's career, then-Governor Price Daniel once told him, "You're about the most colorless guy I met in my life. You need to do something to be more colorful." So Smith promptly went out and bought polka-dot ties and began wearing them exclusively. His life was never without its colorful moments thereafter. Smith once said, "I've found that some people like political jokes and some people do not. My advice is, if you don't like political jokes, don't elect them."

Despite Smith's penchant for victory, he was not elected governor for a third term. Still, observers have remarked that he seemed to enjoy the governorship more than most of his predecessors had. A recent anecdote tells of Smith, having traded his Chrysler in for a Cadillac, cruising around West Texas at about seventy-five miles per hour when a young trooper pulled him over. The trooper asked for his license and noticed that it had one single number (a six) on it. The trooper asked why Mr. Smith had such a low number. "I used to be governor," Preston replied. The trooper paused and then asked, "Governor of what?" How soon they forget!

☆ ☆ ☆ ☆ ☆

TEX-TAX

1973 population: 11 million . . . Legislative appropriation:
$5.8 billion
Per head tax: $524

DOLPH BRISCOE, JR.

Governor of Texas 1973–1979

———— ☆ ☆ ☆ ————

"Give us back the good old days when beef on the hoof wasn't a protest march."

One-liner prayer by the Senate Chaplain, Dr. Gerald Mann

TEXAS LUSTER

· Preferred his seven ranches to the "chicken ranch."
· Never shot at a sitting jack rabbit.
· Sponsored constitutional amendment known as "Texas Tax Relief Act" adopted in 1978.

- Appointed two dead men and one dead woman to state boards (some called this a sign of progress!).
- Started telephone crusades as campaign gimmick.
- Did not cotton to the "kid-the-politicians" game played by the likes of Mark Twain, Will Rogers, and Cactus Pryor (Cactus says Briscoe blushed at the tacky words).
- Best one-on-one man in the business . . . But not good on television.
- Famous for his ranch country cooking — beef with a Spanish touch, side dishes of peppers, chili, hot biscuits and skillet bread.
- Always involved — head of Cattlemen's Association, sheep and goat ranchers, South Texas Chamber of Commerce, etc.
- Last governor to have complete control of the Texas Democratic Party!

☆ ☆ ☆

Reared almost at the knee of John Nance Garner, Dolph Briscoe, Jr., grew up in an atmosphere where politics was a topic discussed almost as often as the weather, a critical element in ranch life. His late father, Dolph Briscoe, Sr., who went broke twice in the ranching business, formed a ranching partnership with Governor Ross Sterling in 1923, the year his son was born. By the time he was grown, Dolph, Jr. was a very wealthy young man. His ranching enterprises covered approximately one million acres of southwest Texas land, and the telephone directory in Uvalde, his hometown, listed seven separate Dolph Briscoe residences. He probably owned more land, as well as more bank stock, than any other individual in Texas.

The handsome young millionaire enjoyed a happy marriage with a charming wife, three fine children, an unblemished reputation, great popularity, and a host of honors gained while performing a variety of volunteer civic work. Always involved in community activities, Briscoe headed organizations such as the Cattlemen's Association, Sheep and Goat Raisers, and the South Texas Chamber of Commerce. Dolph Briscoe, Jr., certainly did not need the job or the money when he tossed his rancher's hat into the governor's race in 1968. In fact he lost money, spending somewhere between $350,000 and $1 million of his own on the campaign.

During that campaign, Briscoe's greatest gimmick involved a telephone crusade. During the two or three weeks immediately preceding the election, households all over Texas received calls asking for votes for Briscoe, enabling the late-entering candidate to finish a sur-

Governor Dolph Briscoe speaking to a joint session of the Texas legislature.
— Courtesy Austin History Center

prising fourth. His 1968 bid for governor was unsuccessful, but his campaign slogan, "Everyone Who Knows Dolph Briscoe Will Vote For Him," proved prophetic. When he ran again in 1972, he defeated incumbent governor Preston Smith.

Briscoe fared well with the legislature and the public during his first years as governor, but some reporters questioned his style, his wealth, and his infrequent press conferences. Briscoe never learned to use the media to his advantage. A Dallas attorney who worked on Briscoe's staff once said Briscoe was "the best one-on-one man I ever saw," and while the governor could be charming and comfortable with people he knew, he was never as impressive on television or before large, unfamiliar audiences. Similarly, Briscoe didn't cotton to the "kid-the-politicians" game invented by Mark Twain, perfected by Will Rogers, and carried on in grand style by Cactus Pryor. According to Pryor, Briscoe left in the middle of his first Headliners luncheon. "He actually blushed at the tacky words. You suspected that he was hearing some of them for the first time." This same distaste for impropriety caused Briscoe to close the infamous "Chicken Ranch" house of prostitution.

Despite occasional grumbling from the press, Briscoe maintained firm control of the state government throughout his tenure. He was probably the last governor to command the Texas Democratic Party. His extended political honeymoon may have been due to the record tax collections for the state, brought about by the unprecedented economic growth enjoyed by Texas and the entire Sunbelt during the prosperous 1970s.

One of Briscoe's most important achievements was the Texas Tax Relief Act. In June 1978, Briscoe called a special legislative session to bring hundreds of millions of dollars in tax relief to the citizens of Texas. As a constitutional amendment, the Texas Tax Relief Act would limit spending increases to ensure that government spending did not exceed the growth of the state economy. Voters overwhelmingly supported it.

Another, less auspicious feat was the appointment of three dead Texans to state boards. In this instance, one of the deceased trio happened to be a woman; some Texans recognized the appointment as a sign of progress.

During Briscoe's tenure as governor, his preference for ranch life over mansion life was well known. He entertained friends and kinfolk by the hundreds. More than 150 guests for the night was not uncommon. Friends came for relaxed talk, fresh air, and ranch country cooking that featured Texas beef with a Spanish touch — side dishes of peppers and chili, hot biscuits, and skillet bread. Many came for the excellent hunting and fishing. Briscoe had a fleet of jeep rangers especially modified to allow the hunter to silently signal the driver with red, yellow, and green lights.

The ranch had no plush blinds; Briscoe believed the quarry was entitled to the sporting chance that came when the hunter was moving along a bumpy road at twenty or thirty miles per hour. One guest remarked that Briscoe's first shot seemed inevitably to miss any jack rabbit that was motionless, but after the rabbit gained full speed, Briscoe's second shot dropped it unerringly. "Dolph won't hit 'em standing still."

Briscoe's love of ranch life may have hurt him as governor, however. Until he'd started thinking of a third term, his inaccessibility was legendary. In fact, his record of absenteeism from the duties of his office was unparalleled in the state's history. Although Briscoe was favored to win another four-year term in 1978, Attorney General John Hill outmaneuvered him and won the Democratic primary. If Briscoe had won, his reelection would have made him Texas' longest serving governor. Instead, Republican Bill Clements would claim that honor.

☆ ☆ ☆ ☆ ☆

TEX-TAX

1979 population: est. 12.5 million . . . Legislative appropriation: $15.5 billion

Per head tax: est. $1,240

WILLIAM P. CLEMENTS

Governor of Texas 1979–1983; 1987–1991

☆ ☆ ☆

"Remind us that America is a country of taxation which was founded to avoid taxation."

One-liner prayer by the Senate Chaplain, Dr. Gerald Mann

TEXAS LUSTER

- First Republican governor in more than a century.
- Last governor to have made his living working on the rigs and eating raw onions for lunch.
- Thought that "getting a haircut and buying new shoes are the two damnedest things you have to do!"
- Called truant senators "Killer Bees" and wanted them to pay for the special sessions they caused.
- Considered his wife Rita his "secret weapon."
- Was a "soup-to-nuts laissez-faire Republican with a certain compelling charmlessness" (*Texas Monthly*)
- A master at handling media!
- Brushed off a football scandal with

Governor Bill Clements

the comment, "There wasn't a Bible in the room."
· Some Democrats now work in the "William P. Clements SOB."
· Zest for dazzling, bizarre sport coats.

☆　☆　☆

Bill Clements was the first Republican governor to occupy the Governor's Mansion in more than one hundred years. And he served longer than any other governor in the history of the state, with non-consecutive terms totaling eight years. When Clements first declared his candidacy, few believed he could defeat John Hill. The Democratic contender was sophisticated, suave, and courtly. Then again, as one writer put it, "Nobody really wanted a gentleman as governor of Texas when it was possible to have a roughneck." Clements certainly was a "roughneck," the last veteran of the oil rigs to run for governor. Clements was that hero out of Texas legend, the strong, bronzed young man who worked the oil rigs, ate a raw onion for lunch, and eventually became chairman of a multimillion-dollar oil drilling firm. What red-blooded Texan would vote for a city boy when he could have a "real" man who embodied the pride of Texas' glory days?

Clements thought government should be run like a business, reflective of his own business orientation and success. Clements was the last governor of Texas *without* a college degree, but that did not hamper him. His business background helped shape both his political campaign and his acts as governor. His $7 million campaign was primarily financed from his own funds, leaving him owing very little to special interests when he assumed office. He was free to devote his energy to his administration's three primary concerns — sound management, accountability, and the business climate of Texas. Within these somewhat narrow concerns, he was considered an effective governor and he spurred economic recovery following the 1986 recession. He lured many business interests to the state, including the controversial SuperCollider, created the Texas Department of Commerce, expanded the prison system, and promoted the deregulation and local control of public schools. His first term saw the remodeling of the Governor's Mansion, an effort spearheaded by his wife. Rita, even more than Clements, was a consummate politician — she knew politics from the precinct level upward. He called her his "secret weapon." For the first part of his term they spent most weekends in Dallas because Rita thought the Governor's Mansion was unsafe — the peeling paint and rickety stairs were no match for her elegant, comfortable home.

Governor Bill Clements and President Ronald Reagan.
— Courtesy Austin History Center

Clements' second term brought the $150 million Capitol renovation and expansion project, controversial due to its expense during the economic recession. During those renovations, which extended well past Clements' tenure, some senators were forced to move their offices to One Capitol Square, a building which had been named for Clements. Some legislators delighted in listing their address as the "William P. Clements SOB" (State Office Building). Although a great deal of money was spent to improve both the Governor's Mansion and the Capitol building, Clements claimed he was not motivated by vanity or greed; it was just "good business."

Clements cared little about "image." Noted for his flamboyant sport coats, he said, "I'm not gonna change my way of dress to create an image." And he complained, "Buying a pair of shoes and getting a haircut are the two damnedest things you have to do." Although Clements was cavalier about his image, he enjoyed a good relationship with the press, and his administration was not marred by excess or corruption. The one scandal to which he was linked did not involve the governorship, but rather a seat he previously held on the SMU board of regents. When Governor Clements admitted he had been part of the pay-for-play football scheme in which illegal payments were made to athletes, he was asked whether he had told the whole truth at the time of the investigation. He responded, "You know, we weren't operating like Inaugural Day with the Bible. There wasn't a Bible present."

Despite this flip remark, Clements was generally very accessible to the press. He practiced the salesman's art of remembering names and faces but did not hesitate to express his annoyance. He told Cactus Pryor that while at first he didn't appreciate the kidding he got from the media, he soon realized that it was part of the game. However, he never enjoyed it enough to attend the Headliners' roasts.

At times, he would hit reporters with verbal jabs or the occasional one-two punch when he thought they deserved it. He maintained this attitude with legislators as well. When certain senators tried to pressure him by hiding out and denying him a quorum for his bills, Clements publicly named them "Killer Bees." He said that he and the other "worker bees" would not allow their legislation to be killed, and declared that if the truants did not return to their duties, he would bill the expense of a special legislative session to them personally.

In spite of an occasional fracas, Clements was popular and won a second term in 1986. This time, observers noted a marked difference in his administrative style. During his first term, he seemed ready to take on the world, but in his second, he often seemed remote, detached, and uninterested. Talk around the Capitol suggested that he had run for the second term only to avenge his previous defeat by opponent Mark White, and that upon winning the election, Clements immediately lost interest in government.

Be that as it may, Clements was a memorable governor. One writer called him a "soup-to-nuts laissez-faire Republican with a certain compelling charmlessness." Clements said of himself, "I'm a nuts-and-bolts guy. I'm a fire-by-friction guy. I'm not long on self-indulgence. I'm a why and a wherefore guy." He didn't consider politics a profession. When pressed to name a vocation, he said, "I'm a drilling contractor."

☆ ☆ ☆ ☆ ☆

TEX-TAX

1983 population: 14.2 million . . . Legislative appropriation:
$20 billion

Per head tax: est. $1,430

1991 population: 15.5 million . . . Legislative appropriation:
$38 billion

Per head tax: est. $2,450

MARK W. WHITE

Secretary of State 1973–1977
Attorney General 1979–1983
Governor of Texas 1983–1987

☆ ☆ ☆

"Teach us the difference between keeping our chin up and sticking our necks out!"

One-liner prayer by the Senate Chaplain, Dr. Gerald Mann

TEXAS LUSTER

· Accused of having had a charisma bypass!
· Purchased the best Mitsubishi in the state fleet — a jet!
· Rode the coattails of Bentsen and Hobby into the Governor's Mansion.
· Designated as a well-meaning political "dilettante." (Look it up . . . We did.)
· Could hold a thirty-minute press conference without answering a single question.
· "Media Mark" — better on TV than in person!
· Vetoed "Kewpie Doll Bill."
· Liked to stop at highway rest areas to ask people about their utility bills.

- Clipped lock off of Governor's Mansion with big clippers and bigger TV crew . . .
- Pushed the "no pass/no play" law with H. Ross Perot.

☆ ☆ ☆

Mark White earned the dubious honor of being the first governor of the state of Texas who came across better on TV than in person. Although Texas country music legend Willie Nelson once described White, the "colorless candidate," as having had a charisma bypass, the governor demonstrated an uncanny ability to manipulate the media. White could get through a thirty-minute press conference without directly answering a single question or divulging a single new piece of information to the press. Some reporters noted that when pushed, White tended to talk faster and faster, until he reached the level of "high babble."

Governor Mark White

White's gift with the media often proved detrimental, however. During his tenure as governor, he frequently appeared in commercials promoting his issues, including the elected Public Utilities Commission, education reform, and the seat belt law. The television spots made it seem as if White were still a candidate, not the governor, and ultimately earned him the nickname "Media Mark." White's perpetual campaigning extended to such activities as stopping at highway rest areas to question people about their utility bills. His first act as governor was to fulfill a campaign promise to "take the lock" off the Governor's Mansion. White snipped off a chain (placed there earlier by his aides) with the largest bolt cutters he could find and with the largest press crew he could muster in attendance.

Such "photo-opportunity" and "sound-bite" antics resulted in accusations of "all style, little substance" from some of his political opponents. Others criticized White for being a well-meaning political dilettante who did not know how to lead. One writer likened the gov-

Mark White and his family shown at the Governor's Mansion during his reign, 1983–1987.

— Courtesy Austin History Center

ernor to an obscure nineteenth-century French minister who said, "There go my people. I must find out where they are going so I can lead them."

Born in Henderson, reared in Houston, and educated at Baylor, White served as secretary of state under Dolph Briscoe and as attorney general under Bill Clements before he was elected governor. White captured only forty-five percent of the Anglo vote, and one observer noted that White had ridden to office on the coattails of a get-out-the-minority-vote drive funded by and for Lloyd Bentsen and Bill Hobby. One cannot ignore, however, that White defeated the lavishly financed and well-known incumbent Bill Clements.

White's record as governor ranks with some of the best administrations in Texas history. He achieved unprecedented advances in indigent health care, water development, and public education. White appointed H. Ross Perot, Dallas billionaire and 1992 presidential candidate, to an education committee, and together they introduced the "no pass/no play" rule which bars failing high school students from all extracurricular school activities, including sports, music, drama, even field trips. Unfortunately for these education crusaders, the law was linked to a direct rise in the teen gang problem. When six-week grade reports were released, gang membership and activity were up fifteen percent.

In another ill-advised move, White persuaded the legislature to purchase a $3-million Mitsubishi jet for his state transportation. The press flew away with it. Among White's other problems was the feud with then-State Comptroller Bob Bullock. The initial clash dated back to White's tenure as attorney general, when Bullock had asked White to rule that the comptroller be allowed to audit state agencies. This duty would have made the comptroller a fiscal czar, with more search-and-destroy power than the governor. White refused; Bullock called him dumb.

In 1985 a bill was introduced allowing emergency vehicles in small rural counties to operate with one technician rather than the required two. White vetoed the bill because a procedure already existed to grant waivers to the rule. The bill would have done no harm, and would have made certain Democrats, many of them White supporters, look good to the folks back home. White also vetoed a bill which would have exempted some carnival games from gambling laws. The innocent "Kewpie Doll Bill," as it was called, was strongly desired by one of White's major fundraisers. White's veto record explains the failure of his reelection campaign — he did not foster loyalty. One political analyst said that there was no advantage to being White's friend and no disadvantage to being his enemy.

Roy Spence, advertising executive and political consultant, proclaimed that White would be the most liberal governor in Texas history. That comment opened the floodgates — it was as if a brainstorm watered White's aides. They leaked stories of White's Lincolnesque greatness, and then let the political rumor mill do its work. However, the strategy didn't work: White lost substantial support from conservative Democrats who had put him in office but were not inclined to condone a liberal ticket for reelection.

One reporter called White a "political windsock" — that is, "another politician who makes necessary changes for direction." White was a poor loser, placing third in the gubernatorial race against Ann Richards in 1989. The week before the runoff election, White called a news conference in Austin to say that he would never endorse, never support, and never vote for Ann Richards. He compared her campaign tactics to those of Nazi storm troopers. What she did, he said "would make Himmler blush." Jane Ely of the *Houston Chronicle* subsequently chided White for whining over his defeat and for not knowing the difference between Joseph Goebbels, the Nazi propagandist, and Heinrich Himmler, the Gestapo chief!

After his unsuccessful bid for governor, White remained in the public eye due to his much-publicized business problems, which included a suit filed by Ross Perot over ownership of two Beaumont radio stations. There was also an accusation of a conflict of interest concerning White's seat on a hospital trust board. It seems that White accepted stock in a private company controlled by a Houston businessman who later received a $15 million contract from the hospital. True to form, when "Media Mark" was interrogated about these troubles, he answered without answering. "Having been in public office — that toughened my hide pretty good," he said.

☆   ☆   ☆   ☆   ☆

TEX-TAX

1987 population: est. 15 million . . . Legislative appropriation:
$30 billion
Per head tax: est $2,180

ANN RICHARDS

State Treasurer 1983–1991
Governor of Texas 1991–Present

☆ ☆ ☆

"Let us remember that women will never be the equal of men until they can be bald and still think they are good-looking."

One-liner prayer by the Senate Chaplain, Dr. Gerald Mann

TEXAS LUSTER

Governor Ann Richards

- First woman governor of Texas since "Ma" Ferguson.
- Has been called everything from "Foxy Grandma" to "The Lady with the Hair" to "A Bubba in Drag."
- Known for her gibes at the Bush administration, including the now famous zinger, "Poor George . . . born with a silver foot in his mouth!"
- Her "New Texas" includes an unprecedented number of appointments of women and minorities to state agencies.
- Did a hard-sell on the state lottery and christened the program by buying the first lottery ticket.
- Compared the legislature's task to a wild mare horse race.
- Considered by some the strongest governor since John Connally.
- Ragged on UT students who drove BMWs and professors who got funding to study "cold fusion."
- Says her biggest perk is her courtside seat at the Lady Longhorns basketball games.

· Compares politics to football: "You have to be smart enough to play
the game and dumb enough to think it's important!"

☆   ☆   ☆

As Texas' first woman governor since Miriam "Ma" Ferguson
nearly sixty years ago, Ann Richards heads what one national magazine
called the "first government matriarchy in the New World" — a reference to not only Richards but the female mayors of Houston, Dallas,
and San Antonio. But Richards' gender is only one of the reasons she
has created a stir in state government. She combines a savvy political
style, progressive politics, and a knack for down-home humor that
have made her one of the most popular and recognizable figures not
only in state but national politics.

Called "Foxy Grandma" by one journalist (Richards has four
grandchildren) and "the lady with the hair" by George Bush, Richards
first came to national attention with her prime-time attack on the
Bush administration. A minor, unknown state official at the time,
Richards delivered the keynote address at the nationally televised 1988
Democratic National Convention in Atlanta. Her memorable speech
included the now infamous observation, "Poor George, he can't help
it. He was born with a silver foot in his mouth!" That punch line catapulted her to national fame.

She hasn't let up on "poor George" either. Other zingers have included: "It surprises me when anyone suggests that Bush is good at
foreign policy. Diplomacy maybe, but not policy. Even a seventeen-
year-old debutante can bow from the waist." About the Reagan-Bush
Republican administrations: "They spent twelve years drilling holes in
our economic boat. And now that we're sinking, they're handing us a
thimble and telling us to bail for four more years." According to Richards, a recent State of the Union address by the president offered "more
of the same meandering — a dribble of this and a dabble of that, sort
of like a Brylcreem commercial: 'A little dab'll do ya.' " She once compared the Bush administration to "a pie crust I used to make in the old
days. Real light, real flaky, real thin. Then when you cut through it,
it was all kind of squashy." And she has equated Bush with everybody's
Uncle Ferd, who wanders in the wilderness for forty years before asking
for directions.

Richards picked up her knack for humorous, snappy comebacks
and her abilities as a master raconteur from her father, who drove a delivery truck in Lakeview, a small town outside Waco. She claims to

have gotten her strength from her mother, who reportedly butchered a chicken just hours after Ann's birth!

Richards graduated with degrees in speech and government in 1954 from Baylor University, which, incidentally, has produced more governors than any other university in the state. She attended graduate school at the University of Texas at Austin, and worked as a teacher, civil rights volunteer, and political campaign volunteer. She worked in the legislative campaign office of Sarah Weddington, the Austin lawyer who helped win the landmark *Roe vs. Wade* abortion rights case before the U.S. Supreme Court. Although she is a proponent of women's rights, Richards once complained, "I am impatient with the term 'women's issues,' which are assumed to revolve around whether we have babies or not. Women's issues are no different from the issues that affect all human beings."

In 1954 Richards married David Richards, a labor lawyer, which in a right-to-work state such as Texas automatically involved them in liberal politics. For nearly thirty years, first in Dallas and then in Austin, the Richards home was a gathering place for liberal activists and bohemian types. Writers, country singers, union leaders, professors, and legislators all came to parties at the Richards place — which were reportedly the best parties in town. For the past eleven years, Richards has attended Alcoholics Anonymous meetings every Tuesday night.

To the disappointment of many of their friends, David and Ann divorced in 1984. Two of her four children from the marriage worked full-time on her 1990 gubernatorial campaign. Richards once said, "My family is no different than anyone else's. That's why my hair is so gray!"

Ann Richards' official political career began in 1976, when she unseated a three-term male incumbent to become a Travis County commissioner. In 1982 she was elected state treasurer, the first woman to hold a statewide office in fifty years. She was reelected to the post in 1986, and her eight years in that office endowed her with an insider's knowledge of the workings of state government. During her 1990 gubernatorial campaign, she claimed, "I have learned this much since I became treasurer. All business is established on personal relationships." Her relationship with Bill Hobby, whom she refers to as her mentor, was particularly beneficial. Hobby held the post of lieutenant governor for a record eighteen years, making him the single dominant figure in state government. During his tenure, he named women to several prominent committees, and Ann says he was "the first man who talked to me about politics as an equal."

When Richards announced for governor in the 1990 election, she entered what would be the most expensive state election in American history. Seven major candidates spent $20 million just to fight through the primaries. Then rancher and oilman Clayton Williams, the eventual Republican nominee, plunked down another $21 million in the general election. Described as "a nasty brawl even by Texan standards," Richards was the early favorite in the Democratic primary with the highest profile and the strongest backing from the party establishment (Hobby and most of Senator Lloyd Bentsen's team). Richards campaigned as a no-nonsense reformer impatient with the "good ol' boy" system of Texas government. She represented herself as a progressive liberal who talked tough. Her campaign slogans included "Don't pass the bill if you can't fill the till," and "If you do the crime, you'll do the time." But Clayton Williams proved himself to be as good a showman as Richards, and he had ten million more dollars to spend on marketing! In a massive advertising onslaught, Williams, mounted on a white stallion, galloped onto TV screens wearing a ten-gallon hat, "strutting his nostalgia for Texas' myths," as one political analyst put it.

Political observers say the race wasn't decided on the issues but by personalities, and many identify Williams' downfall as a crucial moment at a candidates' forum in Dallas, when Williams refused to shake Richards' extended hand. Instantly his image was ruined as the gallant Texan. Others cite an offhand and altogether "politically incorrect" remark he made concerning rape. Whatever the cause, the outcome of the race landed Richards in the governor's office — the first person from the liberal wing of the Democratic party to be elected governor since the early days of the New Deal. She reportedly captured sixty-one percent of the women's vote, and Hispanics voted for her three to one.

Richards was sworn in as the forty-fifth governor of Texas in ceremonies symbolizing her vision of a "New Texas" as a kaleidoscope of people. Her supporters, many of them women, African-Americans, Hispanics, gays and disabled people, marched up the street with her to take over the Capitol. She has fulfilled her promise to appoint women and minorities in numbers that reflected their proportion of the state's population. While state government was once regarded as the playing field for well-heeled "good ol' boys," Richards' appointments at the end of her first year tallied around sixty percent white, fifteen percent black, twenty-three percent Hispanic, two percent Asian — and an astounding forty-five percent female. On the day that Richards revealed

Governor Ann Richards testifying before the Natural Resources Committee in March 1991. — Senate Media Services

Governor Ann Richards with her grand-daughter, Lily Adams.

Texas Governor greets Her Majesty, Queen Elizabeth, during a visit to Texas in 1991.

her choice to replace newly elected State Comptroller John Sharp on the Texas Railroad Commission, Sharp received a call from an irate oilman. "Who the hell is Leonard Guerrero?" the oilman wanted to know. "It's worse than you think," Sharp answered lightly. "It's Lena Guerrero."

Richards' choices for UT and A&M regents settled any remaining doubts about her intentions. No appointments are more prized or more visible than these, or, some claim, more steeped in the "good ol' boy" establishment network. Among the many "firsts" in her appointments, she named the first black man to the University of Texas board and the first black woman to the Texas A&M board. Some critics say many of her appointees are not qualified — especially since it was revealed in September 1992 that Lena Guerrero did not have a college degree, as she claimed (subsequently she resigned her post at the Railroad Commission because of this fact). "We've seen enough of Ann Richards' appointments to know they will be driven by gender, ethnicity and other factors while ignoring experience, qualifications and even demonstrated interest," claimed one critic. Richards, however, dismisses the complaints by declaring, "I don't think we move the cause of minorities and women forward by placing people in positions and have them fail." (One inglorious appointment was made, however, when Richards named Billie Carr to the now-defunct State Board of Canvassers. Political humorists noted that Democratic governors have appointed dead people to state boards in the past, but never to a dead agency!)

Among her many notable accomplishments in her first eighteen months in office were a prison construction program, new environmental protection laws, a shakeup of the notoriously mismanaged Department of Commerce and State Board of Insurance (prompting resignations and installing new heads), and the closure of some dangerously unhealthy nursing homes. She won a stunning political victory by persuading the legislature to put the state lottery on the voters' ballot (a measure that had failed eight times since 1983).

"We've taken on some very powerful interest groups," Richards said after her first legislative session. "We've taken on the insurance companies and the polluters, and we've taken on the bureaucracy." In an address to the legislature, she said, "For the uninitiated among you, {a wild mare race} involves four cowboys trying to saddle a wild horse and then ride it. One of the cowboys has the job of settling the horse down. And the way he does it is to bite the horse's ear. This is called earing it down. It occurred to me that we are undertaking this session much the same task. We are biting the ear of government — settling it down long enough to get a saddle on it and turn it into a workhorse." And in keeping with the cowboy metaphor, an aide of Richards once commented, "She focuses on the horse, not the rider." A reporter concurred, "The ultimate pragmatist, Richards doesn't care where a good idea comes from."

One political observer has commented, "She's probably the first governor since John Connally to convey the impression that she is in charge." Connally himself, who is chairman of the governor's tax equity committee, had high praise for the new governor. He once introduced Richards at a meeting with, "She probably comes to this office more unfettered, more free to act, more free to challenge, more free to question than any governor since W. Lee O'Daniel." Richards quipped, "I thought you were going to say the governor most unfettered since John Connally." Connally reportedly blushed and replied, "I really wanted to say that, but I thought humility prevented it."

Some say Richards is at her best when she is using her office to promote Texas to the rest of the nation. She traveled to Hollywood to encourage the film and television industry to take advantage of Texas as a site for productions. She made a six-day trip through Mexico to bolster support for a free-trade agreement. Richards proved her tag as "the ultimate pragmatist" on one occasion when the president of Mexico was due for a visit and someone noticed that the Mexican flag in Richards' office was drooping from its staff. "Somebody get me a needle and thread," said the no-nonsense governor, who swiftly sewed up the problem. In what Richards regarded as one of the highlights of her first year in office, she played host to the Queen of England in her tour of the state. And in a closer-to-home sales pitch, she devised a plan that is considered to have convinced General Motors, at least in part, to keep their Arlington plant open. Dubbed "The Texas Commitment," its principal incentive was a promise by the state to purchase vehicles from the GM plant that are fueled by clean-burning natural gas produced in Texas.

As a woman governor of Texas, Richards is still regarded as a novelty, and she's proved to be a favorite of the media nationwide. She's been profiled by *Time* and *Vogue* magazine, and *Sixty Minutes* did a flattering piece on her. She deflects the national attention by claiming, "I'm sort of a two-headed cow — kinda like going to the zoo. I just think it's because I'm female and I'm governor of Texas. It's unusual.

It doesn't fit the pattern or the mold." Richards' popularity nevertheless is remarkable. When she emerges from her office at the Capitol, tourists flock to her for autographs. She gets three times more mail than did her predecessor; letters pour into the Capitol at the rate of 6,000 to 7,000 every week.

Still, Richards is not without her detractors. Despite her popularity, some claim she's a "great advertisement for the state but not much of a player in the legislature." Critics say that on at least two of the issues she was most ardent about during her campaign — ethics and education — she has had very little input or effect on relevant legislation. One of her most vocal critics, state Republican chairman Fred Meyer, calls Governor Richards "a master politician" who "has avoided decisions every place she could." Although she visits the House and Senate floors more than any governor since the 1950s, testifying before legislative committees and surprising legislators by dropping by their offices unannounced to chat, detractors say if a bill isn't part of her program, Richards bows out. Sometimes this hands-off approach leads to missed opportunities, and cases in point include the disappointing education and ethics reform bills. Some were particularly discouraged by her approval of the so-called "Robin Hood" school finance scheme in which rich school districts were to pay the poor ones. The state supreme court ultimately called the bill illegal, and many claim that her failure to provide any leadership on the school funding question was a major disappointment since education was the cornerstone of her campaign. She defended her hands-off approach to the education bill by saying, "You don't have to be in the middle of every fight."

She took a lot of heat from higher education supporters when she endorsed a tuition increase for universities and defended her actions by saying, "I think that — after living two doors down from the Beta House for a very long time — it's pretty ridiculous to see kids driving around in BMWs and MGs." Complaining of the dollars spent on research budgets, she went on to say that the average Texan "is more concerned about taking care of the kids and the parents and the bills than about research on cold fusion."

In the other major disappointment of her first year as governor, critics say Richards "talked tough" about ethics reform but in the end settled for a watered-down bill that did not meet half the requirements she had previously insisted were a bare minimum. Critics say her "absolute minimum" of thirteen points for an ethics law vaporized during the legislative session as she passively allowed the lawmakers to set up "loophole after sweetheart arrangement in the name of reform." She reportedly silenced her ethics advisers and signed the "reform" legislation in private, avoiding uncomfortable questioning. She met behind closed doors again with top legislative leaders about budget reform, and in light of her campaign message to bring open government to Texas, one reporter responded, "Sometimes her methods have seemed more akin to the old Texas than the new one she proclaimed."

Predictably, Republican critics accuse her of spending too much money. In signing a $2.7 billion tax bill, she reportedly became the third governor in the past decade who, as a candidate, promised or strongly implied that tax increases could be avoided, only to be left explaining why one was necessary. One observer noted, "I'm not one of them, but there are people who say Ann Richards is just a Bubba in drag." The question being bandied about is whether the governor represents true change or is merely a female version of business as usual. Most say only time will tell. Despite accusations of overspending, Richards saved taxpayer money by reducing the budget on the costly Capitol restoration. She nixed an $800,000 smoke evacuation system and urged the abandonment of plans to replace the building's terrazzo floors with caustic tile. She couldn't "explain to my mama," she said, spending almost $1 million to tear up "a perfectly good terrazzo floor" and replace it with tile just for the sake of historical restoration.

In February 1992 *The Wall Street Journal* published its Governors' Scorecard on Fiscal Policy, and Richards emerged with a grade of "C." A recent article in *The New York Times* reported that Richards has shrewdly practiced the "art of the possible," making deals and compromises when necessary, and only tackling issues head-on when she has picked easy targets such as the insurance industry or the operators of troubled nursing homes.

During an interview marking the first anniversary of her inauguration, Richards said legal maneuvering on redistricting and school finance were among the top frustrations of her first twelve months on the job. Despite the many headaches, however, Richards seems to relish her job as governor of the state of Texas. "This is the most joyous and wonderful time of my life," she said. And George Christian, the former White House press secretary under LBJ who today is perhaps the most influential lobbyist in Austin, concurs. "She enjoys her job more than any governor I ever saw," says the lobbyist who has observed forty years of Texas government at close range. "Being governor of Texas," continued Christian, "is one of the five or six toughest jobs in the nation. And she's coming at a time in history with all of this convergence of massive problems that the state has."

Richards confronts these problems on a daily basis, fulfilling her campaign promise to be a "working" governor, on the job every day. Perhaps due to the twenty-odd cups of coffee that help sustain her through the day, she still has the energy to help paint poor people's houses, escape to a movie every weekend, participate in staff softball games, and cheer on the home team at Lady Longhorns basketball games. On that last diversion she comments, "I think y'all know me well enough to know that I don't stand on a lot of ceremony and I really don't like all the folderol and the perks and the stuff, but I *love* my seats on the floor of the basketball games." A sports fan, she once compared politics to football at a roast for Bum Phillips: "Politics is a lot like football. You have to be smart enough to play the game and dumb enough to think it's important."

Many wonder if Richards has presidential aspirations, especially after a summer 1991 nationwide poll showed noncandidate Richards in fourth place among possible Democratic presidential nominees. She chaired the 1992 Democratic National Convention, but for the time being, Richards plans to stay close to home. She has announced her intentions to run for reelection in 1994. No incumbent governor has been kept in office by Texas voters since Dolph Briscoe in 1974. Richards said she knows the trend is to throw out incumbent governors, but she thinks she can change that.

Regardless of whether she is reelected, Richards acknowledges and relishes her potential influence as a role model. When she took her oath of office, she spoke of the importance of a child of the future thumbing through a history book and seeing a photo of a female governor. In her book *Straight from the Heart*, Richards stressed the importance of all people, regardless of gender or race, involving themselves in politics. "Government touches every part of our lives: the quality of education we receive, the prices we pay at the grocery store, access to medical care, everything from garbage pickup to the most profound questions of life and death on the planet. There is no aspect of our lives so secure that it is shielded from the influence of public policy."

☆   ☆   ☆   ☆   ☆

TEX-TAX

1991 population: 16.9 million . . . Legislative appropriation:
$59 billion
Per head tax: est. $3,470

BONA FIDE
CHARACTERS

"The TV camera is gone, John."
— Courtesy State Representative Neil Caldwell

Colorful

BEN BARNES

House 1961–1964
Speaker of the House 1965–1968
Lieutenant Governor 1969–1972

☆   ☆   ☆

"May all of the wild oats we've sown experience crop failure."
One-liner prayer by the Senate Chaplain, Dr. Gerald Mann

TEXAS LUSTER

- "The golden boy of Texas politics!"
- LBJ predicted the White House for him.
- Trained for politics as door-to-door salesman.
- Second youngest Speaker of the House ever elected (age twenty-six) and youngest lieutenant governor (age thirty)!
- Called then-Governor Preston Smith "a country bum"!
- The young, handsome Barnes was described as "Bedroom Ben, the fastest zipper in the West!"
- Sunk by the Sharpstown scandal.
- Big business bust with John Connally.
- Ann Richards compared him to "an oscillating fan"!

☆   ☆   ☆

Sometimes called the "golden boy of Texas politics," Ben Barnes once seemed destined for national political prominence. Lyndon B. Johnson, who predicted that Barnes would eventually end up in the White House, had this to say about the young political dynamo: "Ben Barnes is a doer, a workhorse. He may look like a showhorse under the lights, but let me tell you, his blue eyes are as tough as steel when necessary."

Born in 1938 in the small town of Gormon, Barnes attended the

72

University of Texas at Austin, receiving his business administration degree in 1960. He reportedly sometimes worked fifty hours a week as a punch-card machine operator while carrying a full load of courses. At the same time, he sold vacuum cleaners door-to-door at night and on weekends. Barnes later said, "I'll never forget the insults and abuse I took as a door-to-door salesman . . . I learned a lot about human nature — and I developed a thick hide, too. And you've got to have that in politics."

Barnes entered politics at the ripe old age of twenty-two, running successfully for a seat in the Texas House of Representatives. As a twenty-three-year-old freshman legislator, Barnes received a telegram inviting him to a meeting to plan John Connally's strategy in his 1962 race for governor. At the time, Connally introduced Barnes as "the brightest young man he had ever known," and the friendship with Connally proved to be an important one throughout Barnes' career. In the 1965 race for Speaker, then-Governor Connally supplanted a reportedly hostile Speaker of the Texas House (Byron Tunnell) by appointing him to the Texas Railroad Commission and installed Barnes in his place. During that last-minute maneuver, Bob Bullock, learning of Connally's preference, called on Bob Ross and me to establish a "command post" at the Driskill Hotel, where we launched a massive thirty-six-hour telephone blitzkrieg to gather pledges for Barnes' election. Barnes won, and at the age of twenty-six, he was the second youngest occupant of that office in the history of Texas. He was re-elected to the post in 1967.

Connally reportedly tried to get the young Speaker to run for governor against Preston Smith (a longtime foe of Connally's) the following year, but Barnes opted to run for lieutenant governor instead. Barnes received a record-breaking number of votes, and broke yet another record by becoming, at the age of thirty, the youngest lieutenant governor Texas ever produced.

As lieutenant governor, Barnes wielded tremendous power and was the heir apparent to Connally's throne as leader of the moderate-conservative power structure. He had won the respect and support of the thirty-one-member Senate, enjoying support from both the liberal and conservative factions of the Democratic party. "His natural power base is the conservative oil-business financial complex that supported ex-Governor John Connally and Lyndon Johnson before him," said one political analyst in 1969. "But despite these associations, Mr. Barnes has won substantial liberal support by solidly backing such programs as a state minimum wage and improved anti-pollution laws."

Lieutenant Governor Ben Barnes

— Senate Media Services

But all was not smooth sailing for Barnes. In 1969 he endorsed a proposal to repeal the sales exemption on groceries. With a deadlock between the House and the Senate, Barnes reportedly drew an imaginary line on the floor of his office one night in mock reminiscence of the scene at the Alamo, and asked any of the fifteen senators present who wanted to repudiate their pledged support of the food tax proposed to step across it. None did. The "food tax" passed in the Senate, but a filibuster won enough time to provoke a deluge of taxpayer objections. As a result, the House filed the measure, putting what some felt was a scar on Barnes' record.

Obvious differences in political philosophies and tastes caused much friction between the lieutenant governor and then-Governor Preston Smith. They disagreed about budget matters, legislative sessions, and political elections — Smith wanting to keep things "status quo" and Barnes often pushing for progressive improvements. They even clashed on musical tastes. Barnes once arranged for Robert Goulet and Carol Lawrence to perform at Smith's inauguration, but at a press conference, Smith (a hardcore country and western fan) mispronounced Goulet's name. Barnes reportedly later described Smith as a "country bum" who didn't even know who Robert Goulet was!

Despite Barnes' good looks and charm, the tall, sandy-haired lieutenant governor did suffer one annoying image problem: his light-colored, sparse eyebrows affected his appearance on TV. I made an appointment with Roy Butler's barber, Roy Grant, and took Barnes out to 38th and Lamar, where we put up a curtain for privacy for the delicate job. Roy dyed Ben's eyebrows. Barnes cussed me all the way back to the Capitol for ruining his life and his career. But when he got out of the car, I knew I was ruined on the hill: No one ever noticed.

During his tenure as lieutenant governor, Barnes, once described as "totally and completely a political animal," accepted as many speaking invitations as possible, often as many as ten or twelve a week. Barnes typically arrived at political dinners thirty minutes late with much fanfare, but one observer noted that one of Barnes' most remarkable assets was his willingness to "have a word" with anyone — friend or foe, and he often remained after speeches and dinners to personally confer with those in attendance.

In 1970 Barnes faced what many considered his most important political decision. Friends and advisers pressured him to run against Senator Ralph Yarborough, the longtime leader of Texas liberals, for a seat in the U.S. Senate. Others insisted that he run against Governor Smith. A private poll showed that Barnes would defeat either candidate in either race. Despite these reports, some considered Barnes to be politically vulnerable at the time, especially in view of an ongoing divorce and the many rumors which surrounded it. Barnes had quite a reputation. Friends and enemies alike reportedly called Barnes "Bedroom Ben, the fastest zipper in the West." And a popular bumper sticker at the time read, "It's 10:30 P.M. Do you know where your Lt. Gov. is?" Cactus Pryor quipped, "Will Rogers never met a man he didn't like, and Ben Barnes never met a woman he didn't . . ." Once, when Barnes sought my advice about some pieces of legislation, he asked me what I thought he should do about an abortion bill. "Pay it," I replied.

Barnes ultimately decided to seek reelection to his post as lieutenant governor, which he won. Two years later, however, Barnes did run for governor against incumbent Preston Smith and contender Dolph

Briscoe, a Uvalde rancher and one-time state legislator. Early on, Barnes was generally conceded to be far out in front in the race. But he was eventually caught in the backlash of the Sharpstown scandal and ended up third behind both Smith and Briscoe, the latter of whom benefited from being far removed from "that mess in Austin" and won the election. To many political observers, Barnes had become the victim of a new ethos, in which his associations with the figures of the Sharpstown scandal became akin to guilt, and unanswered questions about his fast lifestyle and high living became an issue. "I didn't believe that [Sharpstown] was going to rub off on me," Barnes would say later. "I ran a campaign on the issues, instead of talking about Sharpstown. I should have talked about it every day. I should have handled it like John Kennedy handled the Catholic issue." While never indicted, Barnes' political career was aborted.

After his loss, Barnes went into business with a successful builder in Brownwood, Texas, and in ten years established a respectable position in Texas business. In 1981 he went into business with his old friend and supporter John Connally. Sharing a wealth of contacts with bankers and investors throughout the state of Texas, the Barnes-Connally partnership acquired massive amounts of cash, in the form of loans, and initiated bold business ventures which consisted primarily of real estate deals (building apartment complexes, shopping centers, office buildings), but also included the purchase of a commuter airline and an oil company. They reportedly concentrated their efforts on projects that appealed to their expensive tastes. But the collapse of the oil and gas industry devastated the energy holdings of Barnes-Connally, and many of their real estate ventures were, according to experts in the field, ultimately badly timed and badly placed. By the mid-1980s, the partnership had sailed into a legal quagmire with as many as thirty-five lawsuits amounting to $40 million and an indebtedness estimated even higher at somewhere around $200 million. The unincorporated partnership meant that the demands of creditors were crashing down on the two men personally, and Connally eventually declared bankruptcy.

Despite that disappointment, Barnes has continued to remain active on the political front. He reportedly contributed $39,000 to legislative and statewide candidates in 1990. And in 1991, he successfully lobbied for a bullet train proposal for Texas TGV, the French-based consortium, and the state lottery for GTECH Corporation, a Rhode Island lobby service company. He has remained a familiar figure in political circles, maintaining his fast schedule in the fast lane. His energy is notoriously limitless, prompting Governor Ann Richards to once compare him to "an oscillating fan."

BOB BULLOCK

Assistant Attorney General 1967–1968
Secretary of State 1971–1972
State Comptroller of Public Accounts 1975–1990
Lieutenant Governor of Texas 1991–Present

☆ ☆ ☆

"Give us the grace to pay as we go — and the guts to not go if we can't pay."

One-liner prayer by the Senate Chaplain, Dr. Gerald Mann

- "Bob Bullock: State Fossil of Texas" — bill introduced by Bruce Gibson in 1989.
- Best legislative mind under the dome.
- "Bullock Train" (high-speed rail).
- On his knees begging support from black/Hispanic/freshman caucus.
- The lottery — "A sleazy way to raise money."
- Pizza fights with his staff.
- Picnics on his grave site.
- Bullock sayings:
  From a bumper sticker: "Lord give me one more boom, and this time I won't blow it."
  "Government is the first dog kicked and the last dog fed when times get tough."

Lieutenant Governor Bob Bullock
— Senate Media Services

☆ ☆ ☆

Some sing his praises. Others call him the State Fossil of Texas. After more than twenty years of public service, Bob Bullock is a survivor: he was a legislator in the fifties, a lobbyist in the sixties, secretary of state for Governor Preston Smith in the early seventies, and comptroller of public accounts, a statewide elected office, from 1975 to 1990. First elected to the legislature in 1956, Bullock also served as an assistant attorney general and as an aide to Governor Smith. When Bullock was born he was nine years old, politically speaking.

Politics is his first love and his first priority. He has a voracious appetite for information: statistical abstracts, prospective bill drafts, studies, news stories, gossip. According to many sources, including myself, he has the best legislative mind ever seen. As state tax collector, he earned a reputation for knowing more about budget and tax matters than almost anyone in Texas. "You'd better have your house in order before you try to argue with him," Senator John Montford said. "Generally, he'll know more about an issue than you will. I thought I was a workaholic, but I'm a street bum compared to him. I don't know when Bullock sleeps."

Senator Carl Parker says Bullock is close to the people's idea of a perfect politician, "somebody that's tough enough to say what they believe and mean what he says, and not worry about the next election, but worry about the next generation."

Some would call Bullock a Texas-sized Machiavelli, a master of the political game. Bullock probably would agree. He wants respect rather than love and relishes having enemies. His well-publicized feud with then-Governor Mark White during which he called White "dumb" is a perfect example. In the early 1970s, Bullock had a bitter falling out with then-Lieutenant Governor Ben Barnes and, despite some recent fence-mending, Bullock still gives himself much of the "credit" for Barnes' failed bid for governor. Bullock has always stirred up controversy. In a temper fit he threw pizza pieces at his staff. He publicly called the proposed Texas Lottery "a sleazy way to raise money." On the other hand, he got on his knees once to beg support from minority and freshman caucuses, groups typically ignored or overlooked on the political agenda. As comptroller, he was known to switch managers from department to department without warning; while this kept everyone from becoming complacent and gave managers an understanding of every aspect of the agency, it also curtailed any powermongers from creating a personal kingdom.

As lieutenant governor, Bullock presides over the Senate and

Summer 1992 reunion of Gov. Preston Smith's staff members with Lt. Gov. Bob Bullock's staff. Left to right: Jack Roberts, Sen. Bob Glasgow, Lt. Gov. Bob Bullock, Gov. Preston Smith, Sen. Jim Turner, Jerry Hall, Carlton Carl, Mike McKinney, and Jim Oliver.

Bob Bullock, Betty King, Bob Johnson, and staff during a session of the Texas Senate.
— Senate Media Services

wields his gavel like a sword. After Republican Senator Cyndi Kryer of San Antonio backed Bullock's opponent in the 1990 race, she paid a heavy price. In the 1991 regular session, she was frozen out by the lieutenant governor: her bills did not get favorable treatment, and when the time came to redraw legislative lines, she found herself in a new district that she probably couldn't win.

Lawmakers say that Bullock's fast gavel, famous for keeping the legislature on track, can be a two-edged sword. They complain that they don't have a chance to do any independent research or talk to their constituents. When a number of senators were late to work one day, Bullock banged the gavel, adjourned the session, and distributed the names of absent senators to the press.

Born in Hillsboro, Bullock was a high school halfback and a Korean War veteran. While earning his juris doctorate at the Baylor Law School, Bullock was married with two children, commuted thirty-five miles every day, and served in the Texas legislature. His schedule sometimes required him to attend classes at the law school in the morning and speed to Austin before noon for the opening of the legislature.

For his dedication and vision, Bullock has won high marks from government watchdogs, conservationists, and consumer groups. Bullock received several awards for his hiring of minorities and the disabled. When he became comptroller, Bullock traveled all over Texas to meet professors at minority colleges and ask them to recommend their best graduating seniors. Bullock wrote personal letters to the graduates, inviting them to apply at his agency.

Bullock is state government's premier idea man. The high-speed rail is called the "Bullock Train" because of his unswerving support. He was the first to propose revising the state's antiquated tax system. He took a state financial agency with employees who didn't even have calculators and turned it into a state-of-the-art operation. He conducted a comprehensive audit of state government to find ways to eliminate waste and improve efficiency. The audit was so successful that $5.2 billion was created in savings and new revenue, which ironically may have scuttled another controversial Bullock idea: a state income tax.

It's not unusual for staffers to arrive early in the morning to find messages from Bullock already on their answering machines — ideas called in during the middle of the night. That's not to say Bullock never relaxes; he has sent invitations for a picnic on his grave after his expiration. Bullock even has a hobby — making gun shell casings at home.

Texas Monthly in July 1991 explained why no one in Texas politics is as feared as Bob Bullock:

> The combination of an explosive temper, a disdain for conventional civility, and an insatiable appetite for inside information acts as a shield for Bullock. No one wants to go through the hell of taking him on. "He looks at you, and you think, 'He *knows!*'" says a House member. His thirst for information led senators to insist on a provision in the ethics bill requiring lobbyists to disclose their fees. He rebuked a senator for going home on a Friday, even though the senate was not in session, and harassed lobbyists for interfering with his program. "I'm doing the talking," he snapped at one who was trying to explain that he hadn't said what Bullock thought he had said. During a meeting to iron out differences between the senate and Attorney General Dan Morales over who would defend the senate redistricting plan in court, Bullock got toe-to-toe with Morales, patted him derisively on the cheek, and said, according to an eyewitness, "You skinny-assed son-of-a-bitch, you're squealing like a pig stuck under a gate."
>
> Bullock is a driven man. Lack of sleep and a fondness for guz-

zling coffee make him perpetually moody and irascible. He has lived almost twenty years on one lung while continuing to smoke habitually. But there is another side to Bob Bullock. As he gaveled the regular session to a close at midnight one Memorial Day, he said with great feeling, "God bless Texas." One rarely hears that kind of talk around the Capitol anymore.

Amen.

EDWARD A. CLARK

Secretary of State 1937–1939
Ambassador to Australia 1965–1968
Hidden Governor of Texas?

☆ ☆ ☆

"Give us back the days when time was marching on instead of running out."

One-liner prayer by the Senate Chaplain, Dr. Gerald Mann

TEXAS LUSTER

· Personified the old power equation of Texas politics.
· LBJ owed a lot to Clark . . . named him ambassador to Australia.
· Wore a yellow rose in his buttonhole while ambassador to Australia, sometimes had them flown in, packed in Texas ice!
· Had 850 yellow rose bushes on the embassy grounds in Australia.
· His folksy manner and penchant for colorful storytelling initially earned him the sobriquet "Mr. Ed" in Australia.
· Tried to see every one of Australia's three million square miles while he was ambassador there.
· "Kingpin of Lobbyists" with homespun demeanor and manner of speaking.
· 16th floor of the Austin Hotel was his!

☆ ☆ ☆

In 1927, Ed Clark borrowed $150 and came to Austin from San Augustine to seek his fortune. He wound up a successful banker, attorney, ambassador, and "the kingpin of lobbyists," instrumental in passing some of Texas' most important laws, including legislation which significantly restricted labor unions, declaring them monopolies. Active in Democratic party politics since the early 1930s, Clark served as secretary of state under James Allred and was enormously influential in the political careers of Governor Price Daniel, U.S. Senator John Tower, and President Lyndon B. Johnson, among others.

Not above "negative campaigning" tactics, Clark took an active role in his support for Price Daniel in the 1964 gubernatorial race between Daniel and John Connally. Clark reportedly hired a black man to dress in a fancy suit and drive a big, expensive new car throughout rural, poverty-stricken East Texas, buying $2 worth of gasoline at each gas station he came upon. Prominently displayed on that big new car was a John Connally bumper sticker.

Clark's relationship to Lyndon Johnson dated back to the mid-1930s, when Clark, whose law firm had served as attorney for the Lyndon Johnson family for many years, handled LBJ's 1937 congressional campaign. In 1948, when Johnson was elected to the Senate in a close and disputed contest, a legal battle ensued, resulting from charges of vote-rigging and claims that Johnson had no right to run for Senate office while he was still a congressman. During this controversy, Clark acted as Johnson's senior legal counsel. "A lot of people think Ed owed a great deal . . . to LBJ," said one family friend at the time. "In fact, the truth is probably the opposite. Lyndon owed more to Clark than he could ever pay back."

Perhaps in return for Clark's thirty years of loyal friendship and counsel, then-President Johnson appointed Clark U.S. ambassador to Australia in 1965. His appointment became the target of a good deal of criticism; the general impression was that Clark was an overly jovial extrovert who had blundered into the position solely because of his close friendship with Johnson. An Australian newspaperman commented on Clark's direct line to LBJ when he recalled a meeting with the newly appointed ambassador in a crowded Canberra airport lounge. Clark remarked to the reporter, in his famous Texan drawl, "Y'know, I was talkin' 'smornin' to the president, and . . . ." The journalist described a hush as 500 people craned forward to hear what the president of the United States had been thinking. "Whatever it was, it was pretty insignificant," said the reporter. "But when Mister Ed decides to drop a name, he does it from a great height."

Clark's folksy manner and penchant for colorful storytelling ini-

Ed Clark, LBJ's ambassador to Australia. Rode the Democratic "Steer for Texas."

— Austin History Center

tially drew ridicule from the Australian press, thus earning him the nickname of "Mr. Ed." It wasn't long, however, before he'd proved himself to be a shrewd operator and a diligent worker. During his ambassadorship, Clark reportedly averaged a formal speech every five days and continually criss-crossed the three million square miles of Australia, determined to spread as much goodwill as possible. He defended his commitment to his new position by boasting, "There may be a question about the quality of my work — but, dammit, they can't question the quantity!"

In these numerous public appearances, the flamboyant, 200-pound diplomat almost always wore a yellow rose pinned to his lapel. He'd planted 850 yellow rose bushes in his ten-acre gardens at the embassy, and when these were out of season, he reportedly went to extraordinary lengths to keep up the supply, even having them flown, packed in ice, from Texas. Some accused Clark of being the ambassador for Texas rather than the ambassador for the United States. He replied, "That reminds me of the guy who threw a rock at a cat and hit his mother-in-law. It ain't so bad after all."

Clark once addressed his trademark "downhome" delivery. "I used to say that I didn't want to go any place where there was a language barrier," he said. "But my wife, a little unkindly, said, 'Let's face it, honey, wherever you go with that Southern accent, you gonna wind up with a language barrier.' " Clark's homespun demeanor and apparently endless supply of cracker-barrel, Texas-flavored stories once prompted an observer to comment to legislator Pearce Johnson, "You see that son-of-a-bitch over there?," gesturing toward Ed Clark. "That son-of-a-bitch has accumulated more ignorance than anybody I know."

Clark was appointed executive director of the Inter-American Development Bank in Washington, D.C., and was on the Arms Control and Disarmament Agency committees. For six years he was a University of Texas System regent and was a trustee of both Southwestern University in Georgetown and the University of Texas Law School Foundation. He was instrumental in raising millions of dollars for both institutions. He and his late wife donated their 24,000-volume collection of Texana to Southwestern in 1965.

Clark died on September 16, 1992, and the *Austin American-Statesman* reported that at least a thousand people attended the funeral of this legendary statesman.

FRANK ERWIN

University of Texas Board of Regents 1963–1975

☆ ☆ ☆

"We thank you that there's nothing wrong with the younger generation that becoming taxpayers won't cure."
One-liner prayer by the Senate Chaplain, Dr. Gerald Mann

TEXAS LUSTER

· From Waxahachie to Forty Acres . . . Club Scholz, Quorum Club, Headliners Club, etc.
· Lobbied for UT for $10 per year. All he did was:
   increase appropriations from $77 million (1965) to $427 million (1975) — a 453 percent growth;
   act as lead horse in creating LBJ Library, Erwin Center, Memorial Museum, Performing Arts Center, Swim Center, enlarged stadium, etc.;
   help develop one of the best combined academic and athletic programs whichever way you look!

Frank Erwin
— Senate Media Services

· Founder of the Longhorn Club.
· Called Chairman Frank, Big Orange, Emperor, Czar, Poncho Vermin, and a "brilliant, arrogant, imperious storybook villain!"
· A Kappa Sig driver of brightest orange and white on anybody's main street.
· Keeping him quiet was akin to storing gasoline in a tow sack!
· Truly a disciple of LBJ in the belief that you should avoid making permanent enemies 'cause they may someday be your friends.

· Paid no heed to bumper stickers, "Pray for Rosemary's baby and Frank Erwin."
· Died without a will but must have gotten through all right 'cause there is a big orange in the sky most every night.

☆　☆　☆

The name Frank Erwin is legendary in Texas educational and political circles. During Erwin's twelve years on the University of Texas Board of Regents, from 1963 to 1975, the student body increased from 22,000 to 41,500; the annual legislative appropriation rose from $77 million to $427 million; and the average faculty salary rose 112 percent. The Austin campus was the site of fifty-five major building projects valued at more than a quarter of a billion dollars, and the UT System was established, which literally spans the state of Texas.

There was a controversy or two along the way, of course. In fact, Erwin ruefully admitted, he was introduced so often as the "controversial chairman of the Board of Regents" he thought the word was part of the title. Erwin, in fact, had numerous appellations, some respectful and others irreverent. UT administrators and staff generally addressed him as "The Chairman" (he was chairman of the Board of Regents for five years). His (Kappa Sig) fraternity brothers called him the "Big Orange" for his enthusiastic and loyal support of Longhorn athletics, and *Time Magazine* once called him the "Emperor of UT." To his detractors, he was "Czar Erwin," and *The Daily Texan,* the student newspaper, once referred to him as "Frank Vermin." The Austin campus itself was sometimes called "The University of Texas at Erwin."

How did one man garner so much power and notoriety in the operation of an institution as large as The University of Texas? It seems Erwin's love affair with UT began early, when the Waxahachie native entered the university as a freshman in 1937. He was an active student, pursuing interests in football and fraternity activities (serving as president of the Inter-Fraternity Council), and excelling academically as well. He graduated in 1941, served a four-year stint in the Navy during World War II, and returned to UT to attend law school, where he received his degree in 1948. Ranked in the top ten to fifteen percent of his class, Erwin joined an Austin law firm and quickly began to establish himself as a promising young attorney and civic leader, founding the Longhorn Club in 1949. In the early sixties, he became a member of John Connally's inner circle.

Erwin and Connally had been casual acquaintances at UT, but

their friendship primarily developed through state Democratic party politics after World War II. When Connally tapped him for the UT Board of Regents, Erwin had been serving as secretary of the State Democratic Executive Committee. A year later (1964), Connally asked him to assume the chairmanship of the committee. Erwin accepted. UT Student Republicans called for Erwin's resignation from the Board of Regents when the appointment was announced, charging that his new role would politicize the university. It was the first of several unsuccessful attempts to remove him from the Board.

In addition to having a close friend in the governor's chair, Erwin also benefited from Ben Barnes' election to the Texas House Speaker office. Erwin had befriended Barnes during Connally's 1962 gubernatorial campaign, and he was part of "Operation Blitzkrieg," the phone bank set up at the Driskill Hotel to rally support for the young Speaker candidate. According to Larry Temple, a close friend of Erwin's and a former gubernatorial aide to Connally, Barnes' election "really tied Frank into the legislature. It was a big, big plus for Frank's ability to get things done. He could always talk to Barnes. If he couldn't get something out of the Appropriations Committee, he would just go to Barnes and say, 'This is important.' "

Erwin utilized those powerful political connections to become one of the state's most influential lobbyists by the end of the sixties. His advocacy in the Capitol on behalf of the University of Texas began during the 1965 session. While many observers believed that Erwin's power was merely a projection of Connally's and Barnes' power, Erwin, while continuing to remain close to the governor and speaker, carefully nurtured friendships with other influential legislators as well. He would befriend them and drink with them late into the night at the Quorum or the Forty Acres Club. In the fall, he always had football tickets to distribute. Perhaps key to Erwin's success at the Capitol was his habit of acting with respect and deference to the members of the legislature. As Grover Campbell once recalled, "Erwin, no matter how much he'd had to drink, would always stand up for a member of the legislature whenever he came into the room."

The breadth of his knowledge about UT and the education budget was such that he could effectively explain the issues to lawmakers without being forced to rely on university administrators to fill in background and detail. "He got down and got his hands dirty with the politicians in order to get it done. Others before him had found it distasteful," explained lobbyist Howard Ross. Until Erwin's involvement, the UT system had not asserted itself politically, and many consider him the state's first activist for higher education. His efforts to encourage legislators to pump more funds into higher education helped to significantly improve financial support for public colleges and universities throughout the state. "They pulled money out of this state like you can't believe," observed one lobbyist. "Whatever higher education wanted, it got."

Erwin's phenomenal command of knowledge about UT catapulted him to chairmanship of the Board of Regents a mere two years after his appointment. Ordinarily a regent serves four years before anyone considers elevating him or her to chairman. Erwin ascended to a position of influence very rapidly, primarily because nobody understood more than he did or had the facts that he did. Other members realized that when he spoke, he knew what he was talking about because he had done his homework. He relinquished his chairmanship in 1971, but one observer commented, "Erwin was the de facto chairman — always was when he was on the board. It didn't matter if he didn't have the title, he had the power. He had the power because he always had the knowledge." One former president of a UT branch recalled a meeting during which Erwin began recounting statistical information from a report on minority student enrollments. "Frank Erwin started quoting statistics, and the only place those statistics appeared was in the appendix. So he had to have read the appendix to know them . . . He was thorough." Insiders acknowledged that one of Erwin's often-used strategies was to overwhelm his opponents with data, causing them to look unprepared or stupid.

In addition to his close ties with the state's political power structure, Erwin also had White House connections which were to serve the university well during the years of the Johnson administration. Erwin said a "warm personal and political friendship" developed between him and LBJ during the late 1950s, when Johnson was Senate majority leader. Through Connally, Erwin continued to have close ties with LBJ and was considered a Johnson intimate while he served on the Board of Regents. The university would benefit substantially from Erwin's ties with Johnson — federal funds flowed easily to UT. There would be assistance in obtaining federal grant funds, federal surplus property, and federal urban renewal projects. "Whenever we wanted something done, all we had to do was call the President's office," Erwin once remarked as he recounted the days of the Johnson administration. "We could get done by telephone calls to the White House what [the University of] California was having to maintain a twenty-person staff in Washington to do." Johnson's influence had been especially helpful in obtaining several million dollars in federal funds to support construction projects, including the Humanities Research Center. And Erwin was reportedly among those who helped to convince LBJ to build the Johnson presidential library in Austin at UT.

In fact, some see Erwin as the "architect" of the Austin campus, having been instrumental in transforming the original "Forty Acres" into the sprawling campus that exists today. Among the many buildings and expansions (besides the Humanities Research Center and the LBJ Library and Museum) which Erwin helped to create, there are: the Disch-Falk baseball stadium, the enlarged Memorial Stadium, the Texas Swimming Center, the Special Events Center (now called the Frank Erwin Center), the Perry-Castaneda Library, the Graduate School of Business Building, the expanded Chemistry Building, Belmont Hall, the Education Building, Jester Center, the Nursing Building, the LBJ School of Public Affairs Building, the three-building communications complex, and the Fine Arts and Performing Arts Center.

Perhaps an even greater accomplishment during Erwin's reign was the vigorous pursuit of an enlarged statewide focus for UT. It has been observed that in large measure, Erwin's rationale for seeking this broadened political base for UT stemmed from his commitment to one goal: preventing the breakup of the constitutionally mandated and very substantial Permanent University Fund. Regardless of the reasons, as a result of Erwin's efforts the UT System now includes fourteen branches across the state, and the Permanent University Fund, at the time of Erwin's death in 1980, was valued at $1.1 billion, second only to Harvard University's endowments.

Erwin could certainly have never been accused of being a regent who failed to devote the necessary time to his responsibility, nor was he afraid to become involved. Erwin unstintingly devoted himself to the UT System; his efforts, however, often were fraught with controversy. Part of the reason for the controversy lay in the times themselves — his tenure spanned the tumultuous years of student activism and the antiwar movement. While ties to the White House had proved helpful financially, those connections were not without liability politically. As the Vietnam War escalated and became increasingly unpopular, LBJ's ties with the university contributed to some extent to student unrest on the campus. As one professor pointed out, "UT Austin was 'Lyndon Johnson's back yard.' " On one occasion in 1968 when Erwin accompanied Johnson to a function on campus, a crowd of students gathered in protest. Erwin made the following statement: "I am disturbed because a bunch of dirty nothin's can disrupt the workings of a great University in the name of academic freedom. When it comes to the point where 300 armed policemen are needed to keep from embarrassing the President, we need to reexamine the goals of higher education." Students soon began sporting buttons that read, "I'm proud to be a dirty nuthin'."

Erwin did not hesitate to take the heat from the students and faculty for his hardline stands against student demonstrations and other disruptions to the university. As he once boasted, "I've never run from controversy or from anything else." In 1969, at the height of student activism, the regent overcame what was expected to be a difficult confirmation battle for a second six-year term. His reappointment, however, caused one fellow regent to resign in frustration and much consternation among students.

One of the most infamous examples of Erwin's tough stance against student protests was the Waller Creek incident. In 1969 students and environmentalists were concerned about the impact of the $15.6-million, 15,000-seat expansion of UT's Memorial Stadium. The creek would be rerouted and about forty stately old oaks, cypresses, and willows would be cut. On the day the land was to be cleared, protesters climbed the trees and clung to the limbs, warning, "If you take these trees, you take us." While UT President Norman Hackerman pondered how to handle the situation, Erwin acted. Remove the trees, he directed the construction crew, and ignore whatever falls out of them. As the machinery moved in, the protesters scrambled down. When Erwin was asked whether Hackerman had authorized his action, he replied, "Hell, I can't wait on the university administration. Some things have to be done right now!" As the trees fell, Erwin applauded. One protester observed years later, "In the entire history of Texas, a place where being an S.O.B. is a respected art form, there are few finer examples of arrogance on the rampage than Erwin clapping his hands as the trees fell." Some reports say, however, that Erwin may not have relished his role as much as his actions suggested. At the Forty Acres Club that night, he reportedly drank more than his usual amount of scotch while playing "I Did It My Way" and "Is That All There Is?" on the jukebox. Nevertheless, faculty and students were incensed. Within a week, the faculty asked for Erwin's resignation. They didn't get it.

As the campus became increasingly polarized in the late sixties, faculty were allied with students on many of the issues of the day. Erwin openly disapproved of "radical" faculty members and was accused of having had a hand in the dismissal of a few. He sought to assure state lawmakers that radical faculty would not be employed by having a rider inserted in both the House and Senate versions of the 1969 appropriations bill that prevented any state-supported university from hiring revolutionaries. One professor recalled something that Erwin once told him: "You can say anything you goddamned want in that classroom, and I'll protect you. You can leave the campus and say any goddamned thing you want as long as you do not say anything about the University of Texas, and I'll protect you. But whatever you say anywhere on the campus of the University of Texas, you are saying on *my* territory. And I've got your balls in the palm of my hand. And if I don't like what you say, I'll squeeze. And if you don't shut up, I'll rip 'em off."

The most publicized case of Erwin's interference with the hiring and firing of faculty was the 1970 dismissal of Dean John Silber of the College of Arts and Sciences. According to insiders, Silber's crime was not inciting revolutionary behavior in students, but rather the accumulation of too much power. The dean had established the Arts and Sciences Foundation and had embarked on a fund-raising campaign throughout the state. "Meet the Dean" forums were held in Houston, Dallas, and Fort Worth. These events were sometimes hundred-dollar-a-plate affairs, and one of the most notable was held at Dallas' Brook Hollow Country Club. The estimated aggregate wealth of those in attendance was said to have been about $2 billion. Erwin was irate when the Arts and Sciences faculty only a week later urged enrollment limitations. He reportedly told regents, "When a college starts talking about limiting enrollment it's time to break up that college, and when a dean starts talking to country clubs, it's time to fire the dean." Erwin dismissed faculty concerns about unmanageable enrollment numbers; he felt that UT had an obligation to be accessible to all citizens of the state. He did not want the university to become an elite institution. (Some believed that his real reason for opposing enrollment limitations was his law partners' involvement in properties west of campus whose profits depended on large student enrollment.)

Regardless of the reasons, Erwin resolved the situation with Silber by calling a Friday afternoon meeting and telling the dean that he was going to have to leave the university. "If I'm going to be fired from the deanship, when is it going to happen?" Silber asked. The chairman answered: "Just about the time that I cross this threshold out into the hall." The public was not silent on the firing of Silber. Whereas some faculty members were said to have been relieved at the news, one alumnus wrote: "Apparently, Erwin would be content to transform the University of Texas into nothing more than an educationally inferior 'football school,' so long as he maintained personal control of it."

In the wake of the Silber firing, nine faculty members resigned, several of them among the most distinguished in their fields. One resigning professor charged that Erwin had "ruthlessly invaded" faculty autonomy and complained: "A university of 40,000 students and several thousand faculty and staff has become through political chicanery and abusive power, the personal property of one man." The following year, a state representative called for Erwin's immediate resignation from the Board of Regents, citing "the political and psychological domination of Erwin and his lack of restraint in public utterance." The legislator contended that Erwin was causing UT to lose its best professors and depriving students of their teaching. The representative was denied permission to read the resolution in the House.

It seems that Erwin viewed faculty and administrators as "hired hands" working for the Board and for the citizens of Texas. One UT official remarked, "I don't think it's different for other campuses. Frank Erwin was just more vocal, more effective, and more forceful." As Joe Frantz pointed out in his book *Forty Acre Follies,* Erwin "never learned the difference between broad policy and daily operation. A regent sets policy; Frank Erwin set policy, but he interfered in the president's office, in the deans' offices, in the chairmen's offices, in the professors' operations, and, for all I know, in the way the janitors mopped the floors."

In fact, after Erwin's wife June Carr died in 1967, friends said he devoted increasing amounts of time to the university. He "prowled the Forty Acres from sunup until past midnight. No one ever displayed such restless devotion," wrote one historian. In fact, Erwin was said to call Monday mornings (after scouting the campus on Sunday) to ask that various tasks be initiated, such as cleaning dirty windows or other maintenance chores. On weekdays, Erwin would go from office to office, talking with various administrators on the Austin campus and at the UT system. When UT President Hackerman was away on outside consulting activities, Erwin, clearly irritated by Hackerman's absence, would stop at the president's office and leave a note that read: "Norman, you weren't here today and I wanted you."

Erwin's dedication to UT was relentless. During legislative sessions, he frequently would be out lobbying until the wee hours at the Quorum or Forty Acres, then head for his office afterwards to draft legislation for the next day, and would be up the next morning by 8:00 or 8:30 because the telephone would be ringing. Erwin was, in fact, renowned for his long nights of holding court at the Forty Acres Club or the Quorum Club and consuming great quantities of scotch and water. Twice in the 1970s, he was arrested for drunken driving. One night Erwin, Howard Ross, and Bill Barton left the Forty Acres Club at 2:30 or 3:00 A.M. in Erwin's signature burnt orange Cadillac. Erwin insisted they come to his house for a nightcap. Barton said Erwin also insisted on driving. As they headed down 24th Street, a police car stopped them. Recognizing the orange Cadillac, the officer said, "Mr. Erwin, I don't think you are in any condition to drive." Erwin pointed out that his house was just a few blocks up the street, but the officer wouldn't budge. He turned to Ross and asked him if he could drive. *"Suuuure,"* Ross said. The policeman opened the door for Ross, who promptly fell face forward onto the pavement. Deciding that he should perhaps try to keep a lower profile, Erwin had his orange Cadillac painted black the next day. Erwin's DWI trials made history, as each was held on a change of venue. In one trial, his defense lawyer argued that Erwin stayed out late, not to drink, but because he was "a lonely widower looking for someone to have Mexican food with." This excuse for staying out late was reportedly a household phrase for a while.

Erwin decided not to seek a third term on the Board of Regents in 1975. Many said it was because he knew he would not be reappointed by Governor Dolph Briscoe, with whom he had somewhat chilly relations. One legislator pointed out that Erwin's influence — as well as that of the UT System in general — declined to some extent in legislative circles after Briscoe's election in 1973. But Erwin still maintained considerable influence, as demonstrated by Representative Herman Adams who, deliberating over a particular legislative vote, told his aide, "I've got to vote either with Governor Briscoe or Frank Erwin. I'm going to make one of them real mad . . . I'm going with Erwin."

After stepping down from the Board, Erwin became an unpaid lobbyist for the university, laboring especially to protect the Permanent University Fund from being divided among other schools in the state. In 1979 the UT Board, realizing that the Permanent University Fund would be reconsidered during an upcoming legislative session, hired Erwin as the UT System special counsel for legislation at a salary of $10 per year. When Chairman Allan Shivers was asked about the decision, he admitted to the press that it would probably be better if the UT System could get along without the former regent's services, "but we just don't have anyone as capable." As a university employee, Erwin would not be required to register with the secretary of state as an official lobbyist — even though his role differed little from other lobbyists.

Because of the intense criticism he had come under from students, Erwin, in the last year of his life, found it gratifying when a group of students initiated efforts to establish an endowment in his honor. Despite his continuing harangues against them, Erwin was sentimental about UT students. "I regret the fact that there are people who graduated from the University who hate my guts . . . it's kind of sad," he had said near the end of his tenure on the Board. Gifts to the endowment honoring Frank Erwin surpassed $1 million. Two endowed chairs were established at the Austin campus and seven Erwin professorships were established with matching funds. And a Headliners' roast was given in his honor in 1978 with such political heavyweights as Allan Shivers, Ben Barnes, Bob Bullock, and Barbara Jordan delivering speeches about Erwin.

Erwin died in 1980, and while one detractor lamented his death with the wry remark, "We won't have Frank Erwin to kick us around anymore," some 2,000 people attended funeral services honoring the departed former regent at the Special Events Center (now the Frank Erwin Center) on the UT campus. John Connally delivered a twenty-minute eulogy and the Longhorn Band played a solemn "The Eyes of Texas" in honor of the man who, despite his sometimes questionable tactics, had surely done more for The University of Texas and higher education than anyone else in the history of the state.

(See "Headliners Roast of Frank Erwin" in final section of this book.)

WILLIAM PETTUS HOBBY, JR.

Lieutenant Governor of Texas 1973–1990

☆   ☆   ☆

"Our Father, give us the grace to think twice before we say nothing."
One-liner prayer by the Senate Chaplain, Dr. Gerald Mann

TEXAS LUSTER

- Lieutenant governor of Texas for eighteen years, wielding more constitutional power than the governor.
- A soft-spoken, patrician millionaire in a bow tie — so unexcitable he "dropped the meaning of low-key by several octaves."
- Sent Texas State Teachers Association packing and called the business lobby "a bunch of idiots."
- Often forgot to pick up his $2 certificate of election.
- According to Mark White, everybody wanted Hobby's job, but at $7,200 a year, "damn few could afford it."
- Went up against governor Bill Clements during 1987 legislative session . . . Session's theme song: "You can't always get what you want . . ."
- Wrote the foreword for this book!

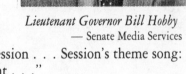

Lieutenant Governor Bill Hobby
— Senate Media Services

☆   ☆   ☆

Bill Hobby served in the office of lieutenant governor for eighteen years, longer than any other person elected to it. When he was first sworn into office in 1973, Hobby continued a family association with state government that extended back more than a century. His grandfather, Edwin Hobby, had been a state senator, and his father, William Pettus Hobby, Sr., had served as lieutenant governor and governor of Texas.

Bill Hobby was born into a publishing empire as well as politics. The Hobby family owned *The Houston Post* for many years, as well as several TV stations; their media fortune was estimated in 1990 to be worth $650 million. The family's wealth once prompted former Governor Mark White to remark about Hobby, "I've probably sipped out of the same silver cup he has. The difference is, he owned it." White added that everyone wanted Hobby's lieutenant governor job, but with a salary of $7,200 a year, "damn few can afford it."

Hobby entered state government as Senate parliamentarian in 1959, and served in several state and federal posts before being elected lieutenant governor. Early on, Hobby built a power base in the legislature for trimming the number of standing committees and appointing key people to the nine remaining committees. During his tenure as lieutenant governor, Hobby was instrumental in the passage of House Bill 72, which changed Texas education with its provision for no pass/ no play, the worker's compensation bill, and particularly the restructuring of the state budget process.

He uncharacteristically flip-flopped on the much publicized ethics reform issue. Initially he announced his stand against ethics legislation, which required disclosure of business ties and investments, then reversed his position after the Sharpstown scandal broke. While detractors accused Hobby of blocking the passage of ethics legislation because of political rivalry with ethics bill spearheader Price Daniel, Jr. (both of whom seemed headed for the governor's office), his defenders claimed the lieutenant governor simply felt that it was wrong to enforce ethical standards. Longtime observer and journalist Bo Byers defended Hobby's position: "It's not that he doesn't care about ethics. His thinking is: 'I'm ethical, but I'm not going to tell other people how to be ethical.'" Many ethics reform supporters, however, complained that by the end of Hobby's tenure, little had changed. Those supporters cited flagrant vote-buying in the summer of 1989, when chicken packing house owner Lonnie "Bo" Pilgrim sauntered through Hobby's Senate, passing out $10,000 checks to senators who would listen to his ideas on the worker's compensation insurance law.

With the possible exception of the ethics reform issue, Hobby has managed to stay out of political scandal — a remarkable feat for a three-decade-long career in government. Many attribute his relatively unsullied image to a patrician manner and a reserved, nonconfrontational style. Hobby's sedate pace prompted one writer to note, "He's so unexcitable he's dropped the meaning of low-key by several octaves." Credited with speaking in eloquent paragraphs instead of "30-second sound bites," Hobby has been described as having a healthy desire for political office without the often accompanying lust for it. In fact, at election time, Hobby reportedly often forgot to pick up his $2 certificate of election.

While maintaining an attitude of calm control, Hobby seemed to inspire a love-hate relationship with those outside the legislature. One day he was praised, the next he was denigrated. *Texas Monthly* criticized some of his faux pas in their Top Ten list of 1985. "His main weakness is his indifference to the details of issues, which sometimes leaves him blind to impending trouble, and his how-ya-doin', good-ol' boy tendencies, which make him at times an easy caricature." However, a 1989 *Texas Monthly* article recognized Hobby's contribution to the office with the observation that "Bill Hobby has had more effect on Texas government for a longer time with a better end result than anyone since Sam Houston."

During Hobby's last term in office, he endured a somewhat antagonistic relationship with then-Governor Bill Clements. Aides commented that Hobby publicly castigated Clements for vetoing a bill that would have added prison space, and their relationship remained strained for the rest of the legislative session. When Hobby endorsed a spending bill that required $3.1 billion in new taxes above Clements' bottom line, political observers suggested that Clements took the size of the Senate bill as a personal affront and an indication that Hobby did not take him seriously. Clements vetoed the bill, and the theme music for the slide show the Senate staff presented on the final night was appropriately "You Can't Always Get What You Want."

It wasn't the first time that Hobby had gone up against some political heavyweights. In 1982 George Strake tried branding Hobby a liberal, but he pulled down that unlikely line before the final stretch. Feeling pressure because Strake had attracted a following, Hobby responded by conducting an all-out campaign, combining forces with Bentsen and White, who all benefited from the liberal down-ballot candidates who had built their own followings and thus strengthened their entire ticket. The situation had its paradoxical side. Some conservative contributors were pouring their money behind Clements,

Bentsen, and Hobby — with the money going to Bentsen and Hobby being used, in effect, to defeat Clements. All the factors had melded together to form a Democratic juggernaut with a full head of steam that was rolling across the Texas political landscape in October of 1982 (Knaggs, *Two Party Texas*).

Despite the lieutenant governor's laconic, reserved manner, he was not incapable of fighting when it was required of him. He proved that in 1984 with the powerful Texas State Teachers Association (TSTA). He reportedly booted the TSTA from his office when the group balked at House Bill 72's required tests for teachers. "He told them to pack their bags and get out of the office and never come back," said one senator who attended the meeting. "It was the second Alamo." And on the eve of a final battle over worker's compensation in 1989, Hobby called the business lobby "a bunch of idiots" for wanting more changes of benefit to them than a majority of the legislature could deliver.

Longtime friend of Hobby and dean of the LBJ School of Public Affairs at The University of Texas, Max Sherman, explained the lieutenant governor's approach to government: "He's a very secure person. He doesn't require accolades," Sherman remarked. "His main purpose is to get the job done." Hobby's commitment to good government earned him an unprecedented four (four-year) reelections to the lieutenant governor post, an office that some claimed was, if not more powerful, at least as powerful as the governor's. Although he did not follow his father's path and progress to the governor's office, many speculate that when Lloyd Bentsen eventually vacates his longtime post as U.S. senator, Hobby will be a likely successor.

GIBSON D. "GIB" LEWIS

House of Representatives 1971–Present
Speaker of the House 1983–Present

☆ ☆ ☆

"Deliver us from politicians who make nothing happen very slowly."
One-liner prayer by the Senate Chaplain, Dr. Gerald Mann

THE WORLD ACCORDING TO GIB:

- "There's a lot of uncertainty that's not clear in my mind."
- His daily briefings were known as "Gib-Gab."
- The nation's capital is located in the "District of Columbus."
- An attempt to amend the Texas Constitution is "one of those things that sounds good and tastes bad."
- In trying out a new budget approach, you sometimes have to "run it up the flagpole and see who salutes that booger."
- In their efforts to "budget the balance," lawmakers are often forced to "not only cut out the fat, we cut out a lot of meat."
- On some votes in the House, "the record reflects itself."

Gib Lewis,
Speaker of the House
(1983–1991).
Senate Media Services

- Sometimes you have to "turn over the first rock" to expose a "sacred cow."
- Considering that the state has a $46 billion budget, the amount of money it would take to give lawmakers a pay increase "would not even be a pimple on a frog."

- Reporters who wrote about the stocking of his ranch with game furnished by the Texas Parks and Wildlife Department were reporting lies and "any-u-windows" (innuendoes).
- He said, "Here it was my first day in office and I was already declared a crook" (because of the Sharpstown scandal).
- "I want this ethics issue dissolved."
- Lewis told reporters, "I don't carry a grudge. If I did, I wouldn't talk to any of you guys."
- "I rent these lips on Mondays, and by Friday noon they're worn out," Lewis said when explaining his malapropisms.
- When reporters ask him "what-if" questions, he responds, "If, if, if — if a frog had a gun he could shoot snakes."
- Perhaps the most famous "gibberish" was the time Mr. Lewis acknowledged a group of disabled people visiting the house gallery. Without thinking, he invited the group — many of them in wheelchairs — to "stand and be recognized."

FAVORITE EXPRESSIONS:

- "I don't have a dog in that fight."
- "If you think you've found someone who gives a damn, you're wrong."
- "Let the big dog eat" — that is, the side that can get the most votes wins.

☆   ☆   ☆

Gib Lewis entered politics in 1969 with his election to the River Oaks City Council. At the time, he was a business-oriented activist in the Fort Worth Jaycees. A native of Limestone County, he had settled in Fort Worth in 1958 after serving in the Air Force. A member of the House since 1971, in the early 1980s Gib Lewis was bored and burned out, telling his staff at a party at his apartment that he would be quitting politics. Instead, he said, they insisted that he seek the Speaker's job. No one told him no. And Speaker Bill Clayton himself insisted that Lewis run.

Lewis was elected by a landslide in 1983, then returned to the chair in 1985, 1987, 1989, and 1991. Rarely did a governor, state official, or fellow legislator criticize or even challenge his leadership, which sometimes was masterful and almost always shrewd.

Throughout his nine years as Speaker, Lewis demonstrated impressive powers of persuasion and bulldog-like determination, both qualities of leadership necessary in anyone who undertakes the thankless job of melding the 150-member, bipartisan House into a cohesive unit that will work together in any semblance of cooperation and harmony.

Neal T. "Buddy" Jones, who served as Lewis' top adviser in his first two terms as Speaker, said Lewis had a knack for turning disagreements into discussions that led to deals. Often he would do so by having warring parties meet behind closed doors that Lewis wouldn't open until a middle ground was found.

Lewis prefers to have others work deals out and bring them to him for enforcement — an approach that worked for tort reform and trucking deregulation but not for the budget.

Some members said Lewis lacked a farsighted agenda. "That was one of his strengths as well as possibly his only weakness. His grand vision for the whole state was to let 150 separate districts create state policy," Buddy Jones said.

Retiring House Speaker Gib Lewis has about $1 million amassed in three political accounts, even as supporters are soliciting donations for him. State law might allow Lewis to convert hundreds of thousands of dollars from his accounts to personal use.

Lewis "has the ethical sensitivity of a walnut," according to columnist Molly Ivins.

In the often tense and tumultuous final days of every session, Lewis would quietly order air conditioners turned down to frosty. "I'd tell them to keep ice cold," Lewis chuckled. "If it's cold, people have a tendency not to get so mad or let their tempers get the best of them."

Although often at odds with the Capitol Press Corps, which he called "the wolf pack," Lewis liked most of the reporters and generally they liked him. Of course, they criticized him constantly for his miscues. News stories suggested he played fast and loose with ethics rules.

Reporters covering the Capitol in 1992 were being buzzed, pecked, and dive-bombed by a rowdy grackle that nested in a tree nearby. During a lull in his daily news conference, Gib Lewis joked with reporters about the grackles. "I have been training them for quite some time to attack reporters, and one of them has learned very well," Lewis said. When he was told that the bird drew blood pecking one particularly aggressive reporter, Lewis quipped, "That's the one I spent the most time with."

Although Lewis is frequently described by the press as all-powerful, ruling by fear and intimidation to advance the cause of the lobby, the truth is far removed from the image. He is less involved in the day-to-day business of legislation than any Speaker in memory. That is just fine with the other 149 members, who enjoy the fruits of the Machiavellian dictum that the weaker the prince, the stronger the barons. Lewis was reelected Speaker without opposition precisely because the rank-and-file member — the sort of person who *can* be ruled by fear and intimidation — knows that he is better off under Lewis than he would be under a more involved Speaker. He is the kind of politician who would rather be liked than respected.

When asked if he would miss the power of being Speaker, Lewis said he always had the philosophy that if you abuse the power, you lose the power: "And that's why the membership overwhelmingly reelected me." He said the best vote of his legislative career was in favor of a bill allowing Texas motorists to make a right turn on red.

Conventional Capitol wisdom held that Bullock and the Senate would run over the House and its weakened Speaker, Gib Lewis, who was awaiting trial on misdemeanor ethics charges. But Lewis' legal troubles had an unforeseen effect. Eager to avoid accusations that he was strong-arming the House, Lewis delegated all the major issues — ethics, education, insurance reform — to his lieutenants. The more power Lewis delegated, the more the House liked him, and the Speaker actually ended the session stronger than he had begun it. Senators angry at the House for burying Bullock's proposal for a natural resources agency looked for Lewis' pet legislative agenda to retaliate against, but of course there wasn't any. The House was too decentralized to be run over by the Senate.

One day after House Speaker Gib Lewis was convicted of two misdemeanor ethics crimes and fined $2,000, he received lavish praise from a group of Texas businesspeople for supporting their causes during his eleven years as Speaker. "You, Mr. Speaker, have been a true friend, and we certainly appreciate it," Larry Milner, president of the Texas Chamber of Commerce, told Lewis at the breakfast meeting.

When asked what he thought about the ethics investigation against him, Lewis said, "They're stomping on ants in the basement while the elephants are stampeding on the first floor."

Gib Lewis has always been a glad-hander with a gift for malapropisms. He developed a fierce group of friends, in part because he was considered bipartisan and fair. He successfully presided over the House during the discrediting ethics investigation by marching in lockstep with Governor Ann Richards, by remembering old allies, and by using his own style of one-on-one persuasion — some would call it "arm-twisting" — when the votes weren't there.

"Gib has got to be the most investigated person in recent Texas history . . . They've talked to friends, enemies, everyone — and if he was as bad as they said he was earlier, I'm sure they would've found something by now," said Lewis' attorney, Bill Willms. Lewis himself said in October 1991, "I would not tell anybody to run for public office. I think it is absolutely ridiculous what public officials are subjected to."

"Entertainment ranks higher with Gib than legislation," says a prominent lobbyist. Under Lewis' predecessor, Billy Clayton, the House frequently worked into the night. Under Lewis, the House adjourns early for legislative golf tournaments. He rows on Town Lake in the early morning, and legislators who want to be insiders have learned to be there too. He loves trips, especially hunting trips. He loves seeing members display their loyalty on their lapels by wearing a tiny, Texas-shaped pin with "Gib" written on it.

A newcomer was at his seat on the floor of the Texas House of Representatives when a handwritten note arrived. "Hello. I'm Mary Jane," it began. "I'm from your district, and I'm a supporter and an admirer of yours. I'm up here in the gallery today, wearing a yellow dress. I would like to see you tonight. If you can meet me, just stand up and casually adjust your tie."

Turning ever so slightly, the freshman legislator spotted the yellow dress at once. It was worn by a voluptuous brunette. He arose slowly, grappling with his tie.

He did not see his colleagues eyeing him. But, too late, he did hear their laughter. Texas House Speaker Gib Lewis and his buddies had struck again.

If Speaker Gib Lewis wants appointment to the Parks and Wildlife board when he leaves the Texas House of Representatives, he did not hurt his chances by helping out Governor Ann Richards in the politically delicate task of deciding which of the thirteen state schools for the mentally retarded should be shut down as part of the settlement of a long-running lawsuit. When Richards marked the Fort Worth State School for closure instead of the Mexia State School, which a task force had recommended, Lewis agreed with the decision to save Limestone County's largest employer. Lewis grew up in Mexia, and his mother still lives there.

BILL HEATLY

House 1955–1982

☆ ☆ ☆

"Teach us that we can't be delivered until we pay the postage."
One-liner prayer by the Senate Chaplain, Dr. Gerald Mann

TEXAS LUSTER

· "The Duke of Paducah."
· Agreed that he was the hardest SOB around.
· His committee votes went in the right drawer for yes and left for no!
· Colorful, vibrant — did not shy from controversy.
· Took more than good care of his constituents!
· Played "you-got-yours-I-got-mine" politics.
· Record number of years as chairman of House Appropriations Committee.

☆ ☆ ☆

Bill Heatly, "The Duke of Paducah," was first elected to the legislature in 1954. By the time he retired in 1982, he had become the dean of the Texas House. During his unprecedented twelve years as chairman of the Appropriations Committee, Heatly never bothered to conceal the joy with which he wielded his immense power.

A legislator remembers how one day Heatly motioned him to come over. Heatly said, "I hear you said such and such about me to somebody." The legislator told him, "I have never said anything about you that I haven't said to your face, with one possible exception. I told somebody the other day that I believe that you are the hardest SOB I ever had any dealings with." Old Heatly sat there and said, "Well, hell, that's right."

Heatly's Appropriations Committee meeting room was an example of the method to his madness. The room was *only* large enough to contain tables and chairs for the members, so when the press came, they had to stand against the wall. He held those meetings on Saturday

afternoons to further deter the media.
One day Dean Cobb attended a
meeting of the Good Neighbor Commission, on which Heatly served as
well. Cobb, patiently biding his time
so he could go play golf, amused himself by observing the actions of the
main players on the committee. The
executive director of one of Heatly's
favored agencies was testifying on the
agency's budget request. If one was
educated in the operations of Heatly,
one would know that only a minimum amount of testimony would be
necessary, if one had done his homework with Heatly before the hearing.

The "Duke" had to leave to go to the
relief room, and while he was gone
the man testifying made it obvious

Bill Heatly,
the "Duke of Paducah."
— Courtesy Bill Malone

that he had little information and was not prepared to undergo extensive examination. Dick Slack, the vice-chairman, was getting more
and more provoked and was insisting more information was needed.
Just before Slack exploded, Heatly returned and kicked Slack plumb
hard on the shins as he sat down. Slack suddenly stopped and sat back
down, saying, "Never mind, I just had it explained to me."

Heatly had a quick wit and did not hesitate to use it. Oscar Carrillo was on the Good Neighbor Commission when Heatly attempted
to describe the commission's success with "our South American and
Mexican neighbors." He recounted how only that week there had been
some Guatemalans in Austin. Carrillo, who had been dozing, misunderstood and thought Heatly had said something about watermelons,
which just happened to be the main Guatemalan export. After a rather
incoherent and confusing comment from Carrillo, Heatly finally said,
"Whether it's watermelon or Guatemalan, you go back to sleep,
Oscar."

Provided that a member attended meetings regularly and stayed
awake, Heatly could be a valuable ally. A member who wanted a favor
would explain the situation to Heatly, who would then write something on a piece of paper. If he put the paper in the lower right-hand
drawer, the member didn't have to worry about anything; the request

would be included in the bill whether the House debated it or not. If he put it in the left drawer, it meant sure death!

Discipline committees of the State Bar of Texas are appointed by the bar director of each district. Heatly's son was on the discipline committee in Denton, and Heatly was dead set to get on the committee for Paducah. When I was executive director of the State Bar, he got on my back pretty good because I could not get this done. The bar director from Paducah said, "This would be like putting the fox in the hen house," and would not do this in spite of my belief that 'twas better to shut him down before bar legislation came under his rebuked eye.

Colorful and vibrant as Heatly was, and always keeping his constituency in mind as he did, Heatly of course did not shy from expressing his thoughts on legislation. In 1981 a newspaper reported that during the 1981 session, Heatly's last, he slipped in a $6.2 million bonus for a drug rehabilitation program in his rural West Texas district. Senators opposed it, reasonably enough, on the grounds that the drug problem is in the cities and that's where the money ought to be spent. That provoked a classic lesson on you-got-yours-I-get-mine politics, Heatly-style:

Heatly: As far as it bein' out in the boondocks, people out there need assistance, too.

Senator: Mr. Heatly, everybody in the state knows why it was put out there. It's because of you, Mr. Heatly.

Heatly: The same was done for you, that upper-level college you got.

Outflanked, the senator surrendered.

BILL MOORE

House of Representatives 1947–1948
Senate 1949–1980

☆   ☆   ☆

"Lord, let us remember that the Devil is always a gentleman,
he never goes where he ain't welcome."
One-liner prayer by the Senate Chaplain, Dr. Gerald Mann

TEXAS LUSTER

- Served in the Capitol for thirty-four years!
- "The Bull of the Brazos."
- An expert in grand jury timing.
- Counts his chips well!
- Made his fortune from the floor.
- Still missed from the "Bull's Pen."
- Almost threw a senator out the window!

☆   ☆   ☆

Known as "The Bull of the Brazos," Senator Bill Moore epito-
mized the "old southern cracker-barrel politician." In a word, Moore
was *colorful*. During a senatorial race against Joe Cannon, Moore said,
"Honesty is no substitute for experience. This li'l ole boy here, running against me, y'all don't know anything about him. But you take
me, I've been before the grand jury and cleared. He ain't never even
been before the grand jury. Vote for somebody that has already been
investigated and cleared."

Moore served his state for thirty-four years; only A. M. Aikin
served for a longer period. As John Knaggs, in his book *Two-Party
Texas,* said, "The 1981 loss of the venerable Bill Moore, Dean of the
Senate, had been a real shocker."

Bill Moore and Bill Patman hated each other. Patman's unmiti-
gated obtuseness on an issue caused Moore to exclaim, "Damn, Senator, I can explain it to you, but I can't *understand* it for you." On another occasion, Moore lost his temper and said, "Why, you young so-

The "Bull of the Brazos," Senator Bill Moore.

— Senate Media Services

and-so, you went out and married all your money. I got mine honest, right here on the floor of this Senate."

When Moore was new in the Senate, he was considered to be very liberal, and seemed always opposed to Hardeman and Lang. Hardeman hassled him unmercifully, and one night Moore took out after him. He yelled, "I'm coming up there and I'm going to grab you out of that chair and throw you out of that window." He was on his way to doing it, with Hazelwood raising the window, when he was restrained by John Dorman, the sergeant-at-arms, and his crew. Alas for the defenestration!

In an investigation of insurance fraud by a Waco insurance company, District Attorney Tom Moore subpoenaed the entire Texas Senate — Ben Ramsey too — to appear before the McLennan County Grand Jury. When "The Bull" went in he said to the press, "There ain't nothing to this. We'll only be in there five minutes." When asked a question by the grand jury he used the fifth amendment. The jury asked if that was to be his answer to every question, and he replied in the affirmative. He was excused and told the press waiting outside, "See, I told you — five minutes." He later made a campaign recommendation to the voters, "Vote for a man who has already been cleared by the grand jury."

On a South Texas deer hunt for state officials, he bunked with Judge Truman Roberts. After a half friendly poker game, Moore made it to his bunk with some assistance. When he awoke the next morning, there was a pile of poker chips on his heaving chest. In an effort to add excitement to the hunt, Judge Roberts observed that there were many more chips in front of him before he was ruled asleep at the table and hoisted to his bunk.

During the medicinal wake-up period, Moore tried to solve the mystery and the concern over the possible loss of a small fortune. His concern faded as ice brought newly revived optimism. He would later recall Judge Roberts as being a somewhat honest judge, but he is not sure about the judges seated at his right and left, and the sheriff who was across the table.

His favorite Ma Ferguson story concerns the wife of the notorious outlaw Raymond Hamilton. She came in barefooted, snuff running down her cheeks, with pillows stuffed in her dress as if she was pregnant, to talk about a pardon for her husband. She was taken to Governor Ma, who not only signed the pardon but reached in her purse and handed her ten dollars and began crying when the wronged mother left.

In talking about the power of the legislature to carve out districts for friends, he too had heard the story about drawing a district for Congressman "Tiger" Teague that stretched from Bryan to Fort Worth. It was said that the district was so narrow, if you drove a taxi from bottom to top and left the front doors open, he would kill ninety percent of the voters!

Yes, the loss of "The Bull" from the Senate has been a long-term shocker. He is missed from his "Bull's Pen." Who knows when he will roar again?

Washington Wranglers

LLOYD BENTSEN

U.S. Senator 1971–Present

☆ ☆ ☆

---

*"Remind us that the best way to starve our doubts —
is to feed our faith."*
One-liner prayer by the Senate Chaplain, Dr. Gerald Mann

TEXAS LUSTER

- When asked if he would run for president in 1992 (at the age of seventy-three), he joked that maybe he should wait and get a little more "maturity."
- Backed by the powerful Connally-Johnson machine, defeated George Bush in a race for Senate seat.
- Once called Texas politics a "contact sport."
- His image is considered so "stiff" by many that they claim he sleeps in a tux!
- Broke wife B.A.'s rib when he threw her over his shoulders in a playful ritual.
- Is he a liberal or a conservative? Cactus Pryor says, "Of course, Bentsen's a liberal. Just as I told that commie Barry Goldwater . . ."
- Famous for his "you're no Jack Kennedy" zinger to Dan Quayle!

*Lloyd Bentsen,
United States senator from Texas.*
— Susan Noonan

☆ ☆ ☆

Lloyd Bentsen was asked at a February 1992 news conference if he were considering running for president. The seventy-three-year-old Bentsen quipped, "You think I ought to wait and get a little more maturity?" Despite encouragement from many of his supporters, U.S. Senator Lloyd Bentsen ultimately decided not to enter that race, which many saw as his last chance to win the office that he's had his eye on since his unsuccessful presidential bid in 1976. In 1988, Bentsen sought the office of vice-president, sharing the Democratic ticket with presidential nominee Michael Dukakis. During that race, Bentsen scored points with his famed "you're no Jack Kennedy" zinger in a debate with the future vice-president, Dan Quayle.

Dukakis and Bentsen, of course, ultimately lost to the Bush-Quayle ticket, but it was not the first time Lloyd Bentsen had faced George Bush as an opponent. In 1970 the two men had vied for a seat in the U.S. Senate. Although Bentsen had served three terms in Congress and then retired voluntarily to enter private business (in which he spent fifteen years constructing a fortune), he was not widely known when his campaign began. He had been part of the inner circle who urged John Connally to run for an unprecedented fourth term as governor, and Connally returned the favor by supporting Bentsen in the primary election against Ralph Yarborough. It was a campaign which, even for Texas politics, was memorable for its meanness. Bentsen painted Yarborough as an "ultraliberal" and with the Connally team behind him, he won the primary. Bentsen went on to face George Bush in the general election. Bush, then a two-term congressman from Houston, had counted on facing Yarborough, and he was put off-balance by Bentsen, a man with whom he agreed on virtually every major issue except party label.

In fact, the similarities between the two men were striking. Both were Houston millionaires who had made their own fortunes, although neither had to do so since they came from wealthy families. Both were war heroes and pilots who had been shot down in combat. Both were members of the River Oaks Country Club in Houston. Although Bentsen's TV image was reportedly less effective than Bush's, he managed to convey the impression that he was addressing issues more directly. Bentsen ultimately prevailed by 200,000 votes, helped considerably by appearances made on his behalf by Connally and President Lyndon B. Johnson. Bush, in fact, later charged that he had to fight the "Connally-Johnson machine" and "the entire Democratic establishment" in Texas.

When Bentsen was running for vice-president, he was in Montana talking to some farmers and ranchers in a high school gymnasium. Since they were not being very receptive to him, he tried to figure out something that would interest them. They began a discussion about the pros and cons of killing wolves and coyotes. Bentsen then launched into a discussion about the screwworm fly program and radiation of the male flies for sterilization purposes. A farmer in the back of the hall stood up and said, "Senator, you don't understand, they ain't screwing our sheep, they are eating them."

Opinions vary as to whether Bentsen should be considered a conservative or a liberal. He's been called a "Tory Democrat," and some of his detractors have accused him of being "the very epitome of an elitist, special interest Senator." Jimmy Carter once said of Bentsen, "I don't think Bentsen likes to work. He goes to a few very small receptions held for very wealthy people, most of whom are Republicans." Some of his staunchly conservative Republican opponents have tried to portray Bentsen as a flaming liberal. Humorist Cactus Pryor may have had the last word on that subject, however, when he commented, "Of course, Lloyd Bentsen is a liberal. Just as I told that commie Barry Goldwater . . ."

Bentsen exudes elegance with his handsome profile, sleek suits, and dignified manners. He has never been known to raise his voice to staff members, and, reports one journalist, is "seldom, if ever, visibly ruffled, even at the end of a (standard) 16 hour working day." A column appearing during Bentsen's 1970 senatorial campaign applies just as aptly more than twenty years later: "Bentsen . . . still as pencil slim as he was as a 23 year old World War II pilot, is a striking, articulate, indefatigable and unflappable candidate." LBJ also had high praise: "Lloyd Bentsen is steadfast, he is a man of integrity, he says what he means, he always means what he says, and he says the same thing in every part of Texas." Bentsen has proven his staying power with the voters of Texas by his election to four consecutive six-year terms in the Senate. His congressional seniority is evidenced by his powerful position as chair of the Senate Finance Committee, a group which must approve any legislation that concerns money.

Bentsen's steadfast and unflappable image, however, has been interpreted by some as bland, solemn, and stiff, with one columnist speculating that Bentsen probably slept in a tuxedo. A story appearing in the *Houston Post* in 1991, however, provided evidence to the contrary. It seems that while visiting a friend's ranch, the then seventy-one-year-old senator slung his wife B. A. (Beryl Ann) over his shoulder and carried her off. Aides insisted that this was part of a frequent bedtime ritual of Mr. and Mrs. Bentsen's — only this time, B. A. suffered a broken rib! Perhaps Bentsen was right when he joked that he wasn't quite mature enough yet to run for president!

Whatever the perceptions and misconceptions about Bentsen may be, he has run the long mile in the Senate and continues to be a popular and powerful representative for Texans. It would be unwise to place bets on his political maneuvers in the future.

BARBARA JORDAN

Senate 1967–1972
U.S. House of Representatives 1973–1978

☆ ☆ ☆

"Teach us the difference between thinking and rearranging our prejudices."

One-liner prayer by the Senate Chaplain, Dr. Gerald Mann

TEXAS LUSTER

· Honor graduate from Texas Southern University.
· Law degree from Boston University.
· Plays a mean guitar around a campfire!
· Known all around as the black woman with the booming voice.
· First law office at the end of a dining table!
· Spellbinder at Democratic Convention in 1976, and did it again in 1992!

☆ ☆ ☆

Barbara Jordan held a national television audience spellbound when she delivered a stirring keynote address at the Democratic National Convention in 1976. Sixteen years later, party officials again called on the imposing black woman with the booming voice, in hopes that she would do for another Southern governor, Bill Clinton of Arkansas, what she did for Georgia's Jimmy Carter in his race against

Congresswoman Barbara Jordan as she waxes eloquent with her resounding voice.
— Austin History Center

Gerald Ford. On July 13, 1992, at the Democratic Convention in New York City, she did it again!

Raised in the fifth ward ghetto in Houston, Jordan graduated with honors from Texas Southern University, got her law degree from Boston University, and returned to her parents' home, setting up her law practice from the dining room table.

Her political career began in 1966, when she became the first black woman elected to the Texas Senate. Jordan was immensely popular with her constituents, and her fellow legislators took a liking to her as well. In her first term, the newly elected senator received an introduction to tequila sours, as well as an introduction to such characters as Bill Moore, Charlie Wilson, J. P. Word, Jack Hightower, and other such makers of the law.

Jordan's reputation as a "good ol' gal" made her a welcome addition to legislators' hunting trips. While her marksmanship shall remain a state secret, she could play a mean guitar. A former legislator recalls that she would sit up all night strumming the guitar and singing, "We Shall Overcome."

"If you can get her started," he continued, "she is pretty damn good at singing. Her specialty is 'St. James Infirmary Blues.' Makes it sound like you are sitting down in the middle of the French Quarter in New Orleans."

After six years in the Texas Senate, Jordan was elected to Congress. She gained national stature as a member of the House Judiciary Committee during the Watergate hearings, but in 1979 she unexpectedly retired from Congress. Some observers have cited health problems as her reason for opting out of politics. Jordan, who uses a wheelchair, reportedly has a neuromuscular disease similar to multiple sclerosis. But Austin novelist Shelby Hearon, who co-wrote Jordan's autobiography, told a reporter that Jordan withdrew because she was uncomfortable with her extreme popularity.

Since her retirement from Congress, Jordan teaches courses in ethics and public policy at the Lyndon B. Johnson School of Public Affairs at UT and serves as Governor Ann Richards' ethics adviser. Jordan says ethics are especially important in raising campaign funds. "The money thing is the toughest part of it because it costs to run for these races. All I can say is, go out there, get the money from anybody who will give you the money, and don't promise anything in return. That's where you get into trouble."

The usually eloquent Jordan was criticized, however, in 1991 for a comment she made at a women's political conference in Austin. An outspoken feminist and advocate for more women in public office, Jordan told the group: "I believe that women have a capacity for understanding and compassion which a man structurally does not have; does not have it because he cannot have it. He's just incapable of it." A number of men's groups demanded Jordan's resignation as ethics adviser. Instead Jordan offered an apology and admitted to "painting with too broad a brush. I plead guilty. I should have spoken with greater specificity — that is, not 'all men,' 'some men.'"

In the final week of the 1971 state legislative session, the automobile dealers association I worked with wanted to resolve a problem dealing with automobile insurance. Several bad automobile accidents had occurred involving automobiles loaned to customers by dealers, and it was not clear whose insurance covered such tragedies — the individual or the dealer. We were anxious to get the law changed to resolve this issue, and we calculated that Jordan was the only senator who could get a bill through in the midst of the inevitable end-of-session panic.

Howard Ross and I drove to Houston to talk to her about the new legislation. Jordan's office was uptown over a laundromat. There, we asked for her help. Although few dealers had supported her, she recognized the problem and agreed to take on a bill to resolve it. No mention was made of contributions, perks, or what should be done to get her support. And when she introduced the bill, not one objection was heard. Everyone trusted and respected her, and she got the bill passed.

Truly, she is a great lady who can harmonize well.

J. J. PICKLE

U.S. House of Representatives 1963–Present

☆ ☆ ☆

"We are grateful that when Moses parted the Red Sea, he didn't have to write the Environmental Impact Statement."

One-liner prayer by the Senate Chaplain, Dr. Gerald Mann

TEXAS LUSTER

- His trademark is a squeaking plastic pickle.
- Has served the 10th District in Congress since 1963.
- Said at seventy-eight that he plans to be in Congress at least fifteen more years.
- Responsible for the "Pickle Special" nonstop flights between Austin and Washington, D.C.
- Labeled by *Congressional Quarterly* "the guardian of Social Security."
- In 1987 was named Austinite of the Year and Most Worthy Citizen.
- Recognized in 1989 as Congressman of the Year by the National Rural Health Association.
- Known as "The Third Senator" of Texas.

Congressman J. J. "Jake" Pickle
— Austin History Center

☆ ☆ ☆

A friend tells it best: "Back before the war, about 1939 or 1940, Jake Pickle and I double-dated one night and the town was full of Aggies. Boots everywhere. Jake walks out right in the middle of the dance floor during an intermission and says, 'All Aggies are bellhops.' They just came pouring out there; I figured we were going to get killed. When the first Aggie came out, Jake held him by the arms and laughed. This went on for maybe a minute and finally it broke out in the damnedest fight."

Congressman Jake Pickle is known as a man who laughs when he fights. The quirky Pickle, thought by some to be the best politician around, drives a burnt orange Chevrolet truck when he's in Texas. During campaign battles, he hands out his trademark squeaking plastic pickles, a symbol that means you can squeeze the man, but he'll never keep quiet. During his 1990 campaign, Pickle explained the value of the symbol. Holding one up, he said, "Kids love these. They love to make them squeak. You know, they tell a story on me that I give them to kids after I've finished speaking. They get to squeaking them and it distracts the audience while my opponent is speaking." He chuckled, winked, and said, "Hey, you know, it works."

Pickle first ran for Congress in a 1963 special election, held when Thornberry vacated his seat. He has represented the 10th District ever since. He is known in Congress as a hard-working moderate who is receptive to all points of view while maintaining a reputation as an independent thinker. *Congressional Quarterly* labeled Pickle the "Guardian of Social Security" for his work on the 1983 Social Security reform bill. He has also fought to improve Medicare.

Pickle has been instrumental in helping to bring the high-tech industry to Austin, Texas. He led the fight to secure federal funds in the first-ever partnership between government and the private sector and to bring Sematech to Austin. The *Dallas Morning News* called Pickle "the driving force behind the project" and Texas Congressman Charles Wilson said, "You can't give enough credit to Pickle."

Pickle was named 1987 Austinite of the Year by the Austin Chamber of Commerce in recognition of his many contributions, and the same year the Texas Association of Realtors gave him the Most Worthy Citizen award. In 1989 the National Rural Health Association recognized Pickle as Congressman of the Year for his efforts in improving rural health care.

Although slowed down for a while this year, by a battle with prostate cancer, Jake Pickle replied to questions regarding his health:

"Any prophecy about my demise or my retirement is absolutely premature." Pickle said he expects to be in Congress at least fifteen more years. Now seventy-eight years old, he is "pickle squeaking" louder than ever!

Pickle requested and received a "letter of exoneration" from the House Bank stating that he had not bounced any checks. The scandal hit the media and the public in 1991, with hundreds of legislators implicated and the checks supposedly numbering in the thousands — for hundreds of thousands of dollars. Pickle voted "aye" on a resolution in October of 1991 to close the House Bank, a "perk" that was seriously abused by many members of the House.

Congressman Pickle wants to "put a human face" on the IRS. In November of 1991 he was busy preparing a "taxpayer bill of rights" that would make the IRS more responsive to people's tax problems. "There is unrest among taxpayers," Pickle said. "Many of them see the IRS as a great bogeyman that is out there to bankrupt someone or to cause them great hardship."

Pickle is especially well known among long-time Texas politicians for what became fondly known as "The Pickle Special." That "Pickle" was a nonstop flight between Austin and the nation's capital. Congressman Pickle lobbied heavily to have such a service available to Texans. Cactus Pryor said, "You were sure to see a lot of familiar faces when you boarded that flight. (Often Pickle himself working the crowd like an extra flight attendant, passengers usually included state officials and the Texas lobbyists winging their way to Mecca on the Potomac). It was a flying Texas party."

Pickle is a long-time politician and was actively involved in LBJ's 1941 campaign for the U.S. Senate against O'Daniel, Dies, and Mann. It came down to a race between Johnson and O'Daniel and the Texas Election Bureau announced that, short of a miracle, Johnson would be the winner. His Austin headquarters celebrated joyously, hoisting the candidate into the air and holding high victory telegrams. But a bitter lesson was to be learned. "You don't celebrate until it's finally finished," Pickle was to say later. "We went to bed after a party with our man, the new senator from Texas. By the time we got down the next day at noon to try to get to work and pick up the pieces, the reports were coming back in that we hadn't won. There had been some change." As victory receded, the Johnson campaign team got together. They were shocked and disbelieving and demanded a challenge. Pickle used the term "electrified" to describe the feelings the campaign team had at the prospect that fraud could overturn the result. Looking ahead to future political efforts, however, LBJ remained upbeat about his political ambitions for the future. Jake Pickle summed up the situation of voting fraud in Texas and waiting for the final count: "You'd better put salt and pepper on it, and go your way." O'Daniel had won by 1,311 votes.

Pickle learned how to "work" Washington politics the hard way. At his first formal social event there, he approached the person he considered to be the most distinguished looking of all the guests and announced, "I'm Jake Pickle, congressman from Austin, Texas. Who are you?" The man replied, "My name is Pierre, and I am your waiter. What would you like to drink?" On the day Pickle arrived in Washington, he was asked what he thought of the Sam Rayburn Office Building, which they were passing. "It doesn't look so hot to me," Pickle responded. Upon being told that the marble was from the 10th District of Texas, Pickle quickly responded, "You know, the closer you get, the prettier it looks."

Pickle has obviously learned a lot about politics and about Washington since those days. In the most recent election, Pickle did not open a campaign office in the district, nor were there Pickle yard signs, billboards, or bumper stickers. He continues on a popular roll!

Between helping his Longhorn buddies, serving as ex-secretary of the Democratic party of Texas, and handling Allan Shivers' campaigns, he became sort of a "Senator at Large for Texans." This started during the days when Ralph Yarborough and John Tower were state senators. Conservative Democrats would go to Pickle rather than Yarborough, and the opposite was true of Republicans. His staff filled a big vacuum.

There is a great story about Pickle and Sherman Birdwell. Before politics, Pickle and Birdwell were together on joint ventures buying property in East Austin. As an undertaker, Birdwell could spot property to be sold under the hammer. They took turns going to the auctions. Birdwell told J. J. about an upcoming auction that he could not make and Pickle went. Pickle, often referred to as "The Late Mr. Pickle," got to the auction early and was standing down front. Birdwell got loose from his other business and also went to the auction, never thinking of Pickle being on time and being there. The result was Pickle bidding from down front and Birdwell from back of the crowd. They bid against each other and raised the price quite a bit!

Pickle chairs a congressional Ways and Means subcommittee responsible for the tax code, the Internal Revenue Service, and the nation's debt management policies. "Congress has now assembled again, and I'm caught," Pickle said by way of explanation for his absence during the election. "I think it's important for me to be here because of the legislation that's involved. I'd rather be out there in the precincts, campaigning and shaking hands. But I've got a duty to do here."

Pickle, approaching his eighties, performs his duty admirably. Even when it's teaching Aggies their place.

In closing, we give a special prayer to his sweet and lovely wife, Beryl: "Lord, remind us that we are as capable of giving a little bit of heaven as well as a whole lot of hell."

JOHN TOWER

U.S. Senate 1961–1985

☆   ☆   ☆

"Remind us that when small people cast long shadows, the sun is about to set!"

One-liner prayer by the Senate Chaplain, Dr. Gerald Mann

TEXAS LUSTER

- After graduation from college, Tower worked as a disc jockey on KTAE in Taylor, where he was known on the air as "Tex Tower."
- Bitter rift between Tower and George Bush caused by vice-presidential ambitions of both men, but they were personal friends.
- Son of a Methodist minister.
- Former professor of government at Midwestern University in Wichita Falls.
- Five feet, six inches tall, eloquent, outspoken, and an entertaining champion of the conservative cause.
- The first Republican U.S. senator to represent Texas in the twentieth century.
- Youngest member of the Senate when he took office (thirty-six years old).
- Made 190 speeches and nine network television appearances in his first ten months in office; rarely wrote speeches — they came out of his head.

- "My name is Tower but I don't."
- Houston native, graduated from Beaumont High School, served aboard a gunboat in World War II, got his bachelor's degree from Southwestern University in 1948 and a master's degree from SMU in 1953. He also did postgraduate work at the University of London.
- Tireless, but did not like campaigning.
- Quipped that he had a Texas Chamber of Commerce permit allowing him to be "one foot less than the legal minimum height for Texans."

Senator John Tower

☆   ☆   ☆

John Tower switched from the Democratic to the Republican party, to the consternation of many people of both parties. He explained, "I decided in 1951 that being a Democrat because Granddaddy was a Democrat was foolish . . . tradition had nothing to do with the current postures of the two parties. Being basically conservative, I felt I should associate myself with the party that most nearly represented my views. And that was the Republican Party, nationally. Then, too, I think I had matured in my thinking to the extent that I felt we should have a two party system in our state instead of an outworn one party system. My being an academic political scientist had something to do with that."

"Friendly" critics have had many things to say about Tower and his style. "While a tireless man, he is not the natural campaigner type. He doesn't enjoy 'feeling the flesh,' mixing with crowds of people and doing those many things that a candidate on the stump must do. He would much rather discuss things with intellectual equals in small groups."

Regarding George Bush and his political possibilities in Texas and the country, Tower said, "I think George is, by far, the strongest candidate we could offer. He has run one statewide race, he's a popular congressman and there was speculation about him as vice-president in 1968. He's got a lot of moxie. He's conservative enough to be sound, so far as the average conservative is concerned, but not dogmatically

Senator Tower being interviewed by Dallas newsmen in 1971. Dave McNeely, then of the Dallas Morning News *and now of the* Austin American-Statesman, *is in the foreground.*

— Courtesy Dallas Morning News

conservative enough to become offensive to the more moderate or liberal element. The liberals would *not* be inclined to mount any crusades against him." In some respects a very perceptive and auspicious prediction for George Bush and the path his career would follow!

In the early 1960s only John Tower remained as the highly visible patron saint of the Republican party in Texas, a lone rallying point. One irony of Tower's career was his attendance at the prestigious London School of Economic and Political Science, an anathema to conservatives at the time. Tower, however, took advantage of his opportunities. He also did his homework in the Senate and became an authority on national defense and the military. Tower opened the door and led the way for development of the two-party system in Texas. John Tower did indeed "tower" over his political adversaries! His untimely death on April 5, 1991, resulted from an airplane crash.

RALPH YARBOROUGH

U.S. Senator 1957–1971

☆　☆　☆

"Teach us the difference between an open mind and an empty head."
One-liner prayer by the Senate Chaplain, Dr. Gerald Mann

TEXAS LUSTER

- "Smiling Ralph" . . . permanent campaigner.
- Third bid for governorship in 1956.
- Subtle as a sledgehammer.
- Long-term feud with Connally . . . and LBJ!
- Wrestling match with Senator Strom Thurmond.
- Called 1969 antiballistic missile system a "big boondoggle packaged in a big hornswoggle."

☆　☆　☆

Described by one observer as "about as subtle as a sledgeham-mer," longtime U.S. Senator Ralph Yarborough feuded with the best of his fellow Texan politicians — including Lyndon B. Johnson, John Connally, and even George Bush. Known to have stormed out of a press conference and to have gotten into a wrestling match in the Sen-ate with Strom Thurmond, Yarborough seems to have saved much of his energy to unleash on his political rivals in the state. He refused to ride in the same car with LBJ and publicly criticized the Johnson administration for budget cuts in domestic programs while Vietnam War costs soared during Johnson's five-year tenure as president. "Talk about student rioting," he told one group. "If the people understood what had been done to them these last five years, the majority of Americans would be ready to riot." Even after LBJ retired to his ranch, Yarborough continued to take jabs at him — once spending more than thirty minutes berating the retired Johnson to a group of labor leaders during his 1970 senatorial reelection campaign.

When Governor John Connally decided to retire in 1967 and

forego a fourth term, Yarborough couldn't resist taking one last swat at him either. He said the governor had seen "the handwriting on the wall" and that he had been popular "only because he was shot with President Kennedy."

Similarly, Yarborough became so upset during his Senate race with George Bush that he continued to denounce the future president even after it had ended. After the votes had been counted, he declared: "I think my opponent ought to pack up his suitcase and go back where he came from. He carried on the vilest and most defaming campaign I have ever seen."

Yarborough has been described as an adamant politician who refused to acknowledge defeat and therefore never quit campaigning. In 1956, as he made his third bid for the governorship, one Dallas reporter noted that Yarborough had never quit running since his 1952 campaign! After his 1970 defeat by Lloyd Bentsen for the U.S. Senate, Yarborough reportedly broke all existing records for the number of press releases issued by a lame duck.

Yarborough had planned to seek the attorney general's office in 1952, but in trying to finance his campaign he discovered that Governor Allan Shivers had already lined up most of the contributors for his would-be opponent. A friend suggested, "If you're going to have to fight the top man, why don't you just run against him?" Three days later, Yarborough announced for governor.

His announcement reportedly triggered some of the most vicious political wars the state had ever known, drawing sharp new battle lines between liberals (supporting Yarborough) and conservatives (supporting Shivers). Shivers' support of Eisenhower provided Yarborough with a "party loyalty" issue which became one of his favorites. Yarborough insisted that he simply could not understand the term "Eisenhower Democrat." "That's like saying you're a Christian who believes in Mohammed," he quipped. During the campaign, Yarborough shocked some of his acquaintances by stopping them on the street and asking them point-blank if they were supporting him or Shivers. "If you even tried to beat around the bush and not give a direct answer," said one victim, "he'd blow his top. He probably lost quite a few votes that way." Yarborough's campaign was significantly aided by the support of Houston millionaire J. R. Parten, whom Shivers had refused to reappoint to the University Board of Regents. Parten was to become one of Yarborough's strongest backers in his gubernatorial races as well as his Senate campaigns.

Senator Ralph Yarborough with "Cyclone" Davis, a perennial candidate for governor in the forties and fifties.
— Courtesy Center for American History, University of Texas at Austin

Yarborough was defeated by Shivers, but that didn't stop him from running again in 1954 and in 1956. In the latter race, political observers predicted another liberal vs. conservative battle between Yarborough and Shivers. But the incumbent governor decided not to seek reelection, and Yarborough's opponent turned out to be U.S. Senator Price Daniel. Daniel's subsequent victory left his unexpired Senate seat open, and Yarborough won that 1957 special election.

In 1958 Yarborough was reelected, and at the end of that six-year term, George Bush challenged him for his Senate seat. Suffering from a lack of identification with the business element in Texas, Yarborough's campaign managers formed a "Businessmen for Yarborough Committee" and listed thirteen millionaires on it. Bush cracked, "A 'Businessmen for Yarborough Committee' sounds about as likely as a 'Barbers for Castro Committee.' " Yarborough won the election, and later, Bush complained that a surprise show of support for Yarborough from LBJ lost him the race. Said Bush, "When President Johnson came to Texas and put his arm around Ralph Yarborough, that was the end of me."

The night after his election in 1958, I spoke to the McGregor Chamber of Commerce Annual Banquet and Yarborough was in the audience. In his manner, he was still running the day after election. My good friend Jack Dillard and I had worked hard on the Shivers side of those campaigns — Dillard took his politics real serious like. Tom Moore (who brought Yarborough to the McGregor banquet) asked me if I would let Yarborough ride back to Austin with me. I did. Tom and I framed Dillard and had him called, telling him that I was seen driving Yarborough after the banquet. Dillard almost had a stroke, saying, "That G.D. turncoat Pittman!" Took me a fifth to restore our longtime friendship.

In 1970 Bush challenged Yarborough once again for his Senate seat. Bush accused the incumbent senator of being "old and out of it. His liberalism is not tied to anything exciting but it's almost a special interest liberalism." Bush went on to say that Yarborough "cries poor mouth but his campaigns are pretty well financed . . . [T]he unions come through big." But the ultimate challenge came from Lloyd Bentsen, who defeated both Yarborough and Bush for the Senate position.

During Yarborough's tenure as U.S. senator, he served as chairman of the Senate Committee on Labor and Public Welfare. He co-authored with Senator Edward Kennedy a bill to revise the draft to a lottery basis, but he said what he really favored was a volunteer army with pay high enough to attract volunteers. In a speech in Washington on May 6, 1969, Yarborough bitterly attacked "war profiteers" and called the anti-ballistic missile system "a big boondoggle packaged in a big hornswoggle." He vehemently opposed the right-to-work law and President Nixon's proposal for post office reform. He favored the oil depletion allowance, but only on domestic production, believing it should be repealed on overseas operations. He also worked for raising the personal income tax exemption.

Yarborough remains one of the state's most colorful and controversial politicians. An amusing anecdote exemplifies Yarborough's penchant for one-upmanship and always having the last word. As a young man, Yarborough had attended West Point; however, despite excellent grades in all of his other subjects, his poor grades in math prevented him from completing his education there. At an SMU-Army football game party many years later, he was greeted by an ex-West Point classmate who remarked, "Too bad, Ralph, that you couldn't finish up. By the way, what are you doing now?"

"I'm United States senator from Texas," replied Yarborough. "What are you doing?"

Mucho Color

CACTUS PRYOR

☆ ☆ ☆

Cactus has been tagged as Austin's Bob Hope . . . the great impersonator . . . a Lone Star movie star . . . and as a great dog and fisherman. He has been in the yard of our Third House for the last fifty years — poking fun at our top hands, writing, helping, grinning and grilling, and giving of his true love of Texans and good humor.

Cactus Pryor

He has the true Texas color that this book is about. Single-handedly (almost), he has given us the joy of poking fun at each other. Austin, perhaps more than any other city, has acquired this trait largely due to Cactus and his disciples — as well as his theater owner dad, "Skinny" Pryor, and his popular brother, Wally Pryor (voice of Longhorn sports and producer of most every social and charity event in Austin).

This book begins with a look at "Ma and Pa" Ferguson. Cactus sold soda water at his dad's Congress Avenue Moving Picture Palace and he recalls Ma and Pa coming to the movie house. Ma would buy an orange soda pop from him and would give him a quarter every time, although the Orange Crush sold for a dime.

Walter Cronkite, in his foreword to Cacti's best-selling book *Inside Texas,* says of Cactus: "He has thus given native Austin a rare gift that few cities anywhere can claim . . . a real live humorist with the sharp eye, quick tongue, the educated pen, and, most important, the warm heart to record in sometimes hilarious detail its fashions and foibles."

We are truly grateful to Cactus for adding to this book. As busy as he is, he jumped up to again give of himself as he has done for Headliners Club projects since Charlie Green designed the club for "those who make and write headlines." The club now has twenty-four journalism scholarships at Texas, Baylor, and A&M universities.

When I remember Cactus' movie career (two movies with John Wayne), I think of the "Road Pictures" of Bob Hope and Bing Crosby. I do believe that if we could get Cactus and Willie Nelson to go on the road with Governor Ann (after she finishes her current job), we, too, would have a winner.

Now, lean back in your porch swing and let's hear from Cacti . . .

Cactus Pryor:

To live in Austin, Texas, and not be a political humorist is like being in the Mother Lode of Gold in the Yukon and not having a shovel. It's just a bird's nest on the ground, and I will forever be appreciative to the likes of Frank Erwin and Ben Barnes, as well as Bob Bullock, Governor Dolph Briscoe, and people like that.

I remember when Governor White succeeded Governor Briscoe, I introduced him as being the most exciting governor to happen to Texas since Dolph Briscoe, which is not very exciting. The first Headliners luncheon that Briscoe came to, he left in the middle of it and had a trooper come and summon him. I don't think there was any urgent message, other than just to get the hell out of there. He was very uncomfortable about humor, and I almost felt guilty for kidding him, because I like Dolph Briscoe. But he took it so personally that it was a little hard to kid him. As a matter of fact, he used to be one of my customers at the K-9 Hilton. A trooper would bring the Briscoes' dog out to our kennel to be groomed, but I noticed after I started kidding Briscoe in my column and on the radio and at banquets that the dog didn't keep coming. He went elsewhere — probably to a Republican groomer.

Frank Erwin was a lot of fun to be with, if you were looking for humor. I remember when he was enlarging the stadium and increasing all the University of Texas athletic units, and they were getting ready to cut down some of the big oak trees in front of the stadium. Some of the students had chained themselves to the oak trees to keep them from being cut down. I wrote a poem that I delivered at some banquet — I guess a Headliners — that went like this (quoting Frank Erwin):

"I refuse to offer apology
For getting involved in ecology.
I'll cut down the trees,
Whenever I please,
So stick that up your physiology."

Of course, having been associated with the radio station and tele-vision station here for so long, I have lots of LBJ stories. *Newsweek* Magazine said that I was the only man that could kid LBJ and get away with it. There were just scores of times when I didn't get away with it. One time we had a staff Christmas party, which Lady Bird and Lyndon always attended, or usually attended, and this was at the time when he was denying with every breath that he was a candidate for the presi-dency. He had appeared on "Face the Nation," and over twenty times during that telecast he'd said: "I am not a candidate for the presidency, I do not intend to be a candidate for the presidency, I have never been a candidate for the presidency," and it was time after time after time. Well, accompanying the entertainment that evening, I produced a film and substituted my own question askers to go with the answers that he had given on "Face the Nation." I know Paul Bolton was one of them. Ray Wadell was another, and Barbara Robinson of our staff was another. We would ask him questions like: "Mr. President, what do you miss the most about being in Texas?" And then we would cut to the clip that said: "I am not a candidate for the presidency, I have never been a candidate for the presidency, I do not intend to be a can-didate for the presidency."

"Well, Mr. President, what is the primary challenge facing the nation?"

"I'm not a candidate for the presidency, I do not intend . . . ."

Well, the group of employees assembled were just having an up-roarious time, yelling and stomping their feet, but then it became quieter and quieter and quieter, and then about the only thing you could hear was the roar of that projector. I knew then that the man was not amused. As a matter of fact, he chewed Paul Bolton out so much that Paul couldn't speak for two days, and I think Ray Wadell feared his job. He chewed them all out individually but never said anything to me, interestingly enough. But I remember feeling so bad that I had hurt his feelings, because he was a very sensitive man. I really wanted to go up and hug him and say, "Mr. President, or Senator Johnson, I really wouldn't kid you if I didn't like you."

Another similar occasion was at the ranch, where he was entertaining Admiral Nimitz, Governor Connally, and about fifteen to twenty other gentlemen out on the lawn with a little barbecue and party. LBJ asked me to bring up some entertainment, which I did, and to emcee it. I brought some folk singers along, I believe. One of the guests was Judge Cofer, who at that time was an attorney representing Billie Sol Estes, and the Estes trial was going on at that very same time. So I figured that this would be a good opportunity for me to introduce a song that I had written for the Geezinslaw Brothers to record on Columbia Records: "The Ballad of Billie Sol Estes," to the tune of "Beautiful, Beautiful Texas." Well, I started singing that, and the audience, I thought, was suitably appreciative because they were laughing and clapping and having a jolly good time. But then they, too, got quieter and quieter and quieter, and again I realized what was happening. They were looking at the owner of the ranch, and the owner of the ranch was not amused. I said to myself: "I am just standing up here, singing myself to death, but I can't stop, I have to go on." Finally, I got to a line that included John Connally's name, and John broke out in the most beautiful, the most gorgeous guffaw that I've ever heard in my life. Well, this gave the audience license to start laughing again, which they did, and Johnson, being the politician that he is, cased the crowd and decided that he had better join the majority. So he started laughing, too, and I survived. But as I told John, "If you run even for Pope, I will be obligated to vote for you for that laugh."

I'll tell you, we had lots of fun at the Headliners Club, and it seemed like whenever Jim Wright would invite me up to speak to members of Congress, or I would be doing the Headliners Club here in Austin, some scandal would break just before my appearance. I was rewriting on the way to almost every occasion that I was to speak at — frantically rewriting because of the change of events. The Sharpstown scandal broke just about two days before the annual Headliners Club party, and I think Walter Cronkite was going to be the honored guest, with all the politicians and all the newsmakers there. I knew that all of those who were involved in Sharpstown would also be in the audience. You know, I don't mind using a scalpel, but I hate to use a bludgeon on people whom I like, and I did like all of those guys. I just didn't know how I was going to handle this, especially regarding Preston Smith, because he had appointed me to the Texas Tourist Development Agency and had always been kind to me.

I got a call from the governor. He didn't use his secretary; he just called in person and said, "Cactus, this is Preston."

I said, "Yes, Governor."

"Can I come to see you?"

I said, "Yes, Governor, but you are much busier than I. I'll be glad to come up to your office."

He said, "Well, I would sure appreciate it."

I figured he was going to say, "Call off the dogs." So I went up there and we visited, socialized for a while. Finally, he says, "Now, Cactus, about the Headliners party . . . You are going to burn my ass, aren't you?"

"Yes, Governor."

And he said, "Well, you've got to. It's expected of you. Would you do me a favor? Would you write me a rebuttal?"

I said, "Yes." So John Henry Faulk and I got together, and we figured out the gag. When I introduced the governor after properly burning him, he came to the podium, slammed down a great big rock on the podium, and said, "Let he who is without stock cast the first rock." It got the crowd to laughing and broke the tension.

The longest laugh I've ever heard didn't involve a politician directly, but it was at another one of the Headliners things. It was regarding Darrell Royal when he was coach of the Longhorns. He held a press conference every Monday. Always the same setting, usually the same type of clothing — casual. Always the same quarters, always the same room. So we duplicated that room and photographed our own news conference. Texas had lost to Oklahoma for yet a third time. So I posed this question to the coach: "Coach, you came from Oklahoma, you are our savior, the Messiah who was going to lead us out of losses, but you've lost three consecutive years to your alma mater, Oklahoma. How do you feel about this?" And the camera came in for a closeup to Royal's very sincere, very believable face. And he said: "You know, I've been thinking about that. Looking for solace. And I've turned to the words of Oliver Wendell Holmes, who said: 'As I look back on my life, I value my mistakes more than my victories, because I learned more from my mistakes, my defeats, than I did from my victories. My defeats were more to my advantage than my victories.' You know, I've been thinking about the words of Oliver Wendell Holmes, and I'd just like to say: 'Piss on him.' "

It took about five minutes for that audience to stop laughing. It was the longest laugh I had ever heard in my life.

Back to Governor Smith. He and I were entertaining a grain co-op dinner, prize-giving, speech making, up in some little town in the

Panhandle. There were about 2,500 farmers assembled. The dinner started at 6:00, and at ten minutes to 12:00 I introduced the governor. The governor stood and said, "Folks, governors have bladders, too. Good night." It was the largest hand that he had ever gotten, and probably the best political speech that he ever made.

Another Headliners story. We used to do a lot of film stuff. Chet Huntley of Huntley and Brinkley News was going to be our honored guest that year, and I was with Channel 7 at the time, as is my brother Wally now. Wally was directing the programs on this particular day, just before the Huntley–Brinkley news. The network always sent down a test feed, and we would see Huntley and Brinkley — Huntley in New York and Brinkley in Washington — talking back and forth, preparing, saying who would read what story and so forth. It was, of course, inside stuff. And Brinkley said to Huntley, "I hear you're going to Austin, Texas, to be on the Headliners' program this Saturday." Well, Wally immediately punched the videotape recorder. And Huntley says, "Yeah, bunch of damn hicks. I got a lot of things I'd rather do than go down to Austin, Texas. Well, I got the word from the boss. He says, 'You gotta go,' so I'm going. But I damn sure don't want to."

At the Headliners show that Saturday I said, "Mr. Huntley, we sure do welcome you here. We really appreciate your coming." And he said, "Well, I have really been looking forward to this." I said, "Hold it! Before you say anything else, we've got a little tape we want to play you." We punched the button and played the tape of the conversation between he and Brinkley. His face was somewhere between burnt orange and scarlet, but he took it in good humor, as everybody did, usually.

Ben Barnes was a bird's nest on the ground, and he always enjoyed being kidded. Bob Bullock did likewise, and we had some good times. One man who didn't enjoy my humor, apparently, so much was Ronald Reagan. I was invited to a fundraiser for John Tower in Dallas. I liked John Tower. He had a sense of humor. I put it pretty hard on Reagan, burned him pretty well, and he came back with good humor also. But one of the Republican leaders was telling me that they were flying from there to Beaumont on a plane with Reagan, and Reagan said, "I do not want to be on the program with that Pryor fellow again." And he was saying it very seriously.

Governor Bill Clements also was generous. Matter of fact, I have done more shows for the Republicans than I have for the Democrats because Republicans pay better. But Clements called me one day, after his reelection, and said, "Cactus, I want you to come down to Houston and speak at my victory celebration."

I said, "Well, Governor, I'm a yellow-dog Democrat."

He says, "I know, but I don't want to sit at the head table and have people praise me all night."

"Well, I can take care of that, Governor."

"Well, come on," he said, "I sure would appreciate it."

So I kidded him. I even auctioned off that old checkered sports coat of his. I think I got $3,500 for it from some veterinarian. It would take the taste of some A&M veterinarian to buy that coat! But I was sitting next to — I forget the man's name — the head of the Republican party for Texas, and there were about 2,500 people there, at $1,000 a head. And he said to me, "Cactus, why aren't you Republican?" And I said, "Well, look out there. There are 2,500 people, and I don't see a black or a brown face." He said, "Yeah, but well, this is a $1,000-a-plate dinner." And I said, "Well, that's my point." Which he did not get.

The LBJ story I tell the most concerns Packal Jack Wallace, who was an all-night disk jockey at Lady Bird's radio station. I was his boss. I would wake up in the middle of the night, just to let Jack know that somebody was listening to him, but I would never call him as myself. I would call and say, "This is Lyndon Johnson. We are up here at the ranch playing dominoes. Would you play me 'Yellow Rose of Texas'?" And he would say, "Yes, sir, Senator Johnson." Then here would come 'Yellow Rose of Texas' out on the air. Then I would call back and say, "Hey, Jack, this is Cactus. What are you doing playing 'Yellow Rose of Texas'? That's not on our play list." He said, "By God, if Senator Johnson wants to hear it, he's going to hear it." This went on for about three months, and Jack finally caught on that I had been pulling his leg. Then one night, the vice-president of the United States flies into the ranch, and there's an election on, and about 2:00 in the morning he calls down to the station and says, "Wallace, this is Lyndon Johnson. Would you read me the latest election results?" Jack said, "Oh yeah, well, this is Martha Washington. Come down and get them yourself." And the next voice he heard was that of the station manager.

Clements and I kind of enjoyed kidding each other. I introduced him at one Headliners banquet, and I said: "The greatest governor this side of Arizona was having gubernatorial problems." And he said, "Pryor, you don't amuse me." I said, "Governor, you sure amuse me."

He had a good sense of humor and I appreciated him.

Connally had, I guess, the juiciest sense of humor, and we have kidded each other over the years. Ann Richards and I have done a lot of shows together. We roasted Charlie Wilson up in Lufkin. That was before Ann was a candidate for governor, but I knew then that she would be elected governor because when she can kid the favorite son of Lufkin, Texas, in East Texas as harshly as she did, and as surgically as she did, and get a standing applause, I knew that she was on the way to being the governor of Texas.★

Thermostrocker Mortimer!

"BICYCLE ANNIE"

☆ ☆ ☆

"Lord, teach us the difference between the gods we have made and the God who made us."

One-liner prayer by the Senate Chaplain, Dr. Gerald Mann

TEXAS LUSTER

· Bike-rider extraordinaire!
· Apparently born in 1893, but refused to give any specific information other than saying, "I may be fat, but I'll never be forty!"
· Reputedly came to Austin in 1938 "to observe what goes on."
· In 1941 started her own periodical, *Up and Down the Drag.*
· In 1948 announced her candidacy as the first woman to run for president of the United States.
· Also known as "The Indian Princess."
· A 1976 newspaper article said, "Austin's best known resident across the years is also the city's least known resident."

☆ ☆ ☆

Zelma O'Riley, better known as "Bicycle Annie," was a recognized and colorful character around Austin for many years. Although she did not serve in any official capacity, local residents probably recognized her more readily than they would their local legislators. "Bicycle Annie" incessantly pushed or rode her bicycle from one end of

Bicycle Annie (Zelma O'Riley) — famed Austin citizen. Ran for president in 1948. Known around the capital as "The Indian Princess."

— Courtesy Austin History Center

Austin to the other, piquing the curiosity of observers who would see her in opposite sections of the city within a very short time period.

Zelma was allegedly born in Durant, Oklahoma, in 1893. But when asked for specific information about her age, she would not give a date, replying instead, "I may be fat, but I'll never be forty." "Bicycle Annie" lived in Austin for over fifty years. She was a familiar and welcome sight to most Austin residents and always remained a figure of mystery and folklore.

It seems that "Annie" fostered the mystery. She was also known as "The Indian Princess" and proudly claimed her heritage from a mother who was Choctaw. She was part Native American and part Irish, but few true facts are known beyond that. There has never been any verification of royalty in her Native American ancestry, but her high cheekbones and her Oklahoma roots helped fuel the legend.

"Bicycle Annie" herself stated that she came to Austin in 1938 because, "It's the capital and I wanted to observe what goes on." Local legend holds that she received several degrees from The University of Texas and had the IQ of a genius. Biruta Celmins Kearl, archivist for the Austin History Center, interviewed her shortly before her death. In that interview, she revealed that she had studied many subjects, including journalism, art, and law. She claimed to have attended The University of Texas Law School to learn how to reclaim Native American lands taken by the government. She also said she had studied at the Boston Museum of Fine Arts. In 1940 she was enrolled at The University of Texas in the College of Arts and Sciences. There is no record of her having received a degree. That same year, she was listed in the telephone directory as an artist. "Bicycle Annie" was undoubtedly an intelligent and talented woman. Many thought her eccentric, and perhaps she was. Perhaps she was just a very private person who did not wish the world to know who she was.

In regard to her periodical, *Up and Down the Drag,* O'Riley went up and down the drag herself, soliciting advertising from merchants and selling subscriptions from 1941 to 1948. One store owner on "The Drag" said that Zelma came into the store for many years and was given ten or fifteen dollars a month for advertising in "what proved to be an imaginary publication" after about 1950 or so. There is a copy of *Up and Down the Drag* dated March 8, 1946, in the Barker Texas History Center.

It was in her publication that she announced her presidential candidacy. She wrote of herself, "She believes it will take a woman to save America and will conduct her campaign on the preparedness plank." She was, apparently, defeated worse than Dewey.

One of the few people to ever be given the opportunity to interview "Bicycle Annie" was Mike Cox, at that time a reporter for the *Austin American-Statesman.* Cox reported that she was unable to leave her home due to an injured foot. She talked to him "in a very guarded manner" and claimed that her injury had been sustained "when a watermelon flew up and struck her down" in front of the Kash 'n Karry Food Store on Guadalupe.

Annie broke a hip once (reports vary from a 1976 article, which states "about eight years ago," to another from 1991, which states "about fifteen years ago"), and apparently broke a hip a second time while attempting to board a bus. From that time on she was seldom seen on the streets of Austin. When interviewed in 1991, she said she was touched that people still remembered her.

When Zelma "Bicycle Annie" O'Riley died in April of 1991, many were saddened to see the real stuff of legend and folklore move into the realm of remembered oral history alone. Austin is a poorer place without "Bicycle Annie" to be seen and wondered about. The truth about her life will never be known — a fact that would probably please her immensely. She remains a mystery, and certainly has a distinct corner among the many colorful characters who have lived under the moonlight towers of Austin!

ROBERT W. CALVERT

House of Representatives 1933–1938
Speaker of the House 1937–1938
Texas Supreme Court Justice 1950–1972
Chief Justice 1960–1972

☆ ☆ ☆

"Our Father, help us to remember that it's always easier to fight for our principles than to live up to them."

One-liner prayer by the Senate Chaplain, Dr. Gerald Mann

TEXAS LUSTER

· State home to state house!
· Political education as student elevator operator in Capitol for two years.
· Made $7.50 first month of law practice . . . $5 the second month.
· Though outweighed by fifty pounds, whipped Representative Abe Mays in men's room fight with a picture-perfect half nelson.
· Accused by Judge Brewster of picking a duck blind with a rattlesnake in it rather than shooting with him.
· Reported by Judge Norvell of seeing two "meece" in Colorado.
· Trouble with Justice Clyde Smith on getting in last word!
· Published excellent book, *Here Comes the Judge.*
· Turned down fast way to make ready cash!

☆ ☆ ☆

From decidedly humble beginnings (spending his formative years in the State Orphans' Home in Corsicana), Robert W. Calvert went on to become chief justice of the Texas Supreme Court. He got his first taste for politics and government operating the Capitol elevator while working his way through UT Law School. After earning his law degree, Calvert joined a firm in Hillsboro, earning the princely sum of $7.50 his first month (and in a less than promising follow-up, $5 his second).

He officially entered state government in 1932, when he was elected to the House of Representatives. During his first term, he chaired the Texas Relief Commission, which issued the bread bonds, and was voted by journalists as one of the five most valuable members. In his memoirs, *Here Comes the Judge* (1977), Calvert described a prophetic incident that occurred on his train ride to Austin to begin his legislative service. It seems a Hillsboro "wheeler-dealer" approached Calvert and described to him a potentially profitable plan: "He told me he knew how we could both make some money. 'You make up your mind how you want to vote on important bills, but don't tell anybody but me. I will then go to the people on that side of the bill and tell them that I will get your vote for a little fee; and then you can go on and vote like you intended to anyway and we'll divide the fee. That way you won't be dishonest — you'll be voting like you intended to all the time.' I rejected the offer. It seemed to me that somebody had been staying awake at night doing some thinking."

Of course, that wouldn't be the last time that Calvert was "propositioned." In a career spanning forty years of public service, Calvert encountered and rejected many such offers. But Calvert is a self-described staunch "law man"; that is, he believes that the law should be applied in a predictable, even-handed manner to all. When an amendment concerning the pari-mutuel betting bill came before the House, Calvert (then Speaker) was offered $25,000 to rule on the side of the issue, which he already supported, but he refused the money. His intolerance of political corruption was evident early in his career. During considerations of a bill backed by "the governors Ferguson," Senator T. H. McGregor, a Ferguson supporter, claimed that the impeached Jim Ferguson had been a victim of dishonest friends and that, like Jesus, Ferguson had had a Judas who betrayed him. Calvert countered by reading from testimony which showed that Governor Jim Ferguson had gotten one-third of a payoff and added, "Now, Senator McGregor, you say that Ferguson was a victim of dishonest friends, and like Jesus had his Judas Iscariot. I fail, Senator, to find in my Bible anywhere an account of Jesus demanding his one-third cut in the thirty pieces of silver!"

When Calvert first ran for Speaker of the House in 1935, he lost to Coke Stevenson. It was a close and vicious race, but Calvert knew he was in trouble when, immediately prior to the vote, his deskmate,

J. D. Duval, a Stevenson supporter, turned to him and said they had him beat. Calvert asked how he could know so and Duval replied, "You and your friends went to bed last night and we didn't." Despite that defeat, Calvert did win the 1937 election and served as Speaker of the House for two years.

In his autobiography, Calvert relates an incident that occurred during that time. It seems that Representative Abe Mays from Atlanta, Texas, had become disenchanted with the new Speaker. As Calvert described it, "I could see him from time to time sitting in his chair grimacing and muttering at me." Late one afternoon after virtually everyone had left, Calvert ran into Mays in the men's room, where the Atlanta legislator said he thought he would give Calvert a "good whipping." The two men scuffled until Calvert ended the fight with a half nelson, forcing Mays (who outweighed him by fifty pounds) to agree not to give him any more trouble. Senator G. C. Morris witnessed the battle, and after the story got around, Mays didn't give him any more trouble — and neither did anybody else!

When Calvert's tenure as Speaker ended in 1938, he made an unsuccessful bid for attorney general. He served as an unpaid lobbyist for the State Bar of Texas in the 1938 legislative session, which passed the State Bar Act, and was elected criminal district attorney in 1942. In 1946 (and again in 1948), Governor Beauford Jester, a longtime friend and supporter, appointed Calvert chairman of the State Democratic Executive Committee — an appointment that upset some of Jester's staunchly conservative supporters. The 1948 Democratic Convention took part in the controversial senatorial race between Lyndon B. Johnson and Coke Stevenson. Calvert devotes an entire chapter of his book to what was facetiously called "the 1948 Johnson Landslide," and the retired chief justice contends that an election fraud had been perpetrated in Duval County (less than 200 votes had been mysteriously added to Johnson's total vote).

In the decade between his years in the legislature and his tenure on the state supreme court, Calvert continued to practice law while serving in various public offices. His influence in state government was recognized by the Honorable S. J. Isaacs of El Paso when, in an introduction to a House audience, he credited Calvert with "having done more than any other one person to chart the course of the Texas Democratic party in the 1940's."

Calvert was elected an associate justice of the Supreme Court of Texas in 1950 and remained for twenty-two years, the second-longest record of service on the Supreme Court in the history of the state. His seniority must have come in handy, for in his book he wrote about the court, "Everything fell into place according to seniority, even the use of the men's room: no matter how urgent the need, those junior had to stand aside for their seniors." Calvert took the oath as chief justice of the Supreme Court in 1961 and held that position until his retirement in 1972. In his memoirs, he speaks highly of his fellow justices, although it is reported that he often became irritated with the "eternally dissenting" Judge Clyde Smith. To solve the problem, Calvert began voting out of turn, so that Smith would be the last to vote. The chief justice would then say, "Clyde Smith, let's see you dissent on this!" On another occasion, in the robing room after a 5–4 vote, Smith ruminated, "I believe I'll change my vote." Calvert snapped, "Well, that's fine, Clyde. I'll just change mine too and it'll come out exactly the same!"

In his book *Here Comes the Judge,* Judge Calvert wrote about many humorous incidents. For example, on a duck hunt near Bayview, he left Judge Brewster in one blind and went to another with a rattlesnake in it (which Justice Calvert hit with a quick shot). Back in Austin, Judge Brewster reported that Justice Calvert preferred a rattlesnake for company! Justice Norvell once reported from Colorado that he had seen two mooses . . . scratched that and wrote "two meece" . . . scratched that for "one moose on one side of the road and one on the other side of the road."

Since his retirement from the bench, Calvert has provided counsel to an Austin law firm, chaired the Constitutional Revision Committee in 1973, and written innumerable articles for various law reviews as well as his excellent memoirs.

Talk about a "colorful character" in our Texas history. This one is red, white, and blue with no yellow at all. Only thing bad I could find after knowing him, and his being plenty of help to me for more than a score of years, is a concern Judge Ruel Walker and I have about him sometimes knocking back a "gimmee" putt before we kicked ours back!

AMANDO CANALES

House of Representatives 1965–1968

☆   ☆   ☆

"Let us know when to rise for the occasion, and also let us know when to sit down."

One-liner prayer by the Senate Chaplain, Dr. Gerald Mann

TEXAS LUSTER

- Had apartment manager in a purple bathrobe put in jail.
- Dueled with pistols at ten feet and missed five shots!
- With Archie Parr, he had 5,000 good votes!

☆   ☆   ☆

Colorful characters make a good tale but don't always make happy neighbors. One night, Amando Canales and some ring-tailed tooters had a party and were raising hell. The apartment manager, who previously had warned them they were flirting with eviction, was awakened at 2:00 A.M. by the noise. The manager, in a purple bathrobe and mad as a wet hornet, beat on Canales' door until finally someone heard him and came to answer. After listening to the manager's threats of eviction and police intervention, Amando spoke a few quick words in Spanish to one of his bodyguards, who immediately left the apartment. When the bodyguard returned, Canales slammed the door in the manager's face. Frustrated as a woodpecker in a petrified forest, the manager returned to his apartment only to find his own door locked, with himself on one side and his keys on the other.

To make matters worse, suddenly the police arrived, arrested the manager, and took him to jail. Evidently Canales not only instructed his bodyguard to close and lock the manager's door, but subsequently phoned the police to report a peeping Tom wearing a purple bathrobe. The Canales party continued without interruption as the hapless manager and his bathrobe spent the night in the pokey.

Landlords aren't the only ones to feel Canales' sting; even those in cahoots with him were playing with a scorpion. In 1965 a legislator was trying to pass a bill for the trucking industry, only to be heckled by a liberal. Canales told the legislator, "I don't like the SOB. Do you want me to take care of him?" Thinking Canales was going to distract the heckler with a few questions, the legislator assented. Canales snapped his fingers and his two big bodyguards, without another word from their boss, started moving toward the troublemaker.

Legislator: "Amando, what are you doing?"

Canales: "I'm going to kill the SOB."

Legislator: "You can't do that."

Canales: "You watch me."

Legislator: "No, really, don't do that!"

So Canales snapped his fingers again and the bodyguards returned. "You killjoy," muttered Canales.

A story goes that A. C. and Oscar Carrillo got into an argument on a South Texas deer lease. They each had pistols, each fired five shots at each other and missed every time. The building was ten feet by ten feet.

Another great story on Amando. He had a bill to close all hunting in Duval County for five years — it was a local bill, of course, one county. Jim Slider was chairman of Game, Fishing. Amando was up talking about passing the bill and Slider said, "Now, Amando, do you want to pass this bill?" He said, "Yeah." Slider said, "But I've got 500 letters here from Duval County opposing your bill. Doesn't that bother you?" Amando said, "No, Mr. Chairman, you see that fellow over there?" He pointed to Archie Parr. "He's 5,000 votes; if he wants this bill, I want this bill." The bill passed and Duval County was closed for five years.

Amando was as convincing as a spade flush and was a "damn good compadre" to have in your corner!

WAGGONER CARR

House of Representatives 1951–1955
Speaker of the House 1957–1959

☆ ☆ ☆

"Remind us that if we've really got it, we don't have to flaunt it."
One-liner prayer by the Senate Chaplain, Dr. Gerald Mann

TEXAS LUSTER

- In 1959 Carr got a big scare when a *Dallas News* headline said "Speaker to be impeached."
- Carr based his attack on John Tower on two items: (1) I'm a Democrat; (2) therefore, I can do better . . . We must.
- It was said that Carr refused to discuss significant issues because he didn't want to say anything which might be used against him when he ran for governor in 1968.
- In the Sharpstown crisis and the Dirty Thirty, Carr flatly denied any wrongdoing and fought through the scandal well.
- Served on Kennedy Assassination Committee.

☆ ☆ ☆

Originally from Lubbock, Waggoner Carr was Speaker of the House for two terms, attorney general for two terms, but was unsuccessful in the race for governor in 1968. While attorney general, he investigated the assassination of Jack Kennedy and attended the Warren Commission hearings. At the time of the Sharpstown scandal, Carr was chairman of Gus Mutscher's Committee of 100, a group of legislators wanting better salaries and facilities.

During the 1959 special legislative session, when Price Daniel was governor, Ben Ramsey was lieutenant governor and Waggoner Carr was Speaker, Carr got an eerie forerunner of the future. He says: "I woke up one morning and saw the *Dallas News* headline: 'Speaker to be Impeached.' Neat way to start a day.

"I didn't want this to bubble and ferment for days, so during ses-

Attorney General Waggoner Carr giving oath of office to now judge/then legislator Neil Caldwell, official cartoonist for this book!

— Courtesy Austin History Center

sion the next morning, I said to the House, 'If you want to impeach me, I'm going back to Lubbock. If you don't, I'm coming back in here and we're going to get to work.' That was the challenge. I walked back to my office feeling very, very lonely. I closed the door, but turned up the speaker on my desk so I could hear what was happening on the House Floor. I thought I had tuned in to my own funeral.

"Well, I heard the call: 'Anyone who would like to remove the speaker, please approach the microphone.' The Floor was dead silent, and since I couldn't see what was happening, I waited, just waited, for a few endless seconds. Then there was a knock on the door. It was the chaplain. He said, 'Sir, I know you're going through a tough time and I think we should have a word of prayer.' So he got started.

"I must confess to you that I resented his interference to my eavesdropping on them. But the Lord works in mysterious ways; over the droning of the chaplain, I heard: 'There being no motion made, we shall move on.' A committee came to get me, and I said, 'Alright, let's get to work.'

"I found out later that the whole thing started with just a knothole of them, including Kinnard and Jerry Sadler, and it wasn't a big deal. They were having a beer and somebody suggested, 'You want to scare the Speaker, let's just try to impeach him. Let's give notice we're going to impeach him.' That's how it developed."

Carr, along with John Connally and Jim Wright, was a potential contender against John Tower in 1966. He was a strong conservative Democrat. Carr had become restless and did not want to serve as attorney general for another term. He announced his candidacy for the Senate on September 18, 1965. LBJ endorsed Carr, and Tower charged that he (Carr) couldn't stand on his own two feet in the political arena. Carr's main strategy against Tower was: (1) I'm a Democrat; (2) therefore, I can do better . . . we must. Carr was also criticized for refusing to discuss significant issues because he didn't want to say anything that could be used against him when he ran for governor in 1968. Tower won by more than 200,000 votes, and Carr even lost in his own Lubbock country. This election gave the Republicans a real boost in politics in Texas. Tom Moore, Jr., said, "Whenever Republicans can raise more than 10,000 votes against a conservative like Carr, and another 10,000 against an old liberal like me, you had better recognize the fact they are here to stay."

Carr was one of the people who flatly denied any wrongdoing and fought through the Sharpstown scandal successfully. He left politics deeply in debt and is now a corporate lawyer in Austin.

BILL CLAYTON

House of Representatives 1963–1982
Speaker of the House 1975–1982

☆   ☆   ☆

"Remind us that the best foundations are built with the rocks people throw at us."

One-liner prayer by the Senate Chaplain, Dr. Gerald Mann

TEXAS LUSTER

- First Speaker to serve more than two terms (served four!).
- Water for West Texas was his mania!
- Ate crow and passed bill, thanks to a political lesson kindly offered by John Connally (who once called Clayton a "goddamned blockhead").
- Slapped a "call on the house" and rounded up truant members at 4:30 A.M. to pass a bill.
- Broke the first rule of political fundraising: never take cash in front of somebody you don't know . . . the result was Brilab!
- Lobbyist for the City of El Paso.

☆   ☆   ☆

A West Texas farm boy from the Panhandle, Billy Wayne Clayton won election to the legislature in 1962 and was reelected in nine consecutive races. Until Clayton, no Speaker had ever served more than two terms. Clayton served four.

One thing always interested Clayton, and that was water in West Texas. A leading spokesman on water issues, he sponsored major legislation addressing the state's need for increased water resources and effective conservation programs. As Speaker, he modernized House operations, providing lawmakers with more support services and advancing computerization of legislative information. He also expanded the role of the standing House committees. He was described as one of fifteen or twenty House members who seldom spoke but nevertheless played crucial roles in lawmaking because of their knowledge and experience.

Clayton learned some valuable lessons in politics early on. The "Hemisfair bill," which involved the use of state monies for San Antonio, provided one of them. It seems Clayton had little respect for legislators from San Antonio; in fact, he thought they comprised the worst delegation in the United States. After a few drinks one night, Clayton made it his business to eliminate the bill. He was soon to learn that in Texas, politics is a blood sport.

When Clayton returned to his room at 1:00 A.M., he got a call from then-Speaker Ben Barnes, who demanded, "What in hell did you do to the Hemisfair bill?" Clayton, thinking Barnes would be proud of him, bragged that he'd killed the son-of-a-bitch bill dead in State Affairs. After an ominous silence, Barnes instructed Clayton to attend the State Affairs breakfast in Governor Connally's office the next morning.

At the breakfast, Clayton watched as Governor Connally greeted Gene Hendricks and others warmly and jovially. When Connally got to Clayton, he said not a word. After breakfast, the governor told Hendricks, "Now, Gene, I know it's hard for you people in Alpine to understand what Hemisfair's going to do," and so proceeded to personally acquaint Hendricks and the others with an outline of the bill. He then turned to Clayton and said, "No use talking to you, you goddamned blockhead." Clayton rightly sensed a gathering storm. A subsequent meeting tied the Hemisfair bill to the water plan bill, a piece of legislation in which Clayton was intensely interested; he *had* to vote for it. Clayton ate crow to keep his constituents from lynching him. It was one of the first political lessons he ever learned — courtesy of John Connally.

Clayton's legislative career was certainly not without controversy. In 1979 the *Dallas Morning News* reported that the Speaker had picked up between $60,000 and $100,000 for what he called "reelection" expenses, though he was not expected to have serious opposition in the next Speaker's race. "Labor is after me," the conservative Democrat explained, but it was generally thought that the money would be used for his political forays around the state both on behalf of his colleagues and in the interest of his 1982 political plans, which at the time seemed likely to include a bid for governor.

Of course, that was before the Brilab scandal. In 1980 Clayton broke the fundamental law of political fundraising: never take cash in front of someone you don't know. The someone in this case turned out

Speaker Billy Clayton and Senator Tom Creighton.

— Senate Media Services

to be an FBI informant. Clayton contended he took the fateful envelope containing $5,000 cash because he didn't want to embarrass the "labor lobbyist" in front of his client, and he insisted that he intended all along to return the "contribution." Within hours of the publication of front-page banner headlines implicating Clayton in the federal sting operation, Gib Lewis announced his candidacy for Speaker. Clayton was ultimately acquitted of the charges, however. Lewis put his speakership ambitions on hold, and Clayton won his fourth term as Speaker the following year.

Despite Clayton's tarnished reputation, he continued to wield power in the House. In 1981 a special session on congressional redistricting was called. After the "Wilson" bill passed in the Senate, Clayton laid it before the House one Sunday night in August, triggering one of the longest, most spirited battles ever waged in that chamber. Through hours of heated debate and parliamentary maneuvering, the Speaker coolly kept the pressure on, working toward passing his slightly more conservative version of the bill. Clayton wanted to work his way through amendments and delay tactics and pass the bill that night, but the rules required a two-hour break at midnight. During the break, the anti-Clayton forces pulled a "Killer Bee" maneuver and persuaded more than fifty of the 150 representatives to disappear for the 2:00 A.M. readjournment, thus denying Clayton a quorum.

Undaunted, Clayton promptly slapped a "Call on the House," empowering the sergeant-at-arms and Department of Public Safety officers to round up the truants from anywhere they could be found. Clayton's loyalists waited patiently, but by 3:00 A.M., some of them were more than a little weary, having had a few libations somewhere near the floor of the House. One in particular had required assistance in finding his desk button for voting during the hassle around midnight. Finally, at 4:32 A.M., a quorum of one hundred members was present, and Clayton rammed home his bill.

Clayton's political longevity shows he acquired the ability to compromise, and retains it even to this day. In 1985 he switched to the Republican party and, four years later, was appointed by Governor Bill Clements to serve as a regent for the Texas A&M University System. But he hasn't stayed away from the House. He recently lobbied for a lottery company bidding for state contracts and currently serves as El Paso's lobbyist in Austin.

DEAN COBB

House of Representatives 1969–1974

☆ ☆ ☆

"Let us do what we must do now;
there may be a law against it tomorrow."

One-liner prayer by the Senate Chaplain, Dr. Gerald Mann

Known as the "Ding-Dong Daddy from Dumas," Dean Cobb often stayed in Austin as the lobbyist for the Texas Trial Lawyers Association (TTLA) and several other clients and causes. The TTLA has had a longstanding barbecue for members of the legislature and their staffs. Phil Gauss, the most popular and successful executive director of TTLA, and his wife Vera worked twenty-four hours a day on the food and drink. Cobb said that Phil was like Jesus of Nazareth — he never ran out of food at his continuous bar and buffet. Perhaps Phil's success came from his knowledge that the staffs around state officials are invaluable as friends. Most agree that "The Trials" are the best under the dome and have been tops for quite a spell.

Cobb, who as a legislator roomed with Gib Lewis, served on the Appropriations Committee chaired by Bill Heatly. Cobb was a close observer of Heatly's style. Dean said you always knew which way Heatly was going to vote on a bill by watching what he did with the file. If he put it in his right drawer, he would allow it to pass, but if he put into the back of the left, it was no-go. I figure that in some manner Cobb used his keen observation in the interest of good government.

When Cobb was a legislator, he sponsored our Motor Vehicle Commission law, for which he says I promised him a flying trip to Las Vegas, which I have never provided. He reminds me of this constantly. I tell him that the promise was made before passage and it doesn't count. And I take the position that such a trip would have ruined his health, so I am doing him a favor by welching. Besides, the new ethics bill forbids an incentive for such!

Dean is a student of the old philosopher who observed, "The best politician is one that can straightforwardly dodge the issues." He, too, is colorful ripe!

JACK FISK
House of Representatives 1951–1952

☆ ☆ ☆

"Teach us that our dreams can't come true until we wake up."
One-liner prayer by the Senate Chaplain, Dr. Gerald Mann

Although Jack Fisk from Wharton didn't get to be "Governor for a Day," he pacified himself for the loss by being a "General for a Day." Gus Straus was Governor for a Day and he appointed Fisk to be a two-star general in the Texas State Guard. Fisk wore the uniform with two stars for the duration of the session. He had a friend who was a colonel in the Texas State Guard, and Fisk mentioned that he would like to go with the Bergstrom group that was taking a trip to practice maneuvers in Germany. His friend was happy to comply, saying, "Just get your stuff together and we'll go out there." According to Bob Ross, the uniform that Fisk's friend appropriated for him was "very fancy and impressive as hell."

They loaded into a seven-passenger Cadillac with a general's flag on the front and as they passed, all the lower-ranking soldiers popped to attention. Fisk and company found out where the Germany-bound group was from a guard at the gate. They arrived at the site and a general approached them. Fisk said, "I would very much like Colonel So-and-So to go along as a representative. How long do you think it would take to make arrangements for him?" The officer said, "Twenty minutes, sir." So off the Colonel and General Fisk went to watch maneuvers over Germany at voters' expense.

According to Bob Ross, when John Connally was informed about the escapade, he was upset with Fisk. He didn't like Fisk to begin with, since Fisk was a "redneck" and supported the segregation of schools. At a meeting called to address the issue of Fisk's "generalship," Connally discovered the only way to take the general's star away from him was to court-martial him. They really didn't have the grounds for a successful court-martial and since Fisk hadn't given his friend monetary compensation for his stars, Connally had to let the situation stand. He instead focused his anger at Crawford Martin, who reportedly signed the papers making Fisk a general.

Ross described Fisk as a "real country hick with a red bandana handkerchief hanging out of his back pocket about four or five inches."

During World War II, Fisk had been a corporal in the infantry. In Germany after the war, he found footlockers full of money. He never did figure out a plan to get the lockers out of Germany. It was said that he set out to be a swashbuckler, but he buckled before he swashed!

GENE FONDREN

House of Representatives 1963–1968
TADA 1972–Present

☆ ☆ ☆

"Let us not settle for the good, if we can have the best."
One-liner prayer by the Senate Chaplain, Dr. Gerald Mann

TEXAS LUSTER

- The "guru" of lobbyists.
- Was a country and western deejay while in school!
- Has the "best-oiled lobbying machine" (TADA) in the state!
- Cites lobbyists' proud heritage by pointing out that the most successful lobbyist in history was Moses, lobbying the Pharoah!
- Lyndon Olson took him on in insurance bill battle and lost . . . said of Fondren, "The guy's got class. He's strong, and he's got a whole army behind him."

☆ ☆ ☆

Gene Fondren, once called the "guru" of lobbyists, is perhaps best described as the representative for the "Brotherhood of the Buick." Fondren has been the chief executive officer of the Texas Automobile Dealers Association (TADA) since 1972. An insurance lobbyist once said about Fondren, "He has to be given the credit for having the best-oiled lobbying machine in the country on a state level." When the insurance lobby went to bat with Fondren over a legislative bill (and lost), Lyndon Olson, Jr., commented, "I'm sorry I can't tell you Fondren's dirty and no-good and low-down, but the guy's got class. He's strong and he's got a whole army behind him."

TADA is indeed a formidable campaign contributor and lobbying force, but many credit Fondren's organizational abilities and know-how for that association's success. Perhaps his experience in the legislature has much to do with his prowess as a lobbyist. After graduating from The University of Texas Law School (and working as a country and western disc jockey), Fondren served as a representative from Taylor from 1963 until 1968. He became a top contender for Speaker, but he was up against a formidable foe in Gus Mutscher. According to Fondren, Mutscher, who was chairman of the House Redistricting Committee, made certain that Fondren had a lopsided district that kept his mind on reelection and not on the Speaker's race.

After leaving the legislature, Fondren moved to Washington, DC, to work as a lobbyist for the Texas Railroad Association. That led to a job as a vice-president of the Missouri-Pacific Railroad. Then, in 1972, Fondren returned to Austin to head the Texas Automobile Dealers Association. Fondren and the association quickly became high-profile as Fondren almost single-handedly worked against approval of a Deceptive Trade Practices Act bill in 1973. Fondren and TADA lost that battle, but they came back in 1979 to push through major changes in the act, and Fondren now calls the law "the strongest consumer protection act in the country."

Fondren has racked up a number of accomplishments along the way. He is a past president of the Automotive Trade Association Executives, a past president of the Headliners Club, and a past president of the Texas Society of Association Executives.

Fondren is true "orange and white" and very generous with advice when speaking to various groups. For instance, in a recent appearance before a group of Aggies, he admonished, "Do not buy a used car if the Cadillac is spelled with a "K"!

JACK HIGHTOWER

House of Representatives 1953–1954
Senate 1965–1975
U.S. House of Representatives 1975–1985
Texas Supreme Court 1988–Present

☆ ☆ ☆

A native of Memphis, Texas, Jack Hightower served two years in the U.S. Navy and at the end of World War II returned to Texas to attend Baylor University. After receiving his law degree from Baylor in 1951, he and his wife Colleen moved to Vernon, where he began prac-

ticing law. The following year, Hightower was elected to the Texas House
of Representatives.

Hightower did not seek reelection to the House, however; instead,
he was appointed district attorney for
the 46th Judicial District, a post he
held for the next seven years. In 1965
he was elected to the Texas Senate,
succeeding George "Cotton" Moffett,
and remained there for ten years, serving as president pro tempore in 1973.
Hightower was elected to the United
States Congress in 1974, and served
until 1985. While in Congress, he sat
on the powerful Appropriations Committee. In 1987 then-Texas Attorney

Jack Hightower
— Guerrero Photographic Group

General Jim Mattox appointed him first assistant attorney general, a
position Hightower held until 1987, when he announced his successful
candidacy for the Supreme Court of Texas. He was sworn in as a justice
in December 1988.

The color grid on this true servant in our house: veteran, district
attorney, state representative, senator, president pro-tem congressman, supreme court justice . . . forty straight years of public service
without a blip. As any clean-cut leader from Baylor is prone to do, he
teaches a weekly Bible class at Austin's First Baptist Church, is a history buff, an expert on his own computer, and eats catfish every week.

He is a former secretary of the Texas Baptist General Convention
and served as Grand Master of the Masonic Lodge in Texas. He does
not believe that dancing the Texas two-step is sinful and wrote the
unanimous 1991 Supreme Court opinion deciding that alcohol manufacturers are not required to use labels that warn consumers of the pit-
falls of the inside juice, saying that such dangers are pretty well known
by now. My personal belief is that the court meant that even the Aggies are up to date on this matter. Around Vernon, Texas, from
whence he hails, this rule decider is known as an honest statute wran-
gler whose hard work keeps the fences mended. We have luck inside
our house to have such elected officials with little color helping us tend
to our business! Amen!

DORSEY HARDEMAN

House of Representatives 1939–1942
Senate 1947–1968

☆ ☆ ☆

"May we love our enemy enough to attend his funeral."
One-liner prayer by the Senate Chaplain, Dr. Gerald Mann

Emotions can run high in the Texas legislature; anger over con-
flicting interests can escalate to personal hatred. In this context, it
would be hard to forget that gruesome twosome — Babe Schwartz and
Dorsey Hardeman. Byron Tunnell remembers a legislator shaking his
head, remarking, "Boy, you can't believe what Schwartz is saying
about Hardeman." Tunnell replied, "Don't worry about it. He can't
say anything about Hardeman that Hardeman hasn't said about
Schwartz!"

After John Connally recovered from the Oswald bullet, members
of the Texas legislature expressed concern that the governor might
leave Texas to serve an appointment in Washington. Preston Smith
would then move to the governor's office, and the Senate president pro
tem would become lieutenant governor of the Great State of Texas.
Schwartz was up for president pro tem. The knives came out.

Many considered Schwartz too controversial for the potential
power of this position. So, although by seniority it was his turn at
president pro tem, he was jilted until the next session. Tom Creighton
was favored instead. Walking out of the caucus that day, Dorsey
Hardeman was button-holed by the press.

"Did y'all make the vote?" they asked.

He said, "Yes, we did."

"Did you elect Senator Schwartz?"

Hardeman replied, "No, we did not."

"Wasn't it his time by seniority?"

"Yes, it was, but we elected Senator Creighton."

"Why did you pass over Schwartz?"

"Write this down," Hardeman said, "this is what you want. We passed over him because he is a goddamn Jew. Now, do you want to print that?" The press never did.

Smith and Yarborough both tried to win Senate confirmation of Hardeman's appointment to the chairmanship of the State Insurance Board. The crusty, tactless, and often rude Hardeman had alienated many of his colleagues during his twenty-two years in the Senate. His appointment was not confirmed. Early in the session, eleven of the thirty-one senators signed a pact agreeing to vote against Hardeman, thus assuring that he would not get the two-thirds majority he needed for confirmation. Until then, appointments of all former members of the Senate had been confirmed almost automatically.

While it seemed that Hardeman was always on the prod, he represented his district full throttle and is truly another in our group of colorful Texans. He died in Austin on August 11, 1992.

GLENN KOTHMANN

House of Representatives 1957–1970
Senate 1971–1980

☆ ☆ ☆

"Our Father, let us not speak today unless we can improve on the silence."

One-liner prayer by the Senate Chaplain, Dr. Gerald Mann

TEXAS LUSTER

- Listed by *Texas Monthly* as one of the worst legislators on the "Furniture List" — those who do so little they just blend in with the furniture.
- Supposedly went through several years in the Senate without ever speaking!
- Vividly portrays the adage "A closed mouth gathers no foot."
- Considered a mental lightweight, but outpredicted professional pollsters and others by knowing the first rule of politics: Get elected, get reelected.

☆ ☆ ☆

Glenn Kothmann has been described as one of the least controversial people to ever serve as a legislator. It is difficult to make enemies or upset anyone if you don't do anything. Kothmann is notorious for being what *Texas Monthly* calls "furniture" in their Ten Best and Ten Worst Legislators list — somebody who does so little, good or bad, that they just blend in with the furniture.

One legislator said Glenn Kothmann "ought to be required to wear a Post No Bills sign. Didn't pass any, which is hardly a surprise, since he didn't introduce any." One poor House member, incensed that Kothmann had blocked his noncontroversial bill in the Senate, waited for weeks for a Kothmann bill to come through the House so he could return the favor. He's still waiting.

Unfortunately, this lack of interest is not entirely uncommon in legislators. That is why it is doubly important that the public be involved and aware of local politics, especially during the session. Kothmann's "indifference to issues is legendary. Never talk about the merits of a bill with him," says a higher education lobbyist. One feminist was startled when Kothmann interrupted her explanation of women's issues with: "You know, I'm a bachelor, and I keep in great physical shape. Want to feel my calf?" It was probably the most animated thing he did all session.

According to a fellow senator, Kothmann went through several years in the Senate without ever speaking! When attempts were made to hold him accountable for his lack of input at the Constitutional Convention, he ventured, "Silence is golden." Or as a wise man once said, "A closed mouth gathers no foot."

Although considered by some a mental lightweight, Kothmann, one of the "Killer Bees," was able to outpredict professional polls, and he knew the first rule of politics: Get elected, get reelected.

HOMER LEONARD

House of Representatives 1931–1939

☆ ☆ ☆

"Thanks for the people who tell it like it is, and thanks more for the people who tell it like it can be."
One-liner prayer by the Senate Chaplain, Dr. Gerald Mann

TEXAS LUSTER

- In a practical joke played on him by Emmett Morse, Leonard was arrested for driving 90 mph and grand theft auto.
- Known as the great unpaid lobbyist for retarded children.
- After his retirement, his brochure of speech topics included "Communist Infiltration into the Texas Screw Worm Program" and "Impact of the Closing of the Chicken Ranch at La Grange on the South Texas Economy."
- Was known for not being overly fond of lobbyists, but he knew how to use their methods to his own advantage.

☆ ☆ ☆

One night Homer Leonard was out around Pflugerville making a speech. He said, "I just want you to know that those lobbyists downtown are not supporting me and Ed Clark ain't supporting me." An ol' boy in the back of the hall said, "And you ain't going to get elected, neither."

Leonard may not have been sympathetic to "downtown lobbyists," but he sure knew how to use their methods for his own ends. Reuben Senterfitt recalled that Leonard's catfish dinners, held in the Stephen F. Austin Hotel, "were quite popular."

Despite the frequency with which Leonard held dinners, he didn't always have an easy time feeding the Texas legislature. During Price Daniel's tenure as governor, Leonard invited the Senate to a state dinner with all the trimmings. Dinner would be at 7:30, and the solons were invited to congregate first at the bar to relax with a drink. Alas, it was not to be; Price Daniel locked the Senate in his chambers. Ever courteous, Daniel had Leonard phoned to tell him the senators would be a little while getting there.

Emmett Morse preceded Leonard as Speaker. Leonard and Morse were renowned for the jokes they played on each other; they often hid each other's cars. Morse eventually took the joke one step further. Knowing that Leonard had to go to San Antonio for a meeting, Morse hid Leonard's car. In the face of Leonard's "emergency," Morse oh-so-kindly lent him his car. Morse then called the police and reported his car was stolen. They arrested Leonard for driving 90 mph, then slapped him with grand theft auto. It took a long time to get him released.

This is not to say that Homer Leonard lacked clout. A friend, Sammy Allred of singing Geezinslaw Brothers fame, was in training for the army, but just *had* to get out for an interview with Arthur Godfrey. He called Leonard for help. Leonard was playing cards with the commanding general from Bergstrom, and asked the general if he could help Sammy get out of training camp and fly back for the audition. The general said not even God could get Sammy out of camp. Contemplating this, Leonard asked the general, "If he does get out, will you furnish a plane to fly him back for the audition?" The general agreed. Homer called LBJ and within an hour Sammy was released on leave. The general put his top plane, a Spider Jet, at Sammy's disposal.

Leonard was also known as the great unpaid lobbyist for mentally retarded children. He had a relative who was in a state home in Austin. He did so much for this cause that the "Lone Star" chapel was named for him in honor of all he had done. He never stopped lobbying for this cause. When he was offered a job in San Antonio ("Name your salary, Homer"), he would not leave because of his work for the retarded.

After he retired, his brochure of speech topics included "Communist Infiltration into the Texas Screw Worm Program" and "Impact of the Closing of the Chicken Ranch at La Grange on the South Texas Economy." He never lost his sense of humor.

DURWOOD MANFORD

House of Representatives 1941–1949
Speaker of the House 1949–1951

☆ ☆ ☆

"Our Father, let us remember that there's always two sides to an argument — until we take one."

One-liner prayer by the Senate Chaplain, Dr. Gerald Mann

After Price Daniel's appointment of Speaker Durwood Manford to the Water Board, Ben Ramsey proclaimed that the governor had decided to abolish the board by appointment but to save the good name of water, Ramsey still worked with Ed Clark in a later appointment of Manford to the Insurance Commission. First, however, in an effort to bring Jean Daniel's bridge group back to Austin, the governor appointed Manford to the Industrial Accident Board where I was serving as chairman. After a few months of having to get to work before noon, Manford maneuvered his appointment to the Water Commission. All he did at the IAB was to seek to have workmen's comp declared unconstitutional . . . which might not have been such a bad idea.

Pearce Johnson served in the House while Durwood was Speaker and became the guardian Speaker on many days that Manford was late traveling the long distance from the Speaker's apartment to the podium by noon call to order. Pearce said that it was not too unusual for him to appear wearing top or bottom pieces to his pajamas.

As Speaker of the House, Manford tried to cut the budget. In so doing he suggested that it would be more cost-efficient if each member would have half a secretary. Colonel Green rose for point of inquiry to ask how they would determine which half the members would get.

Manford's clumsy dealings with secretaries didn't end there. Manford felt it would save time if he would dictate from the bathroom, and have his secretary take notes from outside.

Sam Hanna told how Manford built a new outhouse on his farm near Smiley, presumably one *without* optional secretary attachment. Manford had a carpenter out about 9:00 A.M., and together they examined the old outhouse to determine whether to build a new one or repair the existing structure. Manford spent about an hour debating, then he and the contractor went in to have coffee. About 10:30, he decided to build a new one. They went back outside to see if they should use a new location or keep the old; Manford finally decided to make a fresh start with a new site. The two men took a break for lunch. About 2:00 P.M., Manford said, "Well, we have a decision to make: should it be a one-holer or a two-holer?"

The contractor said, "I have a firm recommendation, Mr. Manford. Let's make it a one-holer, because if you don't, you'll keep changing your mind about which hole to use, and mess your britches every time."

When Manford was Speaker, the legislature didn't adjourn until sometime in July. It was, at that time, the longest session. Late in the session, everything was hung up and a lot of grousing was going on. Someone on the floor came up to Judge Strickland and said, "Don't you think Manford is the sorriest SOB that ever occupied the Speaker's chair?"

Since Strickland was lobbying for a cause, he said diplomatically, "I'm committed to Robert Lee Bobbitt, but I'll keep your man in mind."

Could be that the old Texas political saying, "Where you don't do nothing, you can't be blamed for doing somethin'," was meant for Durwood.

Manford was a true disciple of Murphy's Law, such as "You can't depend on people being wrong all the time" and especially "Indecision is the key to flexibility." If only he had been as pretty and sweet as his ever loving and patient wife, beautiful Joyce. She died in Austin on September 21, 1992.

JIM MATTOX

House of Representatives 1972–1977
U.S. House of Representatives 1978–1981
Attorney General 1982–1989

☆ ☆ ☆

"Lord, if we have to shoot at each other, let it be from the lip only."
One-liner prayer by the Senate Chaplain, Dr. Gerald Mann

Jim Mattox came to the attorney general's office in 1983 calling himself "The People's Lawyer" and promising to wage war on behalf of consumers. He served as the state's chief civil attorney for eight tumultuous years, longer than anyone else in the post. Mattox was considered the most aggressive attorney general in Texas history. His office, which grew from about 500 employees in 1983 to 2,500 in 1989, claimed that it won more than $187 million in judgments and settlement agreements for consumers during Mattox's tenure. A longtime ally of organized labor and trial lawyers (the mortal enemies of businessmen), Mattox took on the Texas Rangers, the insurance industry, prominent charities, auto makers, and even an oatmeal manufacturer.

Mattox went from selling Bibles door-to-door as a teenager in the rough-and-tumble neighborhoods of East Dallas to graduating from Baylor in 1965 as the top business school graduate. He then went on to the dean's list at the Southern Methodist University Law School. After his graduation from SMU, he served as an assistant district attorney of Dallas County for two years. With that training behind him, Jim decided to run for a seat in the Texas state legislature. He won that election in 1972 and gained recognition in the House for his outspoken leadership and for being a champion of legislative reform. In 1975 *Texas Monthly* named Jim Mattox as one of the "ten best legislators."

Mattox won a seat in the U.S. House of Representatives in 1978 and was the only freshman congressman elected to the powerful House Budget Committee. In 1979 he protested the congressional dress code by refusing to wear a coat and tie, infuriating Speaker Tip O'Neill, who would not allow him to speak in the Chamber. He was kicked out three times before he finally conceded to the dress code. Despite that scuffle, Mattox was reelected to a second term in Congress in 1980.

At the end of that term, Mattox ran and won the election for attorney general. Exaggerated advertising was one of Mattox's favorite targets. Such favorite name brands as Carnation infant formula, Quaker Oats, Kraft Cheese Whiz and Mazola Corn Oil all backed off advertising claims because of the attorney general's office. *The Daily Texan* (UT's student newspaper) poked fun at Mattox's battle "to keep our oatmeal safe for democracy." When it was reported that sixteen attorneys (or about 20.9 percent of the attorney general's office legal staff) were working in the consumer-protection subdivision, *The Daily Texan* commented: "Sixteen stalwart souls and Big Jim stand between us and bogus breakfast cereal." Describing Mattox's program as "Oatmealgate," the *Texan* contended that "most citizens fail to perceive oatmeal labeling as one of the gripping social issues of our day."

Mattox had to fend off allegations that he used the weight of his office to squeeze campaign contributions from reluctant givers. In 1986 he submitted an unusual campaign fund report, with each contribution (totaling $750,000) listed on a separate page. At 1,101 pages, it would have reportedly cost an opponent or reporter $165.55 to get a copy from the secretary of state. And critics also questioned the $200,000 he made from a land deal with a Dallas businessman who later was indicted on a racketeering charge because of alleged fraud in a real estate deal.

On the job itself, Mattox probably got some of his sharpest criticism over the unit that enforces court-ordered child support payments. The annual payments collected by the unit jumped from $18 million in 1983 to about $180 million, Mattox said, and he points to awards the unit has received from the federal government for being the most improved. But one group, the Association for Children for Enforcement of Support, still assails him for not doing enough.

Mattox can be combative and often biting — he once called a Williamson County district attorney "the village idiot." With characteristic bluntness, he accused retiring Governor Bill Clements of pursuing "the Pearl Harbor theory" of government: "He acts only when the bombs start falling." He also went after the independently wealthy former Lieutenant Governor Bill Hobby without ever mentioning Hobby's name: "Some of these people have had the gold spoon in their mouth so long that they forget what it's like for the average person." And Mattox has been described as a take-no-prisoners campaigner who has been involved in races unparalleled in their mudslinging and cheap shots. In the 1990 gubernatorial race, he charged Ann Richards with drug use. The strategy backfired, however, as many voters deemed Mattox's negative campaigning as dirty pool. While one former friend and aide described him as a "blunt, mean-spirited SOB," others claim that he is a thoughtful and private man who neither smokes nor drinks, who quotes Scripture, and who looks out for the little guy — the working class and the have-nots of society. Both sides agree that he is not shy of controversy and is always eager for media attention. Mattox defends his controversial image by contending, "The good Lord has given me an extra dose of toughness. I don't have any apologies for that." Paraphrasing Harry Truman, Mattox is fond of saying that a man is known by the enemies he makes. By that standard, he may be the best known politician in Texas. "I am proud of each and every one of my enemies," said Mattox.

After his unsuccessful bid for governor, Mattox and one of his renowned "enemies," gubernatorial opponent and wealthy oilman Clayton Williams, returned to the public stage to debate each other on radio in a program called "The Texas Shoot-Out." Mattox commented, "If I can cut him [Williams] in on this radio deal, maybe he'll cut me in on some of his oil wells."

TOM MOORE, JR.

House of Representatives 1967–1972

☆　☆　☆

"Deliver us from live wires who have no connection."
One-liner prayer by the Senate Chaplain, Dr. Gerald Mann

TEXAS LUSTER

· Drew the battle lines in his first election on purely partisan lines, stating, "How could a Republican possibly be effective in Austin?"
· Remarked, "These Republicans are getting tough."
· Introduced a resolution honoring Albert DeSalvo, "The Boston Strangler."
· Subpoenaed Texas Senate.

☆　☆　☆

In 1971 incumbent Tom Moore, Jr., a former district attorney, defeated Republican Carl McIntosh, a political unknown. McIntosh's well-organized campaign stunned the community when he captured forty-one percent of the vote on January 7, causing a February 4 runoff with Moore, who had garnered thirty-three percent. "The Republicans," said Moore, an articulate liberal, "are to be congratulated. They ran a quiet, well-organized and well-financed campaign . . . [but] no Republican has ever carried McLennan County in my memory . . . and I welcome the opportunity of representing the Democratic Party in this run-off." Moore drew the battle line on a purely partisan basis ("How could a Republican possibly be effective in Austin?") and began marshaling his various forces. Ultimately, he received help from a number of outside sources, including Barbara Jordan, the immensely popular black state senator from Houston, who would help energize the traditional Democratic liberal and black vote.

When all Waco boxes had reported, McIntosh still held a slim lead. All attention turned to the final box to report — from the little community of West, north of Waco. Sentiment in West remained strongly Democratic and the results there crushed the Republican candidate and his cadre of supporters, giving Moore the election by 254 votes out of 21,710 cast. That turnout did indeed exceed the Tower-Carr combined vote by 650 and was about 7,000 more than voted in the first round in which there were seven candidates. McIntosh's $49^9/_{10}$ percentage was identical to Tower's for McLennan County, but McIntosh had received 315 more votes than Tower — a truly remarkable achievement! In his post-election remarks, Moore observed, "These Republicans are getting tough. Whenever Republicans can raise more than 10,000 votes against a conservative like Waggoner Carr, and another 10,000 against an old liberal like me, you had better recognize the fact they are here to stay."

In 1971 Moore introduced a resolution in the House honoring Albert DeSalvo who, among other things, had been officially recognized by the state of Massachusetts for "his noted activities and unconventional techniques involving population control and applied psychology." DeSalvo was the Boston Strangler! The House passed the resolution with as little attention as it usually gives to such matters!

Tom and I were assistants in Gene Madden's office of the district attorney. We shared an office — he ran Yarborough's campaigns on his side, and I worked for Shivers' plans on the other. Our biggest victory was probably the time we set up Shuford Farmer, a well-known defense lawyer, by allowing him to steal the wrong file out of the "cases to be tried" drawer. In the four years I was there, I was the only man to lose a case on a plea of guilty. Watson Arnold and Coy Barret were on board. It was a real interesting and educational time. We had hell keeping Baptist preachers off the grand jury, and we did learn "If You Wanna Go Free Get Frank Tiree," which proved to be true most of the time.

GUS F. MUTSCHER

House of Representatives 1961–1967
Speaker of the House 1969–1971

☆ ☆ ☆

"Remind us that a failure is only the success of discovering one more thing that won't work."

One-liner prayer by the Senate Chaplain, Dr. Gerald Mann

TEXAS LUSTER

· Named Harris County's Outstanding Young Businessman of the Year in 1959.
· A master magician in the House — organized housewives to attend the House en masse to oppose grocery tax bill.
· Convicted of conspiring to accept a bribe in Sharpstown scandal.
· Released from his final year of probation to be appointed Washington County judge!
· Indicted in February '92 by another grand jury on charges of conspiring to defraud investors. When calling the case, the court clerk mispronounced his name "Moocher"!

☆ ☆ ☆

Gus Mutscher is one of the most notorious of the colorful characters. His motto was, "Never quit politicking and never underestimate your opponent." Mutscher could be a supreme strategist when he remembered to cover his tracks. He also attained a reputation as the hardest working Speaker of the House to ever serve. And, while he sometimes overestimated his opponents, he never *under*estimated them.

Mutscher was offered a position on the staff of U.S. Representative Homer Thornberry as a young businessman in Houston. Mutscher had been honored in 1959 by the Chamber of Commerce as the outstanding young businessman of Harris County. Encouraged instead to run for political office himself, he began campaigning and was elected in 1960 to the first of six terms as a state representative.

He used his power in the House to eliminate a rival, Gene Fondren. Mutscher drew a new district to keep Fondren too busy with home politics to run for Speaker, thereby assuring Mutscher's election to that position in 1969. Also in 1969, a bill was presented for a sales tax on food. The House unwittingly allowed a whole weekend for Mutscher to organize, and when the vote came up on Monday, the balcony was full of housewives. Under their watchful eyes, and Mutscher's broad smile, the bill was defeated 149–0.

With Gus Mutscher's guiding hand, the House turned into a Roman circus. During Mutscher's tenure as Speaker, pork barrel spending was shoved through with impunity, prompting Texas Republicans in the legislature to point out that state spending had doubled in just four years and had increased ten times faster than the population in the 1960s.

Of course, those weren't the only tricks Mutscher played; he had a whole deck of 'em. The House Speaker from Brenham made a profit of $105,000 from NBL stock, and was indicted by a federal grand jury on a charge of accepting a bribe. Convicted of conspiring to accept a bribe in what became known as the Sharpstown stock fraud scandal, Mutscher was sentenced to serve five years' probation. He then returned to his home in Washington County.

During the time of the probe and subsequent indictment and conviction in the Sharpstown scandal, Mutscher came under fire in the legislature by a group known as "The Dirty Thirty" (see that section later in the book). The group earned its name after a vote on a resolution sponsored by Sissy Farenthold calling for an investigation of Gus Mutscher. Ethics were almost nonexistent before the Sharpstown scandal and the challenge by this coalition of lawmakers. They called for Mutscher to institute various ethics and reform measures. You can guess how Mutscher responded to that kind of challenge, given his firm control over the House until his resignation! Texas Supreme Court Justice Bob Gammage, a member of the Dirty Thirty, had this to say about the whole episode: "There were many times when I felt like Mutscher was more a victim than a villain in the process. He didn't create it. I think it was the system. It operated that way before Gus Mutscher was speaker."

In 1976 Mutscher was released from the final year of his probation by the Abilene judge who presided over his trial, so he could serve as appointee to the position of Washington County judge. He was re-elected repeatedly to the position until 1990, when he was defeated.

Mutscher recently was indicted by *another* grand jury for conspiring to defraud investors of almost $1.5 million in never-completed land developments in (surprise) Washington and Fayette counties. Charged with fourteen counts of mail fraud, money-laundering, and interstate transportation of fraudulently obtained securities, Mutscher could face up to ninety-five years in prison and fines totaling $3 million.

On a more humorous note, when calling the case, the clerk mispronounced Mutscher's name, asking for the names of the lawyers in the "Moocher" case. From the mouths of babes!

Mutscher's political career has spanned thirty years — from his first campaign in 1960 until his defeat in his last race in 1990. He has lived by his motto of "never quit politicking." Only time will tell if Gus Mutscher will again throw his sombrero into the political arena.

CARL PARKER

House of Representatives 1963–1975
Senate 1977–Present

☆ ☆ ☆

"Lord, remind us that a discussion is an exchange of knowledge, and that an argument is an exchange of ignorance."
One-liner prayer by the Senate Chaplain, Dr. Gerald Mann

TEXAS LUSTER

· Experience has taught us that letting members read the bill only causes problems.
· Won "Best Quip" Award when he suggested that the law allowing Texans to carry handguns should require a "Gun on Board" sign.

- Won "Rudest Behavior by a Lawmaker" Award when he threatened to "annihilate" school districts opposing his "Robin Hood" plans.
- Said that the proposed redistricting plan would "make Richard Nixon proud of his party."
- *Dallas Morning News* voted him one of the seven best in the 72nd Legislature — but compared him to Dr. Jekyll and Mr. Hyde.
- Sometimes tries to be careful. He said, "I don't wish to establish any kind of precedent in voting against fat ugly guys from Port Arthur."
- Called House members "handmaidens of special-interest polluters" regarding environmental issues.
- Stated that grand juries are "as archaic as the rack, and about as useful to justice."

☆   ☆   ☆

Sharp-tongued Senator Carl Parker one day offered to "be nice to everybody for the rest of the week" if his colleagues would attend a reception hosted by his hometown. The room was silent, as if the Angel Gabriel had spoken. Lieutenant Governor Bob Bullock rose to the occasion: "Sergeant-at-Arms, arrest everybody and see that they go."

Parker won "Best Quip" Award when he suggested that the law allowing Texans to carry handguns should require that those licensed to carry a gun must have a "Gun on Board" sign in their vehicles.

He also won the "Rudest Behavior by a Lawmaker" Award when he threatened to "annihilate" school districts opposing his "Robin Hood" funding plans. He wrote in a letter to a Richardson woman that she had a "shallow understanding" of the problem.

But Parker is sometimes more careful. "I don't wish to establish any kind of precedent in voting against fat ugly guys from Port Arthur," he said.

Following a huge ruckus over a minor amendment to a bill, the caliber of arguments prompted Senator Carl Parker to exclaim, "This is the day you pray for a bomb threat." But one aide ascribed the thin skins to more than just an ornery Monday: "Can you tell redistricting started last week?"

In August of 1991, Parker pointed out that the House had "backed us into an ethics bill" and the $85 per diem approved for legislators "would barely cover what it costs for you to be here [in Austin]."

In the midst of a heated debate over the concealed weapons bill mentioned above, Senator Bill Sims, D-San Angelo, allowed that "the cabrito is getting cold down there at Scholz's Beer Garden." Soon into another debate on a different issue, Parker was allowed the floor and asked playfully, "What is cabrito? . . . Is it good cold?" The proposal on the floor was quickly finished and the Senate adjourned to the lunch being sponsored by the Texas Sheep and Goat Raisers Association.

Senator Parker was quoted in "Under the Dome" in the *Fort Worth Star Telegram* as the most quotable with the following, to his philosophical opposite Senator John Leedom, R-Dallas, on the occasion of Leedom's birthday: "I've never seen anyone who is so often wrong and so seldom in doubt."

In January of 1992, the legislature was called into special session to (again) discuss congressional redistricting plans. "This would make Richard Nixon proud of his party," quipped Parker.

In September of 1991, *Texas Monthly* listed Parker as one of the best legislators of the year, stating, "No person made the system work more often this year than Carl Parker. No one knows better how to pass a bill or how to kill one." The article continued, "When Parker grabs his microphone on the Senate floor, belly jutting and nostrils flaring, he brandishes it like a beer bottle to crack over someone's head in a barroom brawl. But his words usually have just enough humor to soften the blows."

Carl Parker was voted one of the seven best of the 72nd Legislature by the *Dallas Morning News*. They said that Parker was "at times the best member of the Senate. He could also be the worst. There is this 'Mr. Hyde' character who keeps turning up in Parker's clothing. A bombastic, physically intimidating man with a devilish sense of humor . . . he knows the rules and players as no other Senator. Most of the time, he exercised his considerable talents on behalf of good bills. But like his humor, which can turn mean and vulgar, the Senator's political performance could turn stubborn and narrow."

When Parker sponsored a bill to create a Natural Resources Conservation Commission, which would be an umbrella agency for the state's half-dozen environmental regulatory groups, he met with resistance and many suggested changes. "I do not think we would do any better in a conference committee," stated Parker. "This way I think we can protect the steps we have taken without the risk of losing what gains we have made. He did, however, call House members "handmaidens of special-interest polluters" and promised to draft other environmental measures and turn the spotlight on representatives.

Under current law, no one is allowed to have a lawyer in the grand jury room when they are being questioned. Parker sponsored a bill to change this situation. When Senator John Montford said that grand juries served as "a buffer between a tyrannical prosecutor and the innocent victim," Parker retorted: "The grand jury has as much to do with justice today and protecting individual rights and freedoms today as the Queen of England has with governing England." Parker, who has been under investigation by three grand juries, and had charges dismissed in all three instances, said that he would abolish grand juries if he could. "The grand jury is as archaic as the rack, and about as useful to justice," Parker said.

All of the above reflect Parker's dedication and dogged determination, as well as his quick wit. Given his popularity, effectiveness and long political career, Texas is sure to be hearing from and about Carl Parker for a long, long time.

Only Ike Harris and Chet Brooks are ahead of Parker in length of time served in the Senate. He is bound to be the most quoted and has no fear of colleagues, the press, or the balcony. His philosophy for service is, "The worst thing a politician can do in a crisis is nothing." The senator does something most every time.

BEN RAMSEY

House of Representatives 1931–1934
Senate 1941–1948

☆ ☆ ☆

"May we not develop wishbones where our backbones should be."
One-liner prayer by the Senate Chaplain, Dr. Gerald Mann

TEXAS LUSTER

· "The sage wit of San Augustine."
· Made Ed Clark look well-dressed.
· Most years ever served by Texas official . . . by any of three top state officials.
· Looked like an unmade bed.
· The "Will Rogers of Texas politics."

• Directed Senate with a loose rein.

☆ ☆ ☆

Ben Ramsey was an unlikely politician. Known for his slouch hat and loose suits, and for his shirt collar overhanging his coat, Ramsey looked like an unmade bed. His wife would insist that the lieutenant governor cut his hair before inaugurations. "She acts like it was her hair," Ramsey grumbled. Called "a political paradox" and the "Will Rogers of Texas politics," Ramsey was disliked by Texas labor leaders because of his "right-to-work" law against compulsory union membership. Despite their powerful opposition, however, Ramsey always emerged victorious.

While on the campaign trail, Ben Ramsey refused to emerge from his hotel in one town. When asked why he wasn't out shaking hands, Ramsey grumped, "None of them is going to vote for me anyway." Five elections later, Ramsey was still lieutenant governor — longer than any other person in history.

Ramsey directed the Senate with what cowboys call a "loose rein." A young reporter asked Ramsey, "When does the Senate come to order?" Without blinking, Ramsey replied, "Young man, the Senate of the State of Texas never comes to order. It just meets."

One night at a Senate committee session, a senator explained to Ramsey, "That man is working under a great handicap. He is stone deaf — can't hear a thing."

Gentle Ben said, "I don't think he's handicapped — he doesn't have to listen to what he's saying."

One day, ten Very Important People stood in line, waiting to see Lieutenant Governor Ramsey. A friend of Ramsey's slipped into the apartment and was surprised to find the Man Himself alone in the living room, casually reading a newspaper. "Ben," asked the friend, "don't you realize there are some mighty important people waiting outside to see you?"

Without lowering his paper, Ramsey muttered, "Well, sit down and be quiet. Maybe they'll go away."

On one occasion when Ramsey was acting governor, he continued to work in the lieutenant governor's office. When asked why he didn't occupy the more elaborate offices of the governor, as he was entitled to do, Ramsey said, "No use going over there. Shivers locked up everything before he went — except the chair." Well, why didn't Ramsey go over and sit in the governor's chair? "This chair over here is more comfortable."

But Ramsey changed his tune when he learned he could draw $35 a day as acting governor, in addition to his $10 a day as lieutenant governor. He remarked, "That's a pretty good deal. Why doesn't Shivers go to Europe?"

In speaking of a wayward senator on a Monday morning, one of Ramsey's great quotes was, "He looks like he was shot out of a cannon and missed the net." Ambassador Ed Clark, a fellow from the same San Augustine, Texas, and a large sponsor of Ramsey, said, "He is as slick as a watermelon seed." Ramsey never eased up on the reins in guiding Texas toward a continuing history of greatness. Read all you can about this man . . . He never missed the net!

BABE SCHWARTZ

House of Representatives 1955–1958
Senate 1961–1980

☆ ☆ ☆

"As we begin this day, may all our hang-ups be drip dry."
One-liner prayer by the Senate Chaplain, Dr. Gerald Mann

A classic confrontation occurred in a debate between newspaper editor Archer Fullingim and State Senator A. R. (Babe) Schwartz of Galveston. Schwartz had long established his liberal-party loyalist credentials. Fullingim warned that liberal Democrats would force the conservative arm of their party over into voting Republican by reelecting John Tower. Schwartz countered, "You can't force conservatives out of the Democratic party by voting against them. What you have to do is build a strong liberal element which will elect a liberal nominee in the primary." Fullingim characterized Schwartz's theory as "weird" and noted, "We [liberals] do not have to follow the suicide course of continuing loyalty to the Democratic Party. We owe no loyalty to a name . . ." Fullingim further characterized the Democratic party in Texas as "nothing more than a group of lackeys for every big business interest in Texas."

Schwartz, a leader of the "Killer Bees," was dubbed "Godfather of the Killer Bees" by *Texas Monthly*. And in 1980 he was characterized as the venerable liberal leader who would become "Dean of the Texas Senate if re-elected." In that election year, Schwartz was involved in a cliffhanger showdown with Buster Brown. Schwartz had a longstanding winning tradition going for him, including not only the traditional liberal-labor forces but a number of prominent business and industrial leaders in Houston. Few believed that Brown could win, and those who thought he might have a chance hesitated, weighing the risk of incurring the wrath of Schwartz should their hope not materialize. Brown supporters hoped his youthful demeanor would provide a welcome contrast to the gray, aging Senate veteran who was known for his acerbic outbursts and whom some considered as having grown out of touch. Brown was given an unanticipated break when Schwartz threw a well-publicized punch at another attorney in a Galveston courtroom. Schwartz lost to Brown by 778 votes. Schwartz refused to blame "the weather, someone else's phone banks or other factors." He said, "I still say Buster Brown is the best person I came up against in twenty years," noting that Brown was "young and intelligent."

Schwartz and Dick Slack were both defeated that election year after each had served twenty-five years in the legislature. When Slack was asked why he would want to spend twenty-five years in the legislature, he replied, "Man, have you ever been to Pecos, Texas?"

In 1957 Babe and I went on a deer hunt to Diboll. I was serving as Shivers' appointed chairman of the Industrial Accident Board and had no idea how to represent an agency before the legislature's appropriations committee. After a thorough briefing by my fellow board member Leonard Carlton, I appeared on behalf of the IAB. I soon learned about putting ten percent cream at the top so the committee would cut back to the amount we wanted. Schwartz kept up with the goings-on, and I quickly regretted not backing up his story that on an East Texas deer hunt he killed a buck 400 yards away on the other side of the hill he shot from. That was the hunt in which the game warden found Senator Warren McDonald to be without a hunting license. We struck camp soon after that!

While it sometimes got as bumpy for him as a twenty-five-pipe cattle guard, the Babe used his great sense of humor and pride to well serve the people he spoke for. He now serves from the balcony, where he continues to earn respect and notice.

REUBEN SENTERFITT

House of Representatives 1941–1951
Speaker of the House 1951

☆   ☆   ☆

---

*"Lord, in the midst of this hectic day, let us remember that the only
people who aren't confused are the ones who are not thinking!"*
One-liner prayer by the Senate Chaplain, Dr. Gerald Mann

TEXAS LUSTER

· Started work in the House in 1941.
· "Mountain went to Mohammed."
· One of the most trusted and popular persons on the hill!
· Fair, honest, but watch his ire!
· Has refused several times to run for mayor of San Saba.

☆   ☆   ☆

Reuben Senterfitt started work in the Texas House of Representatives in 1941, under W. Lee "Pass the Biscuits, Pappy" O'Daniel.
Senterfitt's career encompassed two terms as Speaker of the House,
where he garnered powerful friendships and some memorable moments.

"One time, the House was in a Special Session. Shivers wanted
something done so he called and asked if he could come to see me
alone, without all the hootin' and hollerin' of the House. He walked
over from the governor's office and we sat down and visited a little bit
and we pretty well resolved our problems.

"That was a nice arrangement: I was Speaker, Allan Shivers was
Governor and Ben Ramsey was Lt. Governor. Anyway, we were done
and Shivers started to leave, but all the Capitol press was out there,
sniffin' for blood. Shivers came back in my office, closed the door and
said, 'I am just going to walk out and tell the press that we only discussed the weather and that was all. Kind of a social visit.' I said,
'That's fine, I'll tell them the same thing.' So that's what he told them

and I told them the same thing, but one of them, I believe it was Bo Byers, had a headline the next day, 'The Mountain Went to Mohammed.' "

Yes, Senterfitt wielded great power. Few were willing to risk his ire. After a crucial vote, O. B. Jones approached Senterfitt and said, "Mr. Speaker, I watched that Board real careful, and if you'd needed my vote, you'd have sure had it."

Let it not be said, though, that House Speaker Senterfitt took himself too seriously. Once Senterfitt ruled rather quickly on an issue, and Preston Mangum jumped up on the microphone to raise a point of order: "Mr. Speaker, just a minute. Do you have a precedent for this ruling?"

Senterfitt replied, "No, Mr. Mangum, but my successor will."

JOHN SHARP

House of Representatives 1979–1982
Senate 1983–1984
State Comptroller 1991–Present

☆ ☆ ☆

"Remind us that our critics are using the only talent they have."
One-liner prayer by the Senate Chaplain, Dr. Gerald Mann

TEXAS LUSTER

· Grand croupier of lottery.
· Issues tax-free certificates of citizenship.
· Named "Outstanding Freshman" first year in legislature.
· "Wizard of Odds."
· Looking forward to a bigger government office someday.

☆ ☆ ☆

When John Sharp took over the thankless job of being the chief tax collector for the state, few anticipated that he would soon become the state's conquering hero. He released a plan called the Texas Performance Review, which he promised would save the state billions without raising taxes. A sigh of relief was heard from the Panhandle to the Valley. But praise for Sharp's fiscal prowess quickly died down as government agency officials, schoolteachers, farmers, higher educators, and others began to realize that cutting the deficit would mean cuts that they would feel. As one reporter pointed out, Sharp was praised for his plan but cussed for its ramifications. Nobody ever said it was going to be easy . . .

Besides the deficit, Sharp faces challenges ranging from the "sleaze factor" of the Texas lottery to an avalanche of unsolicited mail requests for honorary (tax-free) Texas citizenship. As if he didn't get enough mail, he even instituted postage-paid cards on which citizens were invited to grade his employees.

The son of an oil field worker and a schoolteacher, and former Aggie student body president, Sharp entered state government in 1979. *Texas Monthly* named him the "Outstanding Freshman" his first year in the Texas House. In 1982 he was elected to the Texas Senate with more than sixty-four percent of the vote. And in 1991 he took over the office of the state comptroller.

A man who "would a whole lot rather go home and mow the lawn" than socialize, Sharp drives a beat-up 1979 Bronco with more than a quarter million miles on it. He thinks most Texans share his priorities of spending on necessities rather than frills. In fact, a Republican group was so impressed with Sharp's plan to cut state government that they wanted the Democrat to join their party. "The public already thinks John Sharp is a Republican. We just want him to make it official," said James Leonard, chairman of the Associated Republicans of Texas.

Another Republican, Texas GOP Party Chairman Fred Meyer, recently welcomed State Comptroller John Sharp home from a seven-day trip to Israel by telling him his lottery operation was in chaos. At a press conference, Sharp brushed off Meyer's remarks: "I like ol' Fred. But my daddy told me never to get into an argument with a man who wears a size 1 hat." When Sharp inherited the administration of the lottery, he quipped that maybe they should change his title to "Wizard of Odds." He promised he would try to "keep it clean," and proposed giving $250,000 a year to the Travis County district attorney's Public Integrity Unit for that very purpose.

A "Doonesbury" comic brought some laughs (and free publicity) to the comptroller's office. Cartoonist Garry Trudeau poked fun at President Bush's claim of residency in state-income-tax-free Texas, and drew a character who, wearing boots and a hat, urged readers to become Texans "just like the Prez." All they had to do was complete a cut-out coupon swearing "my intention to live in Texas at some later date" in exchange for freedom from state income taxes. The coupon was addressed to Sharp and requested a "Texas Certificate of Residency."

Sharp in turn issued "certificates of Texas citizenship" to anyone who filled out the form from the comic strip. The certificate (not printed or mailed at state expense, of course) invited would-be Texans to use it to plea exemption from local income taxes "if you can get away with it."

The certificate proclaimed Texas as the land "where the grass grows tall and the wind blows free and anyone who says 'income tax' gets his mouth washed out with soap." That's what we like to hear from our state comptroller!

JOHN BEN SHEPPERD

Secretary of State 1950–1952
Attorney General 1953–1957

☆ ☆ ☆

"Remind us that the impossible is what nobody can do until somebody does it."

One-liner prayer by the Senate Chaplain, Dr. Gerald Mann

TEXAS LUSTER

· Duval County clean-up of corruption and voting irregularities.
· Chairman of Texas Historical Commission.
· 1984 Texan of the Year by State Chamber of Commerce.
· Odessa Boulevard has his name.
· Expert on chicken-fried steak.
· Mind like a computer before they were invented.

☆ ☆ ☆

In 1950 John Ben Shepperd was president of the National Jaycees. The Jaycees were a godsend to many who, returning from

WWII, were having a hard time getting a job and becoming socially established. For those of us under thirty-five, the Jaycees provided a prestigious but inexpensive way to get involved in civic endeavors. "Jaycees Get the Job Done" was their motto. John Ben was their leader.

Waco Jaycees jumped into poll tax registration campaigns, clean-up projects, barbecue benefit dice games, donkey baseball, and any project that would demonstrate ingenuity and American-style winning ways. They came out with a campaign to give franking privileges to the citizens so that they could write to their congressman for free. This was not a successful endeavor and nearly caused their demise when the Big Boys discovered what was going on.

I was serving as president of the Waco Jaycees and vice-president of the Texas Jaycees. John Ben was secretary of state under an Allan Shivers appointment and had been elected attorney general — he was well on his way to becoming governor of Texas. After Shivers was elected governor, John Ben offered me a job as his executive assistant. We came to Austin.

John Ben was one of the most energetic, ambitious, talented, well-organized leaders the state had ever known. His mind was twenty years ahead of the computer for political purposes. Jo Palmi, a beautiful, six-foot-tall, vivacious blonde, ran the outer office personal files and projects with unmatched efficiency. She had a card file on everyone John Ben came in contact with, classified in an unbelievable number of categories: "Friends of Good Government" (i.e., contributors), "Walkers and Talkers" (i.e., bankers, barbers, mail carriers, and those who moved around and contacted a lot of people), "Introducers" (those who had introduced him at various functions). For almost anything they had done for John Ben, Jo would send a certificate naming them as "Assistant Attorney General for (Introductions, Master of Ceremonies, Arrangements, whatever)." If they visited John Ben's office, Jo had their personal history card in the top drawer of John Ben's desk, coded with every kind of personal history — wife's name, children's activities, etc.

He was secretary of state from 1950 to 1952 under then-Governor Allan Shivers and was attorney general from 1953 to 1957. While he was attorney general, he was a leader against graft, corruption, and violence in Duval County. His investigation of voting irregularities and government corruption in Duval County led to 300 indictments against county and school officials, including county political boss

George Pharr. He also investigated the Veteran's Land Program, which resulted in a prison sentence for then-Land Commissioner Bascom Giles.

He was responsible for creating the state's official highway markers while chairman of the Texas Historical Commission in 1963, and was named Texan of the Year by the State Chamber of Commerce in 1984.

At the Mineral Wells Democratic Convention in 1950, John Ben Shepperd was chairman of the Shivers delegates. Jake Pickle was co-chairman. J. J. assigned me the task of getting telegram proxies from county convention chairmen sent to him so that he could pick up votes. We stayed up with Jack Kultgen, Jack Daniels, and the next morning when the clerk read out total proxies at the opening of the convention, Pickle had more votes than those registered. Pickle never appreciated the overkill, not to mention Shivers. Cyclone Davis was big in the party, and so was Caso March of Waco.

I traveled with John Ben on most of his political trips. One evening after he had spoken at a Fort Worth Chamber of Commerce banquet, the mayor invited us to eat at the Old Cattleman's Restaurant. We were seated at the head table and everyone but yours truly ordered big steaks. Being from Cotulla, I ordered a chicken-fried steak. Afterwards, Shepperd said, "You country bumpkin, the next time you order a chicken-fried steak in public, you can move to the back office."

Without question, Texas lost a great hand when we lost John Ben. He was always ahead of history and was a "Lone Star" who started movement of actions that will continue to benefit us on into the future. He truly lived the motto of his beloved Jaycees . . . He got the job done!

JIM TAYLOR

House of Representatives 1939–1942
Senate 1945–1950

☆ ☆ ☆

"Lord, teach us the difference between free speech and loose talk."
One-liner prayer by the Senate Chaplain, Dr. Gerald Mann

Jim Taylor, House member, senator, and lobbyist, has some colorful stories about his elections.

"One time when I was running for office I ran against Jules Kelse. He had relatives all over that county, and it was already his second term. In those days they would have speakings all over the county; you'd get up on the back of a wagon and they'd have a Coleman lantern hanging up there and you'd make speeches. During one speech Kelse said, 'There ain't anyone supporting this guy Taylor except whores in Corsicana and the racehorse people.'

"Well, when I got home that night, my wife said some woman from Corsicana called and wanted me to call her back — it didn't make any difference how late I got home, I should call. So, somewhat mystified, I phoned.

"She said, 'I heard what Mr. Kelse said about you. If he thinks we ain't got any friends, I can show him. Do you have any of those cards with your name on them? Well, bring me two boxes.' She added, 'But don't come too early because we don't get up before nine A.M.'

"Well, by this time I figured out who she was, and I took her two boxes. She and her gals gave a card to every guy who came in that whorehouse. I'd be way the hell down in the woods somewhere and I'd walk into the back end of a country store where a bunch of guys would be sitting around a stove and I'd say, 'My name is Jim Taylor, and I'm running for the legislature.'

"They'd say, 'I know you,' and one of them would reach in his pocket and pull out that card. Boy, I knew where he'd got it. They elected me to the legislature."

Taylor was serving overseas during World War II when he was

drafted to run for the Senate. "In 1944 a senator from my district died. Bob Barker called Estelle, my wife, and said, 'The guys in the Senate want to elect Jim to the Senate.'

"She said, 'You'll have a hard time doing it because I haven't heard from him in three months.' That was about the time we landed in France.

"They really tried to get me elected, even though I was thousands of miles away and couldn't campaign. I couldn't even file. So the attorney general told them that if they got a petition with twenty-five names from each of the five counties, then they could put my name on the ticket.

"Old Wick Fowler was staying with me at the time because I had the best mess hall and cook. He reported on all the divisions, of course, but wrote twice about me: once about my silver star and then once when I got a bronze star for the operation in southern France. He sent the stories to the *Dallas News,* and when they got to Dallas, an editor would rewrite the lead to say, 'Jim Taylor, who is a candidate for the Senate . . .' Those articles didn't hurt my election campaign any! But I didn't even know I had won until I got a telegram to come home to serve in the Senate."

And speaking of Estelle, Jim's wife, he recalled: "I damn near didn't get married because I went to a 'Pitch' game with her father and almost forgot to ask for her hand!"

General Jim probably has done more for "The Third House" in gathering information on the records and beliefs of candidates than any other person. Being the true Texas philosopher that he is, he often observes, "The worst politician is the one who, after making up his mind, is full of indecision."

BYRON TUNNELL

House of Representatives 1957–1966
Speaker of the House 1963–1964
Railroad Commissioner 1966–1973

☆ ☆ ☆

"Let us flee temptation — and not leave a forwarding address."
One-liner prayer by the Senate Chaplain, Dr. Gerald Mann

TEXAS LUSTER

- Successfully promoted major reforms in industrial and tourist development as well as higher education.
- Pushed Decorum Rules through the House — the doing of which he is the most proud!
- Was without opposition for reelection as Speaker of the House in 1965 when John Connally asked him to fill an unexpired term on the Texas Railroad Commission. Won statewide election for that position in 1966 and 1972.
- In Naval Air Corps but not too good at picking pilots!

☆ ☆ ☆

Byron Tunnell was elected to the Texas legislature in 1957 and served three terms before being elected Speaker of the House for two terms beginning in 1963. As Speaker, he successfully promoted major reforms in industrial and tourist development programs and was instrumental in the formation of the modern, state-supported system of higher education.

He also pushed Decorum Rules through the House. The Senate already had these rules, but the House was in anarchy, with anywhere from 700 to 800 people on the floor at times — wives, kids, lobbyists, tourists, people selling things, etc. The Decorum Rules took all those people off the floor and restored some semblance of order. This is the action of which he is justifiably the most proud.

In 1965 Tunnell was without opposition for reelection as Speaker, but Governor John Connally asked him to fill an unexpired term on the Texas Railroad Commission. He later won statewide elections in 1966 and 1972 for that position. When Tunnell was sworn in as railroad commissioner, Jake Johnson told him, "I want to be the first to shake your hand because this is the happiest day of my life." Tunnell said, "Why? We've never gotten along." Johnson replied: "One, because you ain't Speaker anymore and two, I don't have any oil wells." Jake was the one who once tried to pass a "little civil rights bill" that was defeated. Turned out he had incorporated the Bill of Rights into the bill and then was denied the right to introduce it!

During Tunnell's race for Speaker, former legislator Charlie Murphy flew the candidate to Uvalde for a campaign event. Ben Barnes was with them. Tunnell was somewhat worried about Murphy's ability to find the Uvalde airport in not-too-good weather. Murphy kept saying, "Not to worry," assuring Tunnell that he had plenty of experience flying in all kinds of weather. When they finally started to land, Tunnell was relieved, noting other planes parked beside the strip. They kept taxiing until Tunnell could read the name of the airport. It read "Del Rio" instead of "Uvalde." Tunnell was philosophical, catching his breath with the somewhat comforting thought, "I guess we are lucky he didn't put down someplace in Mexico."

Mas

A. M. AIKIN, JR.

House of Representatives 1933–1936
Senate 1937–1978

☆ ☆ ☆

Even a strong legislator such as Senator Aikin heeds the call of a higher power. While in the Senate Chamber, Aikin was phoned by none other than Allan Shivers, serving his first elected term as governor. Shivers said, "Aikin, now, so-and-so has got this bill and he is just a freshman and doesn't know anything. I want you to go back and sit beside him and when you get recognized, tell him what to say to pass that bill." Senator Aikin said, "But I am not for that bill." Shivers replied, "I don't care whether you are for the bill, I want you to do what I said. I got twenty-six votes." So Aikin went back to sit by the freshman senator and helped him pass the bill. You know what, he had twenty-six votes!

The esteem Shivers had for Aikin has been shared by all who knew him. He was one of the finest gentlemen ever to punch a voting button.

RED BERRY

House of Representatives 1961–1968
Senate 1969–1970

☆ ☆ ☆

"He still had some snap in his garters."

Red Berry was as colorful a character as his name implies, and he himself was not allergic to colorful language. At one point the House was engaged in its perennial debate on parimutuel betting, with old Red carrying the bill. A Baptist minister was testifying, preachifying, and talking a blue streak against the evils of horse racing when Red walked into the rotunda. The Bible-thumper, catching sight of Red, got as lathered up as a preacher with the devil in his backyard. The Lord's deputy got right up in Red's face, shaking his finger at him, spitting on him, hollering at him, and telling him what a mean, vile old man he was. Berry waited a minute, looked at the reverend, and said, "Preacher, screw you," and walked off without an Amen!

Another religious experience, this time a wedding, brought more punishment down on Red's sombrero. During a bachelor party prior to Red's wedding, Red's compadres shaved the doomed man's head. Coke Stevenson, then Speaker of the House and in on the prank, laughed, "A little sweet oil and time will cure everything." One hopes his bride-to-be was as philosophical.

Berry was on his deathbed when a bill on corporate income tax came up. He had told his allies he would vote against the legislature until the day he died, and this time the vote would be close, so they took him at his word. The conservatives got a filibuster going to allow time for Berry to be flown to Austin and put in a back room, wrapped in an old coat, so he could vote on a motion to table the bill. The legislation was defeated 15–14, with one legislator changing his vote twice in the last two minutes.

Once, Red had a plan to lobby for his legislation. As a well-known supporter of horse racing in Texas, he would approach a likely supporter saying, "I am going to the Ruidoso track this weekend and if you give me ten dollars, I will place a bet for you." Come Monday morning, he would always report good luck and he would give his compadre at least one hundred dollars.

H. J. "Doc" Blanchard

House of Representatives 1957–1960
Senate 1963–1974
President Pro Tem 1969–1970

☆ ☆ ☆

Senator "Doc" Blanchard was easygoing but could trim the fat and get to the meat whenever he was ready. Walter Caven and I served as co-chairmen of his "Governor for a Day" celebration in 1973. The only instructions he gave us were, "See that everybody has a good time." He couldn't have cared less about "pomp and ceremony." It is hard to total how much money was raised for Doc — and his friends — but everyone had a big blast and the cost was within budget since there was no budget.

Automobile dealers in Lubbock were crazy about Doc. Mule Dowell was a Chrysler dealer and furnished "wheels" for the senator. P. J. Crimm called Mule once to tell him that Doc had left his car in front of the Austin airport with the keys in it. Mule said, "That is nothing, he left one of the cars we had for him in Lubbock at the airport . . . with the keys in it and the motor running!"

The senator loved the crap shooting in Las Vegas. Mule Dowell was in Las Vegas with him one time when Doc bounced the dice off the table and hit the croupier right on the edge of the eyebrow, where any lick causes blood. Dowell was sitting in the lounge of the Desert Inn when a security man asked him to come with him, as the senator had been in an accident. When Dowell walked into the holding room and saw blood all over Doc's face, he thought, "God, here comes the

Mafia." They quickly flew east toward the safety of Homer Garrison!

WICK FOWLER

☆ ☆ ☆

Wick was one of the most colorful characters that moved around our Third House. He gained worldwide fame for his "Two Alarm" chili mix. A woman once called him, complaining that she had found bugs in her chili mix. Wick asked her, "How many bugs did you find?" She replied, "Three or four." Wick apologized to her, saying, "Sorry about that. You are entitled to five bugs." And he mailed her another package of Two Alarm.

Wick invited all Headliners to go to the Headliners Club after his funeral and have a drink on him. This was a notorious wake!

There are many, many stories about Wick, who wrote a most popular column for GIs during World War II. He was having convulsions about not getting hired to go to Vietnam. Finally, he got *The Denton Eagle* to hire him as its war correspondent. When he returned,

The Wick Fowlers.

— Courtesy Austin History Center

he had lost about thirty pounds. When asked how he had managed to lose so much weight in Vietnam, he said, "From running bent over."

I was in the governor's reception room when someone whizzed by and I asked Wick who it was. He said, "Ben Jack Cage. Did you ever hear of the Kalua bird?" I said, "No." Wick said, "A Kalua bird is a bird that runs in decreasing circles, sticks his head up his own rear and Mr. Cage just made contact." Under indictment in an insurance scandal, Cage left for Rio de Janeiro and no one has called him to come back.

LENA GUERRERO

House of Representatives 1983–1989
Texas Railroad Commissioner 1990–1992

☆ ☆ ☆

Newsweek has called her one of the leading Hispanics in the country. And a *USA Today* story listed her as a potential first female president of the United States. Lena Guerrero is the first woman and the first minority to serve on the 100-year-old Texas Railroad Commission, the powerful three-member panel that regulates the state's $57 billion oil, gas and transportation industries.

The fifth of nine children, Guerrero grew up on the Texas border. Her father died when she was eleven, forcing her family into seasonal farm work. In high school Guerrero became involved in Girls State, and she was one of two girls selected statewide to represent Texas at Girls Nation. There, a pattern emerged. "I ran the campaign for the woman who became president, so she appointed me attorney general," she says.

When Guerrero earned a scholarship and acceptance at the University of Texas at Austin, she immediately immersed herself in student politics. She was the first Hispanic woman to head the state's Young Democrats, and in 1976 she branched out into local campaigns, doing some work for a candidate for Travis County commissioner — Ann Richards.

In 1983, at the age of twenty-six, Guerrero announced her candidacy for the state legislature. She won that election, and two subsequent reelections, serving six years in the House. Her colleagues report that she always managed to break tense situations with her humor. When a committee was scheduled to debate an abortion bill, Guerrero appeared in a hardhat. Her quick wit earned her an invitation to a Washington, D.C. roast of Ann Richards. There, she asked the crowd: "You know the difference between God and Ann Richards? God doesn't think she's Ann Richards."

While in the legislature, Guerrero championed bills for the environment, laborers, child care, and family shelters. Her success with those causes earned her a place in *Texas Monthly*'s ten best legislators list for 1989.

Guerrero served as political adviser to Ann Richards during her gubernatorial campaign and was Governor Richards' first appointment. "Lena, I think, is the epitome of what we're talking about when we say New Texas," Richards said at the time of the appointment. But many in the male-dominated business that the Texas Railroad Commission regulates were less than enthusiastic with the governor's choice. Guerrero had never been involved in the oil and gas business, and being the first woman on the commission was yet another hurdle to overcome. Two weeks into her new job, Guerrero spoke at a luncheon for about eighty men in the trucking industry. During the question-and-answer period, a man stood up and asked: "What's your bra size?" Another man apologized for his colleague, but Guerrero was not to be one-upped. "Wait a minute," she broke in. "Someone finally asked a question I know something about."

Aware of her own inexperience, Guerrero made it her business to learn about the commission. When she was appointed commissioner, she asked for and got an unprecedented four months to prepare before assuming her duties as chair. She pored over reports and gave herself the task of meeting the nearly 1,000 commission employees scattered in outposts across the state, along with as many industry people as possible.

Perhaps the best illustration of Guerrero's unrelenting devotion to her work is the story of the birth of her son. In 1988, when a very pregnant Lena Guerrero went into labor, she headed for the office instead of the hospital. A consultant at the time on an Austin city referendum, she needed to write a campaign budget. For three hours she mapped out a spending strategy, and when the budget was completed she checked herself into the hospital and gave birth to her son a mere six hours later.

For her 1992 reelection campaign, Guerrero reported raising

about $1 million — more than the two Republican hopefuls combined. She seemed a shoe-in, but in September, Guerrero's campaign was besieged by the revelation that she had never graduated from college and that she had never been a member of a prestigious honorary society (Phi Beta Kappa) as was listed on an official biography from her office in 1985. Although she at first claimed to be four hours shy of a degree, the release of her University of Texas transcripts revealed that, due to failing six classes, she was actually nineteen hours short of graduation.

The fan hit the fiction by mid-September 1992. Columnist Felton West of the *Houston Post* wrote on September 17, 1992: "Guerrero's web of lies [is] getting more tangled daily." Juan Palamo wrote: "Guerrero: lying by the numbers." For the *Houston Chronicle*, David Broder, on September 18, 1992, said: "It would be wonderful if politicians instinctively told the truth about their life histories. But they don't, and when they don't journalists have no choice but to press the issue. That's not nitpicking. It's necessary work."

On September 24, 1992, Guerrero resigned as chairman of the Railroad Commission but decided to continue her campaign for a full term as such. History is deciding how much of this sad turn of a great political future is due to "nitpicking" and whether or not she can continue the speed and sparkle of her so-far political life.

RALPH HALL

Senate 1963–1972

☆ ☆ ☆

Speaking to a college graduating class, Ralph Hall said, "You think you have had a tough session? Do you realize that I have sat here for 140 days with Criss Cole on my left and Red Berry from San Antonio, who is deaf, on my right, and all session long when anybody would get up to say anything, all I heard from Criss Cole is 'Who said that?' and from Red Berry, 'What did you say?' "

Observing the benefits of lobby perks, Hall once observed, "I wish I could go down there and sell out on a bill I was already for."

SAM HANNA

House of Representatives 1935–1960

☆ ☆ ☆

History remembers Sam Hanna more for his humor than for his legislating. Waggoner Carr recalls Hanna at the House microphone telling stories just barely repeatable. At one point Hanna mused that if the brains of two particular legislators were put in a field lark's head, a hawk would catch it before 10:00 A.M.

Sam Hanna loved to bait fellow lawmakers. Pat Dwyer from San Antonio had heard rumors that certain legislators were receiving money for their work on the parimutuel bill. Learning that Dwyer was bellyachin' about lobby funds, Hanna and his buddies set their trap. The conspirators got rolls of adding machine tape, dirtied the edges, and wrapped the rolls in one-dollar bills. The result looked like wads of greenbacks thick enough to choke a groundhog. After returning from lunch that day, Pat could find nobody. Eventually he collared someone, who said, "Pat, they're back in the appropriations committee room dividing out the money on the horse racing bill." Dwyer cried, "The SOBs!" He burst into the committee room insisting, "You know that I ought to get most of this. I've done most of the work."

One former Texas lawmaker said Hanna never would read a bill or do anything else, but he'd get up sometimes and talk against one. This legislative trait served Hanna well as assistant manager of a hotel in Dallas. One weekend a woman, without a stitch on, was found asleep in a hall. Assistant Manager Hanna was dispatched. Reportedly, Hanna looked at the woman, nudged her to get her attention, and said, "Lady, if you're going to lay out here you got to lay against the wall; you're blocking traffic."

MANLEY HEAD

House of Representatives 1933–1936
Senate 1937–1940

☆ ☆ ☆

Manley Head tells a story about a little trick he pulled. A representative sitting next to Manley usually had his wife nearby, always knitting or something. Throughout the session, she would constantly turn around and ask everybody near her, "How did you vote? How did you vote?" She also poked through everything on her husband's desk. Manley asked a secretary who wrote in a beautiful, flowing hand to compose a note: "Sweetheart, please meet me tonight at the usual place." Manley gave the note to a page, tipped him, and told him to drop the note on the representative's desk and said, "Above all, *keep moving.*" When the old man reached to pick up this beautifully handwritten note, his wife slapped away his hand and read the note herself. Said Manley, "You could have roped her eyes with a grapevine!" The wife tore into her husband: "So you told me you were going to a committee meeting tonight! I know where you are going now!" She laid him out cold. The bewildered old man turned around and asked Manley, "Do you know anything about this?" Manley quickly grabbed some papers and replied, "I am busy writing an amendment, so don't bother me."

Later Manley laughed, "I watched him at noon when they were going out to lunch and she was still giving him hell all the way, nonstop. If he had ever found out who sent the note, he would have killed me. And I can't say I would have blamed him for it!"

SAM HUDSON

House of Representatives 1973–1980

☆ ☆ ☆

Sam Hudson and Wilson Foreman co-sponsored the change in the law regarding the automatic continuance rule. Only child support cases can now be used as ground for an automatic continuance. Before that change, any legislator could get an automatic continuance on any lawsuit.

S. J. ISAACKS

House of Representatives 1939–1954

MAUD ISAACKS

House of Representatives 1953–1966

☆ ☆ ☆

Like father, like daughter? For the Isaacks from El Paso, that certainly was true. Not only did father and daughter serve at least six terms each in the House of Representatives, but both were more concerned with the quality than the quantity of their mail. During one legislative session in Miss Isaacks' tenure, it happened that many letters were received from schoolteachers. Miss Isaacks, a former schoolmarm herself, every day would gather the letters from her constituents. She would edit each one, in red pen no doubt, award a grade, and send it back. Her father, Judge Isaacks, began this tradition in the 1940s.

OBIE JONES

House of Representatives 1947–1948
Door Keeper 1953–1954
House of Representatives 1955–1962

☆ ☆ ☆

Obie had only one leg. He stood almost full time in front of the Stephen F. Austin Hotel on Congress Avenue. He used one crutch and could regularly be heard coming down the street. He collected campaign money by working his friends on the sidewalks and by often calling on bankers in the downtown banks.

Obie campaigned full-time in every section of the county and at every barbecue. Once, Beryl Milburn ran against Obie. Several of Milburn's friends went with her to a rally being held in South Austin. Obie graciously let Beryl speak first. She lambasted him with both barrels. When it was Obie's turn to speak, he humbly described her as "that sweet pretty young lady" and asked, "How could anyone say anything but good about such an attractive opponent?" Then he sat down. According to Buck Avery, Milburn didn't get a single vote.

In another election, Obie defeated Homer Leonard in a hot race and was a pallbearer at Leonard's funeral.

Yet another time, he ran against Pearce Johnson. Pearce called Obie "Tripod." Pearce said about Jones, "He was clever. He had these little speeches that he gave all over the county. He was out there and we were handing out cards and this, that, and the other. He gave a man one, and a lady reached for a card and he said, 'Oh, just one per family,' and pulled it back. He was tight."

It was said that when he went out "social like," he would wear his artificial leg. But he collected more money without it.

TOM MASSEY

House of Representatives 1973–1980

☆   ☆   ☆

Tom Massey is an example of the adage that power corrupts. During Bill Clayton's tenure as speaker, Massey was chairman of the Calendars Committee, an enviable position. By using it wisely, the best bills can get the attention they deserve and bad bills can be buried in obscurity at the end of the session, where time will hopefully run out before they are heard. By thoughtful and considerate stewardship of this position, a legislator could even forward causes that interest him and his constituency without incurring undue wrath. Not so for Massey.

"Public Enemy Number One" is how he was once described by *Texas Monthly:* ". . . the most hated member of the House as the result of his high-handed, arbitrary chairmanship of the Committee on Calendars. By the end of the session, almost no one would deal with Massey anymore. One measure of his standing came on the last night, when Massey, who considered himself something of an authority on water law, tried — with some justification — to kill a local Harris County water district bill because he had been excluded from compromise discussions. When the results appeared on the voting board, revealing that Massey lost by over a hundred votes, the House broke into spontaneous cheers."

MAURY MAVERICK, SR.

U.S. House of Representatives 1935–1939

MAURY MAVERICK, JR.

House of Representatives 1951–1956

☆   ☆   ☆

The name Maverick is synonymous with fierce individualism, and you can bet the farm that Maury Maverick, Sr., was a colorful character. As reported in the *Dallas Morning News,* House Representative Maury Maverick was known in the 1950s as a champion of racial equality and an enemy of McCarthy-style politics. He took more than 300 pro bono cases, ranging from impoverished black and Hispanic clients to conscientious objectors during the Vietnam War. The American Bar Association honored him as one of the seven national winners of the John Minor Public Interest and Professionalism Awards, which recognize lawyers who have done exemplary pro bono or public interest case work.

Maury, Sr., expected the same honesty and courage from his own son, also a legislator. A resolution was brought for the censure of a University of Texas professor who was thought to be left-leaning. Maury, Jr., and another legislator didn't know anything about the man but didn't want to go on record as being opposed to the resolution, so they went to the restroom, got in the stalls, and pulled up their feet so they couldn't be seen.

Maury, Sr., later called in Maury, Jr., and asked him why he was gone during the resolution vote for censure — why he didn't stand up for a perfectly decent man.

Junior replied, "Jim and I just didn't understand enough about it. There wasn't a committee hearing and we didn't know anything about him."

Turning away in disgust, Dad said, "Well y'all are just a bunch of 'potty liberals'!"

Young Maverick never did lobby, but he could hold his own in the legislature. Reuben Senterfitt was known to raise quite a bit of hell, and one day when Senterfitt was gathering breath to launch a protest, Maverick echoed the sentiments of many other legislators when he said, "Now, Reuben, don't get that hurt-Jesus look on your face. I ain't going to do anything."

THOMAS R. PHILLIPS

Chief Justice, Texas Supreme Court 1988–Present

☆ ☆ ☆

An honors graduate of Baylor University, Thomas R. Phillips earned his law degree from Harvard University in 1974. While an associate trial attorney with Baker & Botts, a Houston law firm, Phillips served as a briefing attorney to the Supreme Court of Texas. It was there, he's acknowledged, that he formed his ambition to serve as a member of the state's highest civil court.

Phillips officially began his judicial career in 1981, when Governor Bill Clements appointed him to the 280th District Court in Harris County, earning him the distinction of being the youngest civil district judge in Texas. Phillips quickly earned a reputation for fairness, impartiality, and diligence on the bench. Running as a Republican, he was unopposed for election and reelection in 1982 and 1986.

Tom Phillips
— Gittings

In 1987, at the age of thirty-eight, he was appointed by Governor Clements to the position of chief justice of the Supreme Court of Texas. Surprisingly, Phillips is not the youngest person ever to serve as chief justice of the state's highest civil appeals court; four were younger. He is, however, the first Republican in modern times to hold that position. Elected in his own right in the general election of 1988, his 56.7 percent margin of victory was the largest of any Republican candidate for state office since 1869. Phillips' colleagues say he is an expert in political and Texas history and reportedly has one of the largest collections of campaign buttons around, dating back to the 1800s.

He was a briefing clerk for Justice Ruel Walker on the Texas Supreme Court 1974–75. Walker praises him as a talented lawyer with deep dedication to his profession. Walker recalls that while other briefing clerks were scrambling for post graduate jobs, Phillips confidentially said "not to worry." He wanted to spend as much time as possible learning as a briefing clerk and would head for Baker & Botts — one of Texas' largest and best law firms — when the time was ripe. A somewhat doubting Walker watched as Phillips did just that.

Known for his even handed approach in the courtrooms, he permits no factual or political "gobbledygook" before or behind his bench. A West Texas cowboy lawyer who knows him from both the Baylor and Harvard environs says "He is book learned and hog smart, and can be as hard as an iron horseshoe." I say that anyone who can graduate *summa cum laude* from Baylor University without training by the outrageous fraternity the "Nose Brotherhood" is truly a colorful character of Texas.

JUDGE CLYDE SMITH

Texas Supreme Court 1950–1971

☆ ☆ ☆

When the Texas Supreme Court justices moved into the new Supreme Court building, there was only one urinal in the restroom and privileges were granted in order of seniority. Clyde Smith had not only a senior kidney, but also an urgent kidney.

It was who went to the Texas legislature to get appropriations for another urinal. They kidded him, saying, "We all know what the Supreme Court is full of," and wouldn't allow the money. The Texas legislature is notorious for denying appropriations for other branches of government, just as the governor's office is known for vetoing legislative salary increases, and the Supreme Court is famous for declaring redistricting to be unconstitutional. The bill took three sessions to pass, but Clyde Smith eventually got relief.

While Robert Calvert served as chief justice, he was irritated by Judge Clyde Smith eternally dissenting. To solve the problem, Calvert started to vote out of turn, so that Smith would be the last to vote. Then the chief justice would say, "Clyde Smith, let's see you dissent on this!" Calvert tried other methods to dissuade Smith from certain annoying practices. In the robing room after a 5–4 vote, Smith ruminated, "I believe I'll change my vote." Calvert snapped, "Well, that's fine, Clyde. I'll just change mine, too, and it'll come out exactly the same."

JOHN PETER STUBBS

House of Representatives 1941–1946

☆ ☆ ☆

Joe Fleming wrote a note just like it was coming from an attractive lady in the balcony. It said, "Mr. Stubbs, I am one of your constituents and would like to know which one you are on the floor. Please take out your handkerchief and wave it so I will know which one you are." Of course, he waved to the delight of most of the members of the floor.

CARLOS TRUAN

House of Representatives 1969–1976
Senate 1977–Present

☆ ☆ ☆

Texas Monthly called Truan "a lethal combination of ego and incompetence." The Corpus Christi representative once took so long to praise a bill that opponents had time to get it killed! Late in one session, Truan took Senator Bob McFarland aside and warned him that he planned to filibuster one of McFarland's bills. McFarland replied, "You'd better get permission from the Speaker of the House about that, because we passed it in the Senate this morning. And you voted for it."

CLAYTON WILLIAMS

☆ ☆ ☆

THE HUEY AWARDS: The campaign's best and worst from *USA TODAY,* November 5, 1990.
WORST JOKE: "Weather's like rape . . . as long as it's inevitable, just relax and enjoy it." Texas GOP gubernatorial candidate later apologized, adding, "If you talk about the weather, you're sure to get into trouble."
BEST COMEBACK LINE: "I am Bubba . . ." after primary rival Jack Rains said Williams "plays to the Bubbas."
MOST INTERESTING CHOICE OF WORDS: "It was the kind of thing boys did at Texas A&M. It was a lot different in those days. The houses were the only place you could get serviced then." On frequenting Mexican houses of prostitution during his college days.
MOST X-RATED EXPLANATION OF HIS CHOICE OF WORDS: "In the world I live in, of bulls and cattlemen, you talk about the bull servicing the cow. I was trying to find a nice polite term for . . ."

The Dirty Thirty and the Killer Bees

☆ ☆ ☆

"Lord, let us be reminded of the lessons of nature.
The bee always fertilizes the flowers it robs."

"Lord, without a quorum, we don't have a prayer."
(Alternate prayer prepared in the event the Bees did not return)
One-liner prayer by the Senate Chaplain, Dr. Gerald Mann

There was almost no such thing as legislative ethics before the Killer Bees and the Dirty Thirty. In fact, some said that the only thing unethical was to be caught in bed with a live man or a dead woman.

Gus Mutscher, often blamed for the excess of those legislative days, in fact did not create the corrupt system; it was alive and well long before his tenure. However, Mutscher was not about to passively relinquish the power or the perks. Jo Beatty recalled, "There is no comparison between then and now. At that time, ethics abuses were rampant. One time, for example, I saw a member come in and this guy put a $100 bill in his pocket for a vote."

Unfortunately for Mutscher, a group of legislators realized that they could hold the House hostage with a never-ending "no" vote, and they proceeded to do so to force Mutscher's hand.

The group earned its name after a vote on a resolution sponsored by Sissy Farenthold, which called for an internal House committee investigation of Mutscher. Farenthold and other legislators were disgusted by the excess in the House and by the lack of respect certain members seemed to have for their office. "Sissy was the nuts and bolts behind the whole thing. She was the brainpower," Beatty said. When thirty lawmakers supported the Farenthold resolution, a lobbyist in the House gallery called them "those thirty dirty bastards," recalled Texas Supreme Court Justice Bob Gammage, a member of the group.

"We could vote 'no' and then leave for Scholz Beer Garten and that about summed up our jobs in many ways," said Bill Bass, who now serves on the 12th Court of Appeals. The Dirty Thirty effectively blocked any and all bills in an effort to force ethics reform legislation on Mutscher.

A searing session of the legislature ensued in the spring of 1971 with the "Dirty Thirty" coalition of Republicans and liberal Democrats challenging Mutscher to institute various ethics and reform measures. Mutscher had the votes to withstand such challenges, but legal questions surrounding his involvement in the Sharpstown scandal, plus the constant publicity generated by the Dirty Thirty, made for a divisive session. Mutscher responded vindictively, directing his cohorts to draw a redistricting plan that would eliminate many of the Dirty Thirty.

Tension ran high during that session. Lawmakers arrived one morning to find that Mutscher had stationed armed Texas Department of Public Safety troopers throughout the House. Just as roll was being called, "Sonny" Jones got up and said, "Mr. Speaker, these guys with the badges and the guns — are they here on the floor to protect us from the people or protect the people from us?"

Mutscher's redistricting plan was declared unconstitutional by the state judicial branch, and the redistricting task was sent to the five-member state redistricting board. Mutscher wasn't beaten yet, though; he had stacked the deck. The redistricting board was composed of Barnes, Mutscher, Attorney General Crawford Martin, Land Commissioner Bob Armstrong, and Comptroller Robert Calvert.

Dora McDonald with Killer Bee garage apartment guests.
— Courtesy Austin History Center

Senate Secretary Dora McDonald, hostess for infamous Killer Bees, with Lieutenant Governor Bill Hobby.

— Courtesy Senate Media Services

After Mutscher's resignation, lawmakers chose Rayford Price as their new Speaker. But, in 1972, Texas voters reacted to the scandal by turning seventy-six veteran lawmakers — including Mr. Price — out of office. The Dirty Thirty had the last laugh.

The "Killer Bees," latter-day Senate counterparts of the Dirty Thirty, used similar tactics to get what they wanted. They started with filibusters and progressed to denying the Senate president a quorum. Senate legislative capability was paralyzed.

It was Lieutenant Governor Hobby versus twelve moderate to liberal senators, who became known as the "Killer Bees." Hobby applied the nickname early on in the session to some of the liberals who would mount impromptu filibusters on other issues.

Late in the session, the Killer Bees found themselves convinced Hobby would break a filibuster on the primary bill, so they conjured up a unique and unlikely strategy. They would hide out for a few days — until forty-eight hours prior to the end of the session, if necessary — and thus deny Hobby a quorum in his thirty-one-member Senate. Within forty-eight hours of the end, the rules were such that the Killer Bees would prevail and the detested bill would be dead as a doornail.

The twelve senators vanished. Nine hid out in a West Austin apartment of Dora McDonald, while the other three maneuvered secretly near their homes or elsewhere, avoiding detection by DPS offices called out by Hobby to search for the "fugitives." The nine who holed up in Austin were Ron Clower of Garland, Lloyd Doggett of Austin, Glenn Kothmann of San Antonio, Oscar Mauzy of Dallas, Carl Parker of Port Arthur, Bill Patman of Ganado, A. R. (Babe) Schwartz of Galveston, Carlos Truan of Corpus Christi, and Bob Vale of San Antonio. Out and about were Chet Brooks of Pasadena, Gene Jones of Houston, and Raul Longoria, who represented the lower Rio Grande Valley. *Texas Monthly* called Schwartz the Godfather of the Killer Bees.

Robert Heard, former AP Capitol correspondent, wrote an earthy book, *The Miracle of the Killer Bees,* which details the frantic five days during which the drama unfolded, including the types of food consumed in the Austin apartment and the fact that it contained a stifling odor of cigarette smoke while the cramped senators sweated out their daring move. The Killer Bees generated intense news coverage statewide and made considerable national news. But it was difficult for the Texan on the street to sort out the split-primary issue with its subjective potential ramifications amid all the hoopla attached to the aspect of twelve state senators hiding out beyond the reach of their furious

"Worker Bee" Bill Hobby tries strong arm tactics on "Killer Bee Godfather" Babe Schwartz while other "Killer Bees" look on. Front row, Schwartz, Carlos Truan, Gene Jones, and Bob Vale; back row, Hobby, Chet Brooks, Ron Clower, Oscar Mauzy, Bill Patman, Glenn Kothman, and Lloyd Doggett.

— Courtesy Senate Media Services

presiding officer. Liberal political activists certainly know the score and they cheered for the Killer Bees. Most Republicans were opposed to the split primary, but they were divided over approving the drastic tactics of the Killer Bees.

Hobby said that the "truants" were neglecting their duty. He spoke of dire measures such as stripping committee assignments, even declaring their seats vacant, requiring special elections. Bluff, bluster, and derision poured from Clements, Hobby, and the "worker bees," the nineteen other senators who were angered by the prospect of their pet legislation dying because of Senate business being held in abeyance. But the five-day phantom strike proved to be effective: the Killer Bees returned to the Senate unscathed, the split primary was dead for the session, and their mission was accomplished.

Senator Babe Schwartz explains a bill to his colleagues.

Senator Babe Schwartz and Lloyd Dogett cancel each others vote.

INSIDE
OUR HOUSE

"Jim, suppose the people get a lobbyist!"
— Courtesy State Representative Neil Caldwell

Texas Automobile Dealers
Association (TADA)

There is a heap of difference between representing and lobbying for a group where membership is voluntary, such as the Texas Automobile Dealers Association (TADA), and one where membership is mandatory, as is the State Bar of Texas. At TADA, at least ninety percent of the dealers are for the program, while at the State Bar at least twenty-five percent are against every action taken by the board of directors. About the biggest "look out" at the average trade association is not to give yourself better football tickets than you give to your president. Not so, representing a bunch of lawyers.

After finishing a six-year term as chairman of the Industrial Accident Board, I decided to stay in Austin but wanted out of the political swirl. I started at the top of Congress Avenue and worked my way down — bank by bank — Mr. Ludecke at the old City Bank, Jack Adams and Leon Stone at the Austin National, E. D. Wroe at the American, and Howard Cox at the Capital National. My message was the same: "If you need a hungry young attorney who is ready to hustle for you, call me. I am fired up and ready to go!" Two weeks later, Jack Adams called me and I went to work as an assistant vice-president of the Austin Bank. This was really my lucky break, as the bank gave me some special assignments and turned me loose to work and serve in the community.

Austin is really a combination of communities: the state (officials, employees, etc.); the university (faculty, students, employees); the business community (Congress Avenue, banks, Chamber of Commerce, etc.); and the miscellaneous (military, retirees, federal employees, etc.). As most towns have cliques, these groups also have their own, but in Austin they tend to mix and mingle. I had seven years of mixing with the state government group and now had the opportunity to mix with the bank social groups. The bank gave me time to serve as president of the YMCA, chairman of the United Way, chairman of the board of the Club; to show off as an after-dinner speaker; and to pursue many other activities.

It was during this time that John Nash called on me to meet with a committee of car dealers. They offered me a job as executive vice-president of the Texas Automobile Dealers Association (TADA). About a week before, I had been offered a job as president at Lamar

Savings. I recall that Rex Shields and Jake Jacobsen touted me on this. But at the last minute (even going to the door to accept), I declined. I didn't know what a trade association was. A mistake I made very quickly was going to an ex-state senator to ask him about TADA. I was quickly dismissed from his office and I later found he was the top contender for the position with TADA.

When I told Jack Adams I was going to accept the TADA post, he told me to go ahead, but warned, "You are probably making a mistake, but it will be thirty years before you realize it." Well, it was not a mistake (particularly when you now look at the banking industry), *and* I learned to appreciate the new car dealers in Texas who personify American ingenuity, enthusiasm, and the free enterprise system. I was more than lucky to have had some greats to work with in developing TADA, such as Bob Bullock, Neal Spelce, P. J. Crimm, and a bunch of all-American dealers.

You quickly learn in trade association work that membership is the most important thing — an active, supportive membership is absolutely vital. When you appear before any legislative body and are asked how many car dealers are in the state and then how many belong to your association, the answer of less than fifty percent doesn't give you a lot of credibility. You are a dead duck because you don't even represent the majority of your own people. At that time, only about 900 out of the 1,900 dealers belonged to TADA, so our first job was to recruit new members. We started a series of statewide meetings to tell the dealers how great we were. After our first supper meeting in Mt. Pleasant (with about twenty-five dealers attending), TADA president Bud Mitchell turned to me and said, "These guys didn't come here to listen — they came here to eat."

So we learned. We immediately started charging for the meals and passing out notebooks explaining our programs. When you do something for nothing, people are skeptical. When you offer books, charts, specialized speakers, and inside information from Austin, they come and participate. We offered every service we could think of: collection agency, discounts on business forms, used car guides, wage and hour information, and used car title warranty programs. By the end of the year, we had 1,700 of the 1,900 new car dealers in the state involved as active members of TADA.

TADA is a dealer "union" protecting dealers from the factories. The factories control distribution and thereby have the dealers at their mercy. "You buy our signs and our batteries — or we ship you nothing but purple pickups." Everybody in the world knows what a dealer has to pay the factory for a car, but nobody — and I mean *nobody* (not even Walter Reuther) — can tell you what it costs a factory to make a car. That is the most closely guarded secret of the auto industry, and the dealers are just as much in the dark as everyone else.

TADA and other state associations work closely together. You learn in the Third House that out-of-state associations are more generous in giving you ideas than most in-state neighbors. There is an area of worry when dealing with local groups in that some are reluctant to pass on an idea for fear you will steal their thunder by using their idea first. Out-of-state executives are less reluctant to give you ideas because you won't be in competition with them on their local turf.

One of the major lessons we learned was that you must be careful before you push the panic button and ask members for help. The first sales tax in our Texas system (enacted in 1960) was on motor vehicles. Under Governor Price Daniel, an increase in the sales tax on automobiles was being considered. As the designated hitter, I put out a cry for help! We mailed a bulletin to all dealers asking them to call, write, or scream to Governor Daniel, letting him know that auto owners were already paying more than their share and that such a tax would bring disaster for many already overtaxed dealers. Claude Holley, a large Chrysler dealer in Tyler, and a large contributor to Daniel, answered my prayers. He wrote a begging plea to the governor, telling him that dealers were in serious straits, that many faced bankruptcy and could not survive a tax increase. As I read his letter, I was bragging to myself about what a great job I was doing and what great points Holley was making. His "P.S.," however, killed me. He had written, "I would come to Austin to see you personally, but we are leaving on an around-the-world cruise." That blew me out of the tub!

Serving as president of the national executive group of TADA was a happy experience. I really learned to like, admire, and respect these gregarious, enthusiastic, generous, conservative con artists. On our first national convention, which was held in Atlantic City, I was told about presidents' speaking fees. President Kennedy was asked to address our convention. Seems that in those days, following an old custom, an elected president reportedly gives his national party executive one speaking engagement to sell — the president will speak and the secretary of the national party gets the fee. Well, according to one insider, the secretary of the Democratic party set up a speech by President Kennedy to the National Automobile Dealers Association convention. After getting his fee, the secretary died and NADA had no speaker and no refund. Tom Abbott of Fort Worth was NADA president at the time, and he immediately yelled for help from the Texas congressional delegation and the Texas dealers. Of course, LBJ wasn't too hot-to-trot to be second choice. Warren Woodward worked with us, and LBJ did accept and speak. The dealers learned, however, not to pay the speaker's fee until after the speech.

The dealers are a great group to have in the Third House. As good businesspeople, they know the value of good sound government and are ever willing to fight for the free enterprise system.

It wasn't hard to get them to participate in local or statewide politics. They like the game and are willing to participate. Especially in the '50s, '60s and '70s, we called on them to help the "good guys" in the legislature by loaning them automobiles to help with their campaigns and with getting their families back and forth from Austin. This was not too difficult, as the beneficiary would pay for insurance and upkeep and the dealer would take the car back into inventory and charge off the decreased value. This was a great benefit to us in working "the Hill." One thing you learn quickly is to have that dealer back home call his legislator from home when you need to get information to the right party. It is sometimes hard to get through when you are in Austin, but they take a call from their local helpful dealer every time.

We had so many cars on "the Hill" it took a staff member to keep tabs. This system is fraught with danger. You have to keep the "reps" from working your hometown dealers without your knowledge. You must be ready day or night to help with repairs, parking, traffic tickets, or misplaced keys.

One weekend, Bill Heatly, also known as "The Duke of Paducah," left his 98 Oldsmobile at Charles Maund's repair shop in Austin. His wife had made note of the mileage on the car and when they got it on Monday, she noted with great dismay that the car had been driven over 450 miles and the "98" insignia had been replaced backward on the automobile's fender. Heatly got me out of a director's meeting on that one and didn't turn me loose for half a session. Maund, as always, was most helpful, although he had to fire a good mechanic.

While Ben Barnes set the record, Gus Mutscher had quite a few vehicles in his entourage. This was good until his trial in Abilene, when the nationwide media coverage of the courthouse noted how many dealers' plates were discharging passengers in front of the courthouse. One of my saddest memories is having to call Sonny Shultz to tell him that in the midst of all their troubles they had one more — all the dealer cars had to go home.

We Love Our Cars

No question about America's love affair with the automobile. There are more "pick-em-ups" in Texas than there are people in many countries on this globe. We wash, polish, grease, tune, and love to show off our "wheels." As our history is written, the changes in motor vehicle transportation are being chronicled. Remember the days of not so long ago when your "Lizzie" was gassed, oiled, washed, repaired, and updated at the same location? Now we have to go to about five different places, not counting the places we have to go for loans and registration. The automobile is the second largest purchase the average family makes.

Numbers Tell a Lot

- If we applied the idea of parity to automobiles as we do to feed and grain, a typical economy car would cost at least $40,000. It has been estimated that a 1910 Nash Rambler would cost $43,987.50 in 1990 dollars!
- In 1990, 154,407 cars were stolen in Texas, worth more than $750 million.
- Texas has 8.4 million cars registered, about half of California's 16.4 million. But when it comes to pickup trucks, Texas closes the gap with 3.9 million trucks, compared with California's 4.8 million.

Other Numbers May Tell You Even More

Most of us have at least heard of odometer fraud. Most of us probably also think it won't happen to us — that we could not be rooked in this fashion. The facts speak otherwise. Odometer fraud is a $3 billion-a-year industry. It is estimated that at least one in five odometers gets "rolled back," for an average of 30,000 miles on three million vehicles a year.

In attempts to counteract odometer fraud, legislation has been enacted making it illegal. The federal Truth-In-Mileage Act made it mandatory for all states to require odometer readings on car titles as of 1989. It also makes odometer tampering a felony. The punishments can range from a possible three-year jail sentence and/or a $50,000 fine to a ten-year prison term and a $250,000 fine. A car title is considered a security, and the stiffer sentences are imposed under securities fraud convictions.

Passing laws and enforcing them are sometimes two different things. One outcome of all this legislation to protect the buyer has been the growth of another illegal business, the extremely lucrative "title washing" operations. The car is (theoretically) sold out-of-state, generating another title on which the reduced mileage is then recorded. A lengthy paper trail can be generated, making it difficult sometimes to find out the true mileage of the car. Apparently, the risks are worth it. The National Highway Traffic Safety Administration (NHTSA) estimates that it costs $300 on average to get a title laundered, but the price of the car can be jacked up $1,000 or more.

Colors May Tell Even More

The color of car you buy tells a lot about you. Many studies have been done and conclusions drawn about the significance of car color. A few results may provide some insight:

Red: Considered aggressive and attention-getting. Drivers of red cars are viewed as intense, impulsive, and animated. Several studies have shown more red cars are involved in accidents than any other color.

Brown: This is the color of the conservative, cautious, analytical consumer. Your CPA could well drive a brown car!

White: The sign of a neat, critical, detail-oriented person who is cautious and likes the high visibility of this color for safety reasons.

Blue: The color of consistency. This one is for the introverted or those who like to be able to count on the stability of certain things.

Green: The favorite color of sophisticated Europeans — remember British racing green? This is for the socially conscious, including conservationists and the ecological-minded. It is also the color of the highly intelligent and the romantic. Green symbolized life and love even in the Middle Ages.

Teal: This is one of the hottest new colors and appeals to trend-setters, extroverts who like attention, admiration, and novelty.

Neutrals: Beige, gray, taupe, etc. These are the colors of noncommitment and are preferred by those who don't want to take a stand or to stand out.

Metallics: Silver and the metalflakes. These colors are the choice of the confident, understated extrovert. Subtle but smashing!

Black: Still the ultimate power color. Reflective of the self-confident, sophisticated consumer who wishes to be taken seriously.

Yellow: Yellow is for the active, the artistic, and those willing to try something new. It is bright and easily seen, so is a favorite of the safety conscious.

Orange: With the wild new neons, orange is the color of youth, fun, excitement. It reflects the gregarious, the good-natured, those willing to take a ribbing.

(Adapted from Parade Magazine article by Paul A. Eisenstein, October 6, 1991)

Keep in mind that the fastest-moving target in America may be the salesman's calculator *(TADA Dealers Choice,* Winter 1991). While some could sell a double bed to the Pope, ice cubes to an Eskimo, or snow shoes in San Antonio, by and large, you can count on your dealer friends for political savvy, community participation, and team work in patriotism, as well as a deer hunt or a gin game. In most cases they deserve our accolades. Certainly, they more than pay their own way as valued members of our family inside our Third House. Our sombreros are off to what may be the last of the vanishing independent merchants.

State Bar

First off, I invoke the seldom quoted doctrine of "argumentum ad-judictum," which said doctrine was given full meaning by Judge Roy Bean. Translated into Westex jargon, it means "Don't argue with the judge." Few did!

Since I am writing this "brief," and you have read to here, I rise to try to explain the difference in representing an organization where membership is voluntary (TADA) and a group whose membership is mandated by law (State Bar). It does not take long to figure out that when somebody *has* to join any group, at least twenty-five percent are going to be against the team. Sorta like the rich Texan who, when asked "How long has your maid

Leroy Jeffers,
President of the State Bar, 1973.
— Photo by Gittings

been with you?," replied, "Never, she has been against us all the time."

The "great and more than modest" Jim Bowmer, certainly one of the truly great presidents of the bar (he hired me), shared the glowing pride of Bell County with another past president, Leroy Jeffers. Jim has some great stories about Leroy. Jeffers was proud to tell how one of his lawyer uncles always referred to federal court as "the post office court," since he could make all his appearances before the feds through the mail.

A favorite story of Jeffers was about a couple of happy lawyers who got to celebrating in the early hours and sleeping the night on a bench in the town square. When the town clock struck at 6:00 A.M. one of these characters counted thirteen strikes on the big clock and, in a fuzzy fright, started shaking his partner, saying, "Judd, Judd, wake up! It's later than it has ever been!"

One classic about Leroy has him representing a client before the Supreme Court and, with Yankee cockiness, the barrister in the pin-striped suit suddenly rose and cited a Latin precedent, "injuria fit ei cui convictum est vel de eo factum" (or something like that). A justice looked at Jeffers and asked, "Mr. Jeffers, are you familiar with this doctrine?" With care and confidence, Jeffers slowly replied, "Your Honor, back in Bell County, Texas, from whence I come, the people speak of little else."

In May 1978, Jeffers wrote an article for the *St. Mary's Law Journal* entitled, "Let the Sun Set on the Statutory Bar." He strongly urged the Texas Bar to "petition the Supreme Court to exercise its inherent power by unifying the legal profession in Texas and providing for the government of the bar by order of that court." This recommendation is still on hold.

Of the thirty senators in our Texas Senate, fifteen are lawyers and ten are in business. Of the one hundred fifty members of the House, fifty-two are lawyers. Before Briscoe, the top three state offices (governor, lieutenant governor, and Speaker of the House) were mostly occupied by lawyers.

In 1991, the State Bar of Texas received 6,000 complaints, tops for all state agencies. More than 230 lawyers were disciplined, and the bar paid $400,549 to clients from the security fund which is maintained to cover such deadbeat characters.

It is so easy to file a lawsuit these days, and it costs a lot to prepare a defense. Trial lawyers prey on this, while insurance companies know that most of the time it is better to settle out of court. These costs go into insurance premiums for members of our Third House. Such fact became obvious when suits began to be filed against judges for failure to "keep proper decorum." Their insurance companies took settlements as the cheapest way out! The *Dallas Morning News* (August 7, 1991) reported that the "nuisance value" makes settlement more practical. I don't know of anything worse than practicing law if you don't love it!

How long would it take for an average citizen to receive justice if he had to use the court system for relief? Take the sad situation of the docket backlog in our courts and the average life expectancy, and relief could be a long time coming. The bar handles these sad cases well . . . considering the alternative!

The State Bar of Texas is the third largest lawyers' association in the U.S. A price tag of over $87.5 million was placed on volunteer pro bono hours contributed by members of the bar in 1990.

The election of officers of the State Bar operates in a unique manner. It has been said that only lawyers could make it so complicated. The bar presidency alternates between nominees from metropolitan areas one year, from areas other than metropolitan counties the next year, and from any county the third year. In the not so recent past, lawyers from big firms in the big cities ran for election with big budgets, airplanes, and all. The junior bar (under age thirty-five) elects its own leaders. As far as I know, only James Watson from Corpus Christi, who in 1972 lost his life in an automobile accident while returning home from a State Bar meeting in Austin, served as president of both groups. The James C. Watson Inn of former officers and directors was created in his honor.

The first year the law creating the Sunset Commission was in effect, we played a losing game with Lloyd Doggett, who chaired the Senate committee. He was anti-bar for his own reasons! The bar was winding up the campaign to raise money from lawyers to complete construction of the building of the Law Center. Under the newly adopted Sunset rules, state agencies were to be reviewed in alphabetical order. We were pleased, as that would bring the bar up for review the next year, and we would be able to complete the highly successful fundraising campaign without lawyer donors worrying about the bar being abolished. Doggett would not hear our plea for delay and insisted that the bar appear before his committee on the first hearing date. Bennie Bock was a member of and chaired the Sunset Commission. He was very supportive of the bar's request to be treated like other state agencies. I was bugging the devil out of him to keep the bar's hearing date in the usual alphabetical order. He would check each night to see if we were in the "S" spot and kept me posted. This went on for several nights before the meeting of the conference committee. Apparently every night, Doggett would move the bar back up and Bock would help us get it back down to the "S" slot. Doggett saw to it that we lost that battle. The only thing he ever said to me was, "I appreciate your enthusiasm!"

The bar lost this initial skirmish but won the battle when the lawyers of Texas raised some $7 million of their own money, and on the 4th of July, 1976, dedicated the Law Center for the benefit of all Texans, without one dime of tax money being used. The Law Center now has an appraised value of over $10 million.

One great show of pride and support came on that July 4th from the beautiful and loyal Martha Greenhill, wife of then-Chief Justice Joe Greenhill. A crop-busting thunderstorm hit at the exact time of the ceremony. In all of this bedlam, the electricity went out, and Martha, in the rain, saved the occasion by holding together the extension cords

Pittman (right) with Judge Charles Barrow and Jack Dillard (left) as they congratulate each other on opening the Texas Law Center. Judge Barrow had just been notified by Governor Dolph Briscoe of his appointment as a justice of the Texas Supreme Court.

for the speaker microphone. How are you going to beat that for dedication?

Joe Roddy was tremendously colorful. He died last year while heading the Information Section for the University of Texas System. When I was executive director of the bar in 1977, Roddy placed a phone call to me. When told that I was not in, he asked my secretary if she would give me a message: "Dr. Obolster called to tell him that his Wassermann test was positive." My secretary was on the side of those who did not like me very much, and she was an expert in spreading bad news. When I returned, she had three floors organized to spread the word! By the by, this story was repeated at the wake held at the Headliners Club after Roddy's funeral!

There were many "sui generis" phenomenon during my stay with the bar. Many said that "bartender" was an excellent title for me. Current FBI head Judge William Sessions granted me immunity after I had his car towed to a pound . . . I forgot to put out a chair for John Hill at the Law Center dedication . . . We gave Sarah Weddington the usual plaque for outstanding support in the legislature. Unfortunately, the plaque read "for 'his' excellent service." She called a press conference to show what she termed a sample of our research capabilities. I apologized, telling her, "After all, it was a close question."

An old East Texas philosopher once said, "The sure by-product of man's inhumanity is lawyers!" Around the same country store, another cracker barrel wit says, "Practicing law may not be the oldest profession but the results to the clients are the same."

Judges can be adroit. I have been lucky enough to hunt with several presiders through the years. Judge Thomas Stovall, a cantina player, always instructs a female witness, "The lady will state her age and then be sworn."

Now, if I can waive cross-examination, I will take an oath on information above furnished!

Associations

Associations can be considered unusual businesses. There are more than 350 in Austin alone, which contribute a great deal to the capital city and to their own individual members. These associations are in the thick of things during legislative sessions, lobbying, and working to promote bills in the best interest of their membership.

Such associations include the Gulf Intercoastal Canal Association, the State Bar of Texas, and Sportsmen Conservationists of Texas. There is even a Texas Society of Association Executives (TSAE), which is an association for people who are paid to manage associations.

"Whatever you can think of in your wildest imagination, there will be an association to represent it," said Marilyn Monroe, president of TSAE.

Austin, being the capital, attracts a large number of these groups. Fifty-five own their headquarters buildings in the city because they need proximity to the legislature and other state agencies. The liaisons they form with these groups are an important function, giving a voice in government to their membership.

John Devenport, director of communications for the Texas Automobile Dealers Association, said, "We, of course, represent the interest of dealerships before the legislature and the appropriate regulatory agencies."

Mike Bently, director of marketing for the 6,000-member Texas Restaurant Association, noted that one of their most important activities is lobbying for members' interests at the city, state, and national level.

Members' interests can include legislation pertaining to directors' liability insurance or the bed tax (tax paid on a hotel room). These associations may also serve to set standards by which excellence in a field may be gauged. Awards are based on criteria often including continuing education and references from colleagues.

Other services provided to association members include insurance packages, publications, and continuing education and management training programs. Conferences, workshops and symposiums are planned to bring members important information concerning their area of expertise.

The fact that many of these association activities take place in Austin is a coup to the city's economy. TSAE is currently conducting an economic impact study focusing on associations and their contributions in Austin, Houston, and the Dallas-Fort Worth area. The location of many of the associations in the capital also assists organizations like the Chamber of Commerce and volunteer groups by providing members and leaders.

Chief Justice Joe Greenhill and Justice Ruel Walker.
—Senate Media Services

"SHUCKING"

"Mr. Chairman, I'm afraid I can't answer that question."
— Courtesy State Representative Neil Caldwell

To PAC . . . Or Not to PAC

"Remind us that power is never good except he be good who has it."
One-liner prayer by the Senate Chaplain, Dr. Gerald Mann

PACs, or political action committees, were officially established in Texas in 1973 when newly elected House Speaker Price Daniel, Jr., introduced an extensive reform legislation program following the Sharpstown scandal. Actually, a few PACs existed before the passage of HB4, the "reform" bill which tightened Texas' rather weak laws governing reports of campaign expenditures and contributions. The 1973 law might have driven PACs out of business because they could no longer offer privacy to donors. Instead, however, PACs proliferated and whereas "far less than 100" PACs existed in the early 1970s, as of 1992 there are a total of 1,072 PACs registered in the state. The reform laws requiring PACs to report their financial activities "had the impact of kind of legitimizing PAC operations," contended one lobbyist.

The average citizen might wonder why groups form PACs rather than rely on lobbyists to represent their interests in government. The Texas State Teachers Association, for example, had enjoyed moderate success for years with strong, locally based lobbying. In the early 1970s, however, the association formed TEPAC (Texas Educators Political Action Committee) when it identified a need for a stronger effort on behalf of teacher pay raises and recognized that gubernatorial candidate Dolph Briscoe was not completely sympathetic to their goals. TEPAC poured thousands of dollars into opponent John Hill's unsuccessful race for governor.

Lobbyists often encourage their clients to form PACs. A lobbyist fares better if backed up by letters, telegrams, and telephone calls to legislators from members of his or her client group in their districts, and PACs can be instrumental in generating that type of activity from constituents. Also, as one lobbyist pointed out, PAC contributions "have been able to get me in the door. I think candidates are very aware of where the big contributions come from and probably scrutinize those contributors' issues a little more closely."

Ironically, the 1973 reform legislation was intended to curb big business influence on the government and to insure accountability and control. PACs were originally created to provide a way for small contributors to pool their funds and give money to those political candidates who best represented their group's interests. But things have

222

gotten somewhat out of hand, say PAC critics, and that original lofty goal of granting small donors a louder voice through collective contributions has been subverted. Corporations and labor unions, while prohibited from contributing directly to political campaigns, can form PACs and donate funds legally through them. "While a few PACs are truly amalgams of small donors, many PACs are clubs comprised of the wealthy and powerful who want to control politics in Texas," Tom Smith of Public Citizen/Texas recently told the *Dallas Morning News*. And whereas political action committees were originally designed to represent "the little guy," today they receive their biggest contributions from utilities, banks, lawyers, oil and gas, and transportation interests and can no longer be considered a "grassroots" approach to involvement in government.

PACs wield influence on a national level as well. According to a 1991 Common Cause study released in Washington, the top eleven special-interest political action committees invested $49,952,584 in current members of the U.S. House of Representatives during the period from 1981 to 1990. Area congressmen receiving substantial contributions from leading PACs include: U.S. Rep. Charles Wilson, $786,840 Business PAC; U.S. Rep. Ralph Hall, $26,650 Automobile Dealers PAC; and U.S. Rep. Jim Chapman, $27,000 Trial Lawyers PAC. Political action committees gave a total of $63.5 million to congressional candidates in the first fifteen months of the 1990 election cycle. Topping the fundraising list was the Teamsters Union PAC; American Telephone and Telegraph's PAC was the leading corporate political action committee.

Governor Ann Richards received her largest single contribution to her gubernatorial campaign in 1990 from a national political action committee called EMILY'S List. EMILY's List is the seven-year-old brainchild of Ellen Malcolm, who created the donor network as a system of raising money for selected pro-choice, Democratic women candidates. The catchy name derives from the PAC's motto: "Early Money Is Like Yeast" (it makes the dough rise). In the 1990 elections, the 6,000 members of EMILY's List raised $1.5 million for the fourteen women candidates it supported; nine won. EMILY's List is now in the top one percent of all political action committees in the country, and it is the largest single financial resource for women candidates.

Campaign contributions are, of course, the primary "raison d'etre" for political action committees. Most incumbent politicians believe that a heavily funded campaign war chest is essential for political

survival, and PACs are often the primary means by which those chests
are filled. Lobbyist and political consultant Buck Wood described the
importance of PAC donations:

> More and more money is demanded, and the only way to get it is
> from the PACs. It's a phenomenon, feeding on itself, like the price
> of gold. It doesn't relate to the cost of campaigning . . . It has a mo-
> mentum all its own. If you find the other guy is raising $500,000,
> you feel you've got to raise $500,000; if he raises to $1 million, you
> feel you've got to raise to $1 million. It has nothing to do with the
> effectiveness of the money spent.

Of the eight contenders to replace Gib Lewis as Speaker of the
Texas House of Representatives, seven have received more than fifty
percent of their campaign funds from political action committees. In
some cases, special interests represented by PACs or lobbyists contributed nearly all of the key legislators' political funds. While there's
nothing illegal about political candidates accepting money from PACs
— PACs are entitled to make contributions and politicians are entitled
to seek them — many critics worry about the impact large contributions have on legislators' votes. According to Tom Smith, "The PACs
contribute because they know it buys access. And they are particularly
intent on contributions to those who are going to have control of the
House in the future."

The Speaker candidates involved maintain that PAC contributions to their campaigns represent smaller donations from individuals
who work in certain professions or belong to particular organizations,
and they insist that most of those contributions are not solicited.
"PACs are made up of individual contributions. I can see why the per-
ception is that they are special interests, but many PACs are simply individuals contributing to a committee. It's just another way to make
campaign contributions," said one candidate. Another agreed: "PACs
represent people. A lot of my constituents use PACs to make campaign
contributions — they donate to their PACs, and the PACs donate to
me." Another representative defended the practice as the only way
working individuals can become involved in politics. And another
Speaker candidate insisted that he doesn't pay attention to contributions from PACs. "Those things aren't solicited. They just come into
the office. On some occasions, I have sent some campaign contributions back."

One representative, however, acknowledged the purpose of the contributions as a way of gaining some influence over legislation. "I look at political action committees as groups that join together to have some influence . . . Ten guys can give me $25 apiece and I have $250, or they can put it in a PAC. These are people that are giving to their groups to have influence in Austin."

The Texas Medical Association, representing the state's physicians, was the biggest single contributor to Texas politicians last year. Candidates that TEX-PAC, the political arm of the Texas Medical Association, favored tended to oppose groups that allowed doctors to be hired on salary, and they opposed letting chiropractors receive payment under medical insurance policies. According to filings with the Texas Secretary of State's office, the Medical Association spent $711,013 on political contributions to Texas officials between January 1990 and May 1991. The recipients included Lieutenant Governor Bob Bullock, House Speaker Gib Lewis, and Chet Brooks, chairman of the Senate Health and Human Services Committee and a member of the Senate Finance Committee.

Texas Trial Lawyers Association and its political arm, LIFT (Lawyers Involved for Texas), is generally considered the best-funded and most powerful political action committee in the state. Its members primarily make their living representing clients against insurance companies; they therefore back candidates who oppose no-fault auto insurance, since lawyers receive a typical twenty-five percent of the auto injury benefits paid.

In fact, you can name any interest you want and it's a safe bet their concerns are represented by a political action committee or a lobbyist in Austin. Among the more well-known PACs are the AFL-CIO, Texas Brewers' Institute, Texas Automobile Dealers Association, State Bar of Texas, Texas Manufacturers Association, TREPAC (the funding arm for the realtors of Texas), and the National Organization for the Reform of Marijuana Laws (NORML).

A PAC's acronym often sheds little, if any, light on the interest group behind it, and to those political action committees that want to conceal their true identities and purposes, this can be an advantage. PAC names can also lend them a friendly public image; as one observer pointed out, perhaps it feels better to give to or get from a group that calls itself LIFT, HELP (Hospitals Express Legislative Preference), PAL (Pharmacists Assist Legislators), or PEACE (Private Employment Agencies Committee for Education). The use of cryptic acronyms can backfire, however, particularly when a PAC expects a politician to show his gratitude later on. A reporter once asked Senator O. H. "Ike" Harris of Dallas to identify some of the PAC donors to his campaign, and the senator "could not think offhand what PEACE, HELP, and SWAC (Spirits and Wine Political Action Committee) stood for."

The recent ethics reform legislation did little to regulate the influence of PACs. In fact, some lobbyists complained that the new bribery law succeeded in granting more power to PACs. They pointed out that political action committees' large campaign donations are exempt from bribery prosecution; whereas, less powerful lobbyists' attentions, such as treating legislators to lunch, were more firmly curtailed in the new laws.

Some legislators advocate abolishing PACs altogether. "The only way you can have meaningful campaign finance reform is to do away with PACs completely," commented one key House leader. Abolition of PACs has been debated on the national level for months. Whereas most political insiders admit that the elimination of PACs is impractical or at least unlikely, some support establishing stricter limitations. Under existing Texas law, individuals and PACs are allowed to make unlimited contributions. Rob Mosbacher voiced criticism of the laxity of the new ethics reform bill on PACs in a recent interview: "I think it's a disgrace that Texas doesn't have limitations on how much individuals and PACs can contribute to political races. If you think that someone who contributed $10,000 or $20,000 speaks louder than someone who gave $1,000 or $500, you're absolutely right . . . We have no limits on PACs in Texas — the ethics bill that passed the Legislature, in my judgment, is evidence of the inability of legislators to reform themselves." Further criticism of PAC legislation stems from the fact that failure by a PAC to report a campaign contribution is only a Class C misdemeanor, punishable by a fine of up to $200. And publicized reports have detailed some legislators' flagrant misuse of PAC campaign funds, using those campaign donations to buy houses, take vacations, and supplement office expenses.

Despite these criticisms of the enormous influence of political action committees, it seems they're here to stay — at least for the time being. And if, as some PAC supporters insist, they are the only means by which "the little guy" can obtain a voice in government, perhaps the solution is for more "little guys" to form political action committees. A distinction is made between specific-purpose PACs, which may be formed on behalf of (or sometimes against) specific candidates in a particular election or ballot propositions (such as the Bob Bullock for

Lieutenant Governor Committee or the Save Our Springs Coalition in Austin), and general-purpose PACs, which make up most of the union-, corporation-, and occupation-related committees. The process of forming a PAC is relatively simple, and the newly formed Ethics Commission office can furnish the necessary paperwork.

The Third House: Who Lives There and Who Does the Housecleaning?

"Don't let us believe all that we hear, but let us believe all that we say!"
One-liner prayer by the Senate Chaplain, Dr. Gerald Mann

- Lobby maxim: "There are hundreds of ways to kill a bill but only one way to pass it!"
- 1989 session: $1.86 million spent by lobbyists on legislators' meals, drinks, golf junkets, hunting trips, and vacations!
- Typical Monday night outing for eight lawmakers (including one on a committee to study lobby-sponsored entertainment) consisted of an expensive dinner, a stretch limo, and Cher!
- During a Workers' Comp debate, chicken magnate Bo Pilgrim hands out $10,000 checks to senators on the Senate floor!
- One lobbyist shucked off $100 bills to legislators in the men's room!
- Ann Richards' reform-heavy opening speech to 1989 legislative session sent out a warning, according to one House aide: "If you don't own a lobbyist, get one!"
- When one senator played golf with lobbyists from the Texas Chemical Council and a few days later blocked an environmental bill, someone commented, "That smells as bad as the air over Freeport!"
- Bullock gaveled the ethics bill into passage with a golf club! Some say $50 per day spending limit for lobbyists was set so golf games could continue unreported . . .
- First thing Ethics Commission did was raise the legislator per diem because they said lawmakers were "starving to death" from lack of lobby-paid lunches!
- Presiding officer of ethics reform session (Speaker of the House Gib Lewis) under indictment for allegedly allowing lobbyists to pay delinquent property taxes! Lewis, whose ranches were reportedly stocked with game by the Texas Parks and Wildlife Department, often told battling legislators: "Let the big dog eat!"

· Some say "legislative-proof" Ethics Commission's power is limited to prosecuting infractions such as using Canadian coins in a parking meter!
· Laments one representative: "The people elect us, but the lobbyists instruct us . . ."

☆   ☆   ☆

There's an old saying around the Capitol: "If you can't eat the lobby's steaks, drink the lobby's whiskey, sleep with the lobby's women, and then vote against the lobby in the morning, then you don't belong here." But can our legislators partake of the lobbyists' hospitality without returning the favor by voting according to their "hosts'" wishes? As Molly Ivins pointed out, "You got to dance with them what brung you." For many years now, "them" has increasingly consisted of organized, specialized interest money.

Texas is not alone in the problem; that is, if you think of it as a problem. The number of registered lobbyists throughout the country has more than doubled in the past twenty years as other states join the heavy lobbying trend long alive in Texas. Here at home, according to a 1991 survey, the Texas legislature has 1,429 lobbyists registered, with a ratio of 7.9 lobbyists per legislator.

Who are these lobbyists and whom do they represent? The law defines a lobbyist as anyone who directly communicates with a member of the legislative or executive branch of the state government for the purpose of influencing legislative or administrative action. Our 1991 "ethics law" further defines a lobbyist as one who spends or is paid at least $200 per quarter to do so. These "professional" lobbyists must register with the newly created Texas Ethics Commission, pay a registration fee of $300 per year, and, of course, as all good government agencies require, complete a stack of forms. Many registered lobbyists are former legislators. As one political journalist remarked, "When the brightest bulbs in our Legislature burn out, they go to work as lobbyists and become zillionaires."

But what do lobbyists *do*? Lobbyists are watchdogs for their clients' interests, and their clients constitute nearly every interest group and cause imaginable — corporations, unions, universities, teachers, automobile dealers, environmentalists, plaintiff lawyers, defense lawyers, gun control advocates, anti-gun control advocates, pro-choice groups, pro-life groups. A rise in "public-interest" lobbying by groups other than businesses and unions accounts for part of the surge in lobbyist numbers. In what has become a common practice, hundreds of Texan cities and towns are paying free-lance lobbyists to protect their interests; in 1991 the city of Austin spent a reported $140,000. Says one senator, "We have created a subculture in Austin, where if you want something done, you don't go to your $7,200-a-year senator. You go hire a $50,000 lobbyist so he can get done for you what your senator and representative ought to be doing."

While anti-lobby groups may fear the increase in lobbyist numbers, one positive result of the massive influx is that there are too many interest groups for one to become dominant. Gene Fondren, a lobbyist for automobile dealers who has been called a guru among lobbyists, agrees: "[I]t would appear that lobbying is objectionable only if there are too few, rather than too many lobbyists — if only a few have the ear of government and only a few interests are represented . . . . The more points of view represented, the better the legislator is able to evaluate and determine what is in the 'public interest.' "

Sounds good, in theory. But, unfortunately, the one thing that can undo the balance is money. Legislators and lobbyists always say that lobbyists' money buys access — a chance to have their cases heard. But it stands to reason, then, that lobbyists who spend lots of money have better access than the ones who don't. Lawmakers argue that a few fancy dinners can't buy them, but those dinners buy the legislators' undivided attention and help. And as Travis County District Attorney Ronald Earle points out, "If money is the only way to get a legislator's attention, then the only issues that get attention are fights between monied interests." He said the public "pays the price" on education, health care, crime, and other issues that are not promoted by wealthy special interests.

Some lobbyists and legislators object to the distinction made between "special interests" and "public interests." As former House Appropriations Chairman Bill Heatly said, "Everything we pass besides the appropriations bill and the tax bill is special interest legislation."

Some view the lobby as corrupt and evil. However, certain unacceptable actions by the lobby have been called — and stopped. An example involves the "one-lie rule," which refers to a lobbyist furnishing false information to or about a legislator. Anyone doing so is branded in the open and his credibility destroyed. A most notable result of such rare action was reported in January 1991, when State Comptroller John Sharp called a press conference to report such action by Mark Hanna, lobbyist for the Texas Nurses Association. Sharp charged that Hanna falsely reported to members of the association that Sharp was planning a fee increase for the nurses' group. Sharp decried this false reporting as unforgivable.

Nevertheless, some view the lobby as necessary to modern legislation. Fondren points out, "The members of the legislature simply do not have the time to study every legislative proposal or to know the impact, or potential impact, of each of several thousand pieces of legislation." Lobbyists do the legwork that legislators never have the time to do, which includes conducting research to explain why a bill is (or isn't) good public policy. But, cautions one longtime legislative observer, "What you gotta know is their facts support their cause." Longtime respected railroad lobbyist Walter Caven pointed out, "Most members don't have any interest in ninety-five percent of the bills. They'll do what you ask if you get to them early."

What lobbyists usually ask is that a prospective bill be voted down. Most of the business-oriented lobbying, says one business lobbyist, "is killing, not passing. If the Legislature did not go into session, that'd be fine." After all, the lobby's maxim is: "There are hundreds of ways to kill a bill but only one way to pass it."

How can lobbyists wield so much power? Some contend that lobbyists fill the void created by the apathy of the average voter. Others say that if a legislator is a puppet for a PAC (political action committee), or trades votes for lobby-sponsored hunting trips, then the real problem is with that legislator.

But what about the paltry $600-a-month salaries of Texas legislators? The disparity between legislators' and lobbyists' salaries helps justify taking the gifts, some legislators say. "The lobbyists are down here making $200,000 or $300,000 a year, and so it won't hurt them to pay for some of these extra things," one lawmaker contended. Some argue that higher pay could reduce the lobby's temptations but that argument sounds hollow when you consider that House Speaker Gib Lewis, one of the legislature's wealthier members, reportedly enjoys partaking of the lobby's largesse as much as anybody. Besides, said one lawmaker, "It looks terrible to voters if you say, 'Give me a pay raise and I'll become an ethical person.' " Many legislators reportedly view perks as part of their compensation.

What exactly are those perks? Free lunches and golf junkets seem to be the most common invitations made to legislators. For years, lobbyists have lined up outside the chambers of the House and Senate at lunchtime to whisk legislators to Austin's best restaurants and private clubs. Legislators routinely receive passes to movies and free tickets to virtually any state college or university football team. But the favors often go further than that. According to one highly publicized report, during the five-month regular legislative session that ended in May 1989, lobbyists spent $1.86 million on entertainment and gifts for Texas lawmakers: meals, drinks, golf junkets, hunting trips, and vacations at a rate exceeding $12,800 a day. That's more than $10,300 in entertainment and gifts per legislator, if the money had been spread evenly among the 181 lawmakers. It wasn't, of course — most perks are lavished on the more powerful and influential lawmakers. This spending spree followed lobbyists' $1.35 million expenditure courting legislators in 1988, when the legislature wasn't even in session, according to an *Austin American-Statesman* review of records in the secretary of state's office.

One lobby-paid excursion that year involved tobacco lobbyists who treated eight members to dinner at an expensive Austin restaurant and then drove them in chauffeured white stretch limousines with moon roofs and bars to a Cher concert at the Frank Erwin Center. It was a typical Monday night outing for legislators, said one insider. Included in the outing were the chairmen of the two committees studying new restrictions for lobbyists entertaining lawmakers.

The highest roller, Neal T. "Buddy" Jones, a former executive assistant to the Speaker of the House who now represents twenty-four large corporate clients, was the top-spending individual lobbyist. Jones reported spending almost $7,000 a month on entertainment and gifts. But just as not all lawmakers are recipients of such generosity, not all of the registered lobbyists spend that kind of money. Big spending is concentrated in the hands of a few; in fact, one report shows only fifty lobbyists accounted for almost $1 million of the $1.5 million spent on entertainment and gifts in 1990.

In a recent divorce case, details of lobbyist Emil Pena's lifestyle emerged. He stocked the bar and refrigerator at a $2,000-a-month suite at Austin's Radisson Plaza Hotel, courting legislators who downed more than $6,000 in food and liquor in five months. Despite these lavish expenditures, Pena is not even in the top twenty-five highest spenders. One senator admitted to living for seven months in a lobbyist's Austin apartment without paying any rent. In a much more blatant case of vote-buying, East Texas chicken magnate Lonnie "Bo" Pilgrim passed out $10,000 checks to senators on the Senate floor during a heated battle over worker's compensation in 1989. According to Texas' lax ethics legislation of the time, his actions were not illegal.

These examples of subtle and not-so-subtle influence-peddling are not limited to recent times. A 1981 story in the *Dallas Times Her-*

ald reported a legislators' annual dove hunt in northern Mexico sponsored by the Texas Chemical Council, which provided shotgun shells, meals, whiskey, servants to retrieve dead birds, and transportation if desired. Then-Lieutenant Governor Bill Hobby, Hobby's executive assistant, the House parliamentarian, the UT president, lobbyist Don Adams, and a number of senators and representatives attended the hunt.

In the 1970s, Governor Preston Smith reportedly received booze for the Governor's Mansion and a plane from the liquor lobby. Several years before that, a coalition of business interests was rumored to keep several rooms in an Austin hotel for senators to consort with women. One source said he watched lobbyists on a hunting trip in the Rio Grande Valley peel off bills for House members to use in a visit to a border brothel. One lobbyist used to carry a stack of crisp $100 bills "and they were shucked off like a deck of cards to members in the restroom," according to a knowledgeable Senate source. A poker game among senators and lobbyists during legislative sessions was said to be luckier for those senators who ate with the lobbyists. Some lobbyists paid for legislators to go on a three-day junket to see a Las Vegas prize fight. A longtime lobbyist recently told one of his most interesting experiences in trying to persuade legislators. The lobbyist, who wanted to find out from one lawmaker what it would take to get his vote on a pending bill, asked, "How about a suit of clothes? Tickets to the football game? Weekend in Las Vegas? A job for your daughter-in-law?" After no positive response the lobbyist tried once more by asking, "Just what will it take?" The lawmaker readily replied, "You haven't tried *money!*"

One difference noted in a recent *Texas Monthly* article between lobbyist perks in the old days and today is the change in attitude on the part of new members. A veteran legislator observed that the new lawmakers have a different attitude about the legislature: "They're here to see how much they can get out of it." No longer do members wait to be invited out to dinner by lobbyists; they call a lobbyist, ask for a credit card number, and go to dinner with friends but without the lobbyist. They make weekly searches for lobbyists who will pay for a group night on the town without asking to come along. The legislators' most coveted perk, the out-of-town trip, however, is still by invitation only. Typical destinations are the "Honey Hole," as legislators call Houston Lighting and Power's fishpond on Cedar Bayou, prime hunting leases around the state and in Mexico, and Pebble Beach for golf.

A critic of the recent ethics reform legislation complained that focusing on golfing fees and lunches is silly, because the real payoffs in the ethics and influence game are the lawyer referrals that come to attorney-lawmakers from business or law firms that have direct interest in legislation in the Capitol. The referrals are not limited to attorneys but include other lawmakers who have businesses that may benefit as well. For years, legislators privately complained that special interests were steering business to their colleagues or, in the case of attorneys in the legislature, putting them on retainer.

Several lawyers in the legislature have reported receiving hefty fees to appear before state agencies for their clients. One of them, Bob Glasgow, a co-author of the recent ethics legislation, reported making $45,000 to $105,000 in ten cases before state agencies. Longtime state senator O. H. "Ike" Harris of Dallas has worked as an attorney for at least two insurance companies involved in sensitive negotiations with state regulators. "They're scared to death of Ike Harris," said a high-ranking administrator of his colleagues on the state board. "He comes up here in his shorts and T-shirt and struts around like he owns the place." Harris countered that Texas law does not bar a legislator from acting as an attorney for a company involved in litigation with state agencies.

Joint business ventures between legislators and lobbyists are also not uncommon. The House parliamentarian, Robert Kelly, was a business partner in a $500,000 Gulf Coast sports lodge with several big-name lobbyists, some of whom had opposed an insurance reform measure which was, incidentally, scuttled by a parliamentary ruling. When Austin lobbyist Kraege Polan needed a loan on his Tarrytown house, he turned to his old friend, Representative Tom Craddick of Midland. One legislator owns a 300-acre farm and vineyard in West Texas with three business lobbyists. A representative has invested in land and several oil and gas ventures with lobbyists, and a senator bought a South Texas radio station with lobbyists. In their defense, one legislator argues, "I have every right in the world to choose my friends and who I do business with." The state's new ethics law requires legislators for the first time to disclose business dealings with lobbyists, but does not make them illegal.

Some ethics experts say that if ethics laws are to be effective, they must address campaign reform. One lobbyist describes himself a "broker," getting politicians and campaign contributors together. The politician gets the money, the contributor gets the influence, but always through the lobbyist "because that's his bread and butter." Political action committees, such as Tex-Pac (the political arm of the Texas Medical Association) and LIFT (the political arm of the Texas Trial Lawyers Association), often show up on campaign financial reports of candidates who favor the legislation those organizations desire. In a recent column, Molly Ivins commended public-interest lobbies such as Common Cause and Public Citizen for making campaign finance reform their number-one priority. "It doesn't matter what else we do to try to clean up politics — term limitations, ethics laws, financial disclosure," Ivins contended. "Unless and until we change the way campaigns are financed in this country, our elected representatives will continue to dance with the special interests what brung'em — and the rest of us will take the hindmost."

A Sacramento lobbyist for California Common Cause says, "In the real world, incumbents get very few contributions of note from their real constituents. Instead they get money from political action committees, wealthy individuals, industries and corporations with business before the legislature." One representative from Orange County says, "I don't think there's anything inherently evil in receiving contributions from interest groups. I know there's been plenty of times when I received contributions from specific organizations, and then I voted against them when they had a big bill before the legislature because I was philosophically opposed to it. If you can ever make a tie between a sudden shift in [a legislator's] voting behavior and large contribution, that might be suspicious."

The public does seem to be suspicious about all the behind-the-scenes maneuvering of lobbyists, political action committees, and legislators. Max Sherman, a former state senator who is now dean of the LBJ School of Public Affairs at University of Texas–Austin, observed in 1989, "It would appear that the public perceives the influence of lobbyists is undue — and that's a strong feeling. If you're a member, I'd say you'd have to be concerned about that now. Legislative ethics becomes an issue in cycles, every few years, and the public is very interested in it again." Sherman, who served in the Senate from 1971 to 1977, was involved in the last major overhaul of legislative ethics, after the Sharpstown stock scandal.

Before reforms resulting from the Sharpstown scandal, the lobby ruled the legislature more than it does today. Back in the 1960s and early 1970s, the legislative process was dominated by the Big Four lobbyists, who represented the oil industry, the petrochemical industry, the railroads, and big business (the Texas Manufacturers Association). The reach of the Big Four extended beyond their clients' immediate concerns. They in essence determined the political climate of the state: low-tax, low-service, pro-business, and anti-union. Lobbyists reportedly plotted strategy over poker games with the lieutenant governor, and the legislative agenda typically consisted of a series of special-interest bills.

Sharpstown brought on reforms that ended the reign of the Big Four, and by the early 1980s, their influence at the Capitol had passed to a group known as the Hired Guns — a dozen or so lobbyists, most of them former legislators, who specialized in single-shot issues with major economic effects, such as tort reform or interstate banking. The obviously tainted special-interest bills that passed routinely in the days of the Big Four, writes one political analyst, don't even get introduced anymore.

Some observers insist that lobbyists wield as much power as ever; in a recent survey, Texas House members said lobbyists are as powerful as legislative committees in deciding which bills get passed. Representatives said the House Speaker has the most influence in the House, but lobbyists tied with committees for second place. In the Senate, lobbyist power was rated third behind the lieutenant governor and Senate committees. According to House Speaker Gib Lewis, "The education lobby, on a scale from one to 10, is probably a 10. Now when you get down below, the next one is probably the trial lawyers, and they're only a six."

Lieutenant Governor Bob Bullock readily acknowledged the enormous influence that lobbyists in general have in terms of which bills pass. "There's no question in my mind," Bullock said. "The Lord strike me dead right now without even a funeral if I don't believe that. You ain't going to whip them on the floor of the House and the Senate. The lieutenant governor is not going to do it. The Speaker is not going to do it."

Bullock proved the value of lobby support when he sought their help with the passage of his tax plan in the 1991 legislative session. Bullock called sixty to eighty lobbyists together for a private meeting in which he requested their support and reportedly gave them "extra incentive" to back his tax bill. He inserted a clause which stipulated that if the bill failed to get a majority, five additional contingency taxes would be imposed to make up for the lost revenue. The contingency taxes targeted the hotel, cigarette, insurance, car wash, and sand

and gravel industries, most of which have considerable lobbyist representation. The lobbyists immediately swung into action, and the bill passed. Said Representative Al Price, "What we have here before us is proof positive that the people elect us, but the lobbyists instruct us." Bullock's spokesman defended the lieutenant governor's action by saying that neutralizing the lobby would be a step toward passing a tax bill. "If we get to where the lobbyists don't get up in the House gallery and give hand signals to kill it, we've made a lot of progress." The irony of "lobbying the lobby" was not lost on one political observer who remarked, "When you have to get lobbyist permission to write a budget and tax bill, you have a real serious problem in terms of the quality of government you are offering."

The 1991 legislative session, supposedly dedicated to ethics reform, showed that the lobby was still going strong. In a speech to the 1991 legislative session, Governor Ann Richards urged passing tougher campaign laws, consolidating certain agencies, taking on insurance companies, and reworking franchise tax laws on corporations. Afterwards, a consultant and a House aide discussed the likely repercussions. "It was a lobbyist's full-employment speech," one said. "If you don't own a lobbyist, get one." At the close of the session House Speaker Gib Lewis made the comment that he had "never seen such pressure from the lobby" as during that session. Representative Dan Kubiak elaborated, "The lobby totally controls the House. I didn't see anything happen that the lobby didn't want."

In the subsequent summer special session, Senator Buster Brown blocked an environmental bill from immediate consideration just days after he had played golf with lobbyists for the Texas Chemical Council — the bill's leading opponents. Brown said lobbyists were on the golf outing but didn't sponsor it. Tom Smith of Public Citizen remarked, "This smells just about as bad as the air over Freeport. This was what the ethics battle was supposed to be all about."

So what was the ethics battle all about? Prior to the ethics reform legislation, Texas laws requiring disclosure of lobby spending were some of the most lax in the nation, requiring lobbyists only to report lump sums they spent — not on whom they spent it or how. The new bill, which took effect January 1, 1992, requires lobbyists to report food and entertainment expenditures exceeding $50 per day on officials, limits lobbyists to spending no more than $500 a year on gifts on each official, and requires lobbyists to accompany officials when they spend money in those categories. The bill requires legislators to report when they represent clients in front of state agencies, bans lobby-paid pleasure trips, and requires disclosure of lobby-sponsored trips that are work-related. The bill also established the Ethics Commission, with eight members appointed by the governor, lieutenant governor, and Speaker.

When Lieutenant Governor Bob Bullock gaveled the ethics bill to passage, he did so with a golf club. His purpose was to rib the ethics bill sponsor, Sen. Bob Glasgow, about the fact that Glasgow, among other legislators, occasionally tees off at lobby expense. Everyone laughed. But some say the reason Glasgow and others put the $50 ceiling on disclosures was so that the golf games can continue unreported. In some cases, the greens fees are bumping up against the $50 limit, so insiders predict the senators will have one lobbyist pay the green fees and another pay for the golf cart.

The ethics bill has been criticized as full of loopholes and questionable stipulations; the $50-per-day limit could allow a lobbyist to spend just under that amount every day for a year, totaling more than $18,000 on one member without reporting it. "No one wants to be with someone that much," argued one bill researcher. Others complain that it lacks adequate reporting requirements for legislative and state officials. Caps on how much lobbyists could spend on food and drink for legislators were dropped in the last-minute drafting of the bill. Senate staff members insist that the negotiators voted in public to limit a lobbyist to spending $500 per year on each lawmaker and blamed the oversight on hasty staff work, but many are skeptical. Others ridicule the provision that a lobbyist (besides the unlimited wining and dining) can also give up to $1,500 a year to a legislator in three other categories — $500 for gifts, $500 for mementos, and $500 for entertainment.

The ethics measure was written behind closed doors in the final hours of the session, and most legislators were forced to cast votes for the controversial measure sight unseen. (Incidentally, Keith Oakley, who two years prior had asked lobbyists to pay for a special birthday dinner for his wife and later a three-day anniversary weekend in Galveston, was on the subcommittee writing the bill.) Government leaders urged Governor Richards to amend the bill, but Richards declined to add any more items to be considered during the special session. Referring to another item taking precedence on the legislative agenda, Tom Smith of Public Citizen commented, "If they've got enough time to decide whether to sell beer in a stadium . . . we've got enough time to fix the ethics legislation."

Even lobbyists were unhappy with "the bureaucratic, form-completing, recordkeeping nightmare" required by the new laws. Ethics expert Buck Wood agreed with the lobbyists who complained about the amount of recordkeeping the new law seemed to require. Wood said he liked the approach of former Travis County D.A. Bob Smith: "Anything you can consume in one sitting, I don't care — even if it costs $300." Some lobbyists have also complained that the new bribery laws have shifted the balance between the haves and the have-nots within the lobby. Lobbyists with wealthy political action committees can afford to give large campaign donations, which are exempt from bribery prosecution. Those funds can be used to support a lawmaker's lifestyle under the guise of political expenses. Many lobbyists in trade groups do not have the funds to donate large sums to a campaign, instead relying on lunches, dinners, and other tokens to establish relationships with lawmakers.

Additional complaints were registered about the Ethics Commission, a body one journalist described as "one more revenue-absorbing albatross to be run by those masters of efficiency — the government." Commission guidelines allowed for it to cloak its early inquiries in secrecy and to defer investigation of candidates until after their election. It was revealed that a complaint filed during a campaign for the March primary would not be investigated until after the November general election. Furthermore, the commission saves its harshest penalties for people who leak information. As one political reporter humorously pointed out, "The Ethics Commission could fine a legislator who breaks finance rules up to $5,000. But there would be a fine up to $10,000 for people who bring ethics complaints later deemed frivolous. Isn't there a disparity there? Well, what could the Ethics Commission act on? Using a Canadian coin in a parking meter, that sort of thing."

In addition, critics bemoaned that all eight members would be screened and nominated by the legislature, the very body the commission must regulate. A hefty six of the eight commission members would have to vote to take an investigation to a public hearing. "What you have created is a commission that will be legislative proof," says one critic. Some even decry the bipartisan make-up of the commission; with four Democrats and four Republicans, some say it could be difficult to reach agreement on anything related to a subject as touchy as ethics — unless it were so watered down as to be meaningless. Besides, not all Texans are Democratic or Republican. To top it all off, one of the first things the newly formed Ethics Commission did was to increase the per diem pay for legislators from $30 to $85. One commission member joked, "The emergency is the legislators are starving to death because the lobbyists can't buy them anything."

One political reviewer observed that the legislature figuratively thumbed its nose at the public's concern about its ethics by allowing House Speaker Gib Lewis — under criminal indictment on ethics charges for allegedly allowing a lobbyist to pay some of his delinquent property taxes — to be in charge of the session to reform ethics. Observers say the Texas House cannot adopt a meaningful ethics reform bill while under Lewis, who has a history of involvement in questionable activities. According to an article in *Texas Monthly,* Lewis' modus operandi generally consists of letting legislators and lobbyists fight out the issues. When asked to intervene, he often replies, "I don't have a dog in that fight." Another favorite expression: "Let the big dog eat," that is, the side that can get the most votes wins. What does he care about? "Entertainment ranks higher with Gib than legislation," says a prominent lobbyist. Lewis reportedly enjoyed a lobby-paid trip to Manzanillo, Mexico, and he was one of several state officials whose ranches were stocked with game by the Texas Parks and Wildlife Department.

Lewis recently announced that he would not seek reelection to the House, and his campaign funds (totaling a reported $1 million) are of considerable interest to a citizens group which has asked the Texas Ethics Commission to rule on how Speaker candidates can dispose of leftover money. Despite the hefty bank balance, Lewis and his allies have not stopped raising money. Hours after his announcement to not seek reelection, Lewis met with a dozen lobbyists at the office of TADA president Gene Fondren. Speaker race accounts are governed by a special state law which allows candidates to spend the money for expenses directly related to a campaign, but Lewis reportedly has been using his Speaker race account to pay for his defense against the two misdemeanor ethics charges.

In what one writer described as "the hilarious world of ethics," the House Appropriations Committee voted to cut off state funding for the Travis County district attorney's Public Integrity Unit which has been investigating Speaker Lewis. And under a bill already passed by the full House, public officials who are convicted of such crimes, including bribery, probably would escape with nothing more than a fine and a "work punishment" sentence. Public Citizen's Tom Smith says,

"It sure does look funny when they eliminate prosecutors' funding and concurrently reduce the penalties for official misconduct. And it happens at a time when the Speaker is under indictment and there are persistent rumors of additional investigations of House members."

Lewis' announced retirement has opened up the powerful position of Speaker of the House. While some argue that "this is probably the most non-lobby oriented speaker's race" because "to have the lobby wrapped around your neck would be a huge detriment" in the atmosphere of ethics reform, others contend that the lobby will be knee-deep in the fight. One editorial writer laments, "It is tragic that the average citizen in Texas will not know about the campaign behind the scenes to decide who the next speaker will be. The media will not be able to keep up with the private phone calls or the private hunts held in ranches deep in South and West Texas."

Since the enactment of the ethics reform bill, reports show that lobbyists have significantly reduced the amounts they are spending on legislators. Some are even writing (anonymously) to the Texas Ethics Commission to find out which lobby-paid perks are forbidden under the state's new ethics laws. Lobby-paid hunting trips are a top concern. Commission members say a typical letter whines, "My buddies and I have been doing this for years. Can we continue doing it?" Well, that depends. While it is illegal for lobbyists to give lawmakers lodging or transportation for non-work-related trips, it is legal for legislators to accept such freebies. Advice? Go dutch. As one commission member put it, "Anybody can go hunting with anybody. You only get into a problem when people aren't paying their own way."

While some lobbyists take the reform measures seriously, others have their doubts. By noon on the last day of the legislative session enacting the ethics reform, liquor already was seen arriving at the Capitol. Crews unloaded cases of Coors beer and Jack Daniels, bound for the offices of state lawmakers for one last party in the final hours of the session. One representative, referring both to the lobby-paid refreshments and to the session itself, commented: "Business as usual."

Reform supporters may bemoan the diluted ethics bill and the undisturbed power of lobbyists and political action committees, but there's another old saying up on the Hill: "If Christopher Columbus had not lobbied Queen Isabella, America would never have been found." Or funded!

PRATTLE

The lobbyist is a good listener and his true feelings aren't always apparent!

— Courtesy State Representative Neil Caldwell

Lingo

This section on "lingo" demonstrates that this is not a new phenomenon. Those involved in politics and government have been at the art of creating a new language for a very long time. And you *do* have to be an insider to understand it!

advise and consent: Confirmation by the Senate of certain appointees.

amateur night: When local citizens come to town for one night of lobbying.

argumentum adjudicum: Judge Roy Bean's motto; translated it means, "Don't argue with the judge." Few people ever did.

astronaut bag: Allows male legislators to speak longer during filibuster without leaving the room when nature calls.

bad bills bin: Senator Carl Parker was given a be-ribboned "Bad Bills Bin" in which to store bad bills.

bedlam: A place or condition of noise and confusion.

bedroom communities: Where people live in one taxing district and vote in another.

brain drain: Taking Texas' best out of the state.

Buzzin' Dozen: Killer Bees.

canned hunts: Killing exotic animals in an enclosed area.

carry-over bill: Legislation introduced in one year which may be considered for passage the following year without reintroduction.

cash cow: Something seen as a source for revenue (comment made in reference to public transportation).

catbird seat: Hot seat.

cheat sheet: A laminated card in the shirt pocket of a legislator with bill numbers and topics so legislator will know which bill to kill and which to save.

chubbing: A House practice that sets limits on debate. A planned group undertaking whereby members organize to delay a vote by parliamentary tactics. It happens particularly at the end of the session, when members debate at length on bills they don't necessarily oppose, to prevent the House from reaching a bill they do oppose but suspect will pass.

clean-up bill: Going back to redo a bill; "companion bill."

consultant (or expert): Any ordinary guy with a briefcase more than fifty miles away from home.

Democratic Square Dance: Dancing Democrats.

242

doable: In the house — "braggacious." Stress Diet . . . Catch 22.

do pass: The affirmative recommendations made by a committee in sending a bill to the floor for final vote.

engrossment: The preparation of an exact, accurate, and official copy of a measure passed by the House of origin containing the proper endorsements of said House and including insertion of all amendments. The measure is then forwarded to the other House for its consideration.

feeding frenzy: The equivalent of "piling on" in football; refers to sharks and legislators.

feedlot: The name in the House for the Kent Hance Award. It was awarded in the 1960s when Rep. Tom Holmes of Granbury had a bill to help feedlot owners; it got only fifteen ayes of the 150 House members.

filibuster: A Senate practice allowing unlimited debate. In a filibuster, a senator talks at great length to prevent a vote on a measure that he opposes but which is likely to pass. This is an attempt to make the Senate put off the bill to get on to other matters. The practice is particularly effective late in the session.

flaking: Promising to vote one way, then voting another!

flim-flam: Double-talk.

floor reporting: Committee approves a bill without public hearing or rational discussion.

fluid coalition: An example is minority groups with Republicans.

"for personal reasons": As in "resign for personal reasons," to resign because you know they are going to fire you.

four-fifths rule: In last seventy-two hours of a session, all bills are considered dead unless tentatively approved by the entire House or reported from committee in Senate.

franking privilege: A privilege accorded members of Congress to post "official business" mail without charge.

French perfume: It is "French perfume" to stand up and say that someone else's bill stinks.

friends of good government: Contributors.

FUBAR: Fouled Up Beyond All Repair.

furniture: Term first used around the legislature to describe members who, by virtue of their indifference or ineffectiveness, were indistinguishable from their desks, chairs, or spittoons.

futility: "It's like walking on a woodpile."

gerrymandering: Maneuvering political boundaries.

get-even time: Five members banding together can knock a bill off consent calendar with ten minutes debate, forcing it to go the regular route.

ghost vote: Rep. Larry Evans died on August 8, 1991. Other members voted him present and voting on other legislation. He was found dead in his apartment at 2:55 P.M.

gibberish or gibberisms: Gib Lewis slang.

grandfathering: Forgiving all that has happened before.

grizzly owls: Capitol Press Corps.

grousing: Complaining.

harem: A senator's office staff comprising the "damnedest assortment of beauties."

heroes and zeros: Two kinds of members.

hopper: A box on the desk of the clerk of the House where representatives deposit the bills which they sponsor.

the "I" word: Sticking one's neck out.

"It's a glitch": This means "We will go forward with the appeal."

judicial thicket: Redistricting problems.

keeper of the gate keys: Law passed for LBJ so he could run for two offices at the same time.

lame duck: An elected official whose term of office continues after he has failed to be reelected.

Lawyers Full-employment Bill: This is a bill so technical that we may never figure it out, but people with law degrees will get rich trying.

lay on the table: Temporary postponement of a matter before the legislature, which may be brought up for consideration by motion from the floor.

legislators getting wobbly knees: What it says.

line item: Gib Lewis' pet zebra.

Linoleum Club: A tiny basement cafeteria that was in the Capitol for years.

litmus test: Putting forth a measure to see how later proposals will be received.

Lobby Full-employment Act: John Sharp's reference to the many effects of his proposed consolidation of game, racing, liquor agencies.

logjam: The effect of Democratic lawyers in the Texas Senate.

log rolling: Political slang for the practice whereby elected officials help one another to get their pet bills passed.

loose herding: Coke Stevenson's refusal to assert tight control over the 150 legislators.

low caller: One who is answering calls but not doing much about them; likely to avoid political decisions.

man of letters: Known by initials!

mark up legislation: Fool around with legislation.

minor technical amendment: All you will recognize from your bill after this will be its caption.

moving target: Play dumb and keep moving!

nibble to death: Pick to pieces the opposition.

no record vote: Allows members to vote without the record showing how they voted.

non-substantive recodification: Something is about to happen to you, and you will not be kissed first.

note and initial: Let's spread the responsibility for this.

OTB: Off-track betting.

Oklahoma Guarantee: If it breaks in two, you get both parts!

on the table: Laid out for all to see.

paired: When changed legislative boundaries put two incumbents in the same district. (*Dallas Morning News,* May 16, 1991)

pairing: A procedure whereby two opposing voters in the legislature "pair" their vote by previous agreement. Both members can then be absent when the vote takes place.

pawed sand: Referring to Connally's delay in announcing his intent to run in 1967.

penthouse to outhouse: Going from top to bottom.

pit bulls: Representative Rudd had pit bulls on his committee, ready to kill bills.

point of order: Motion calling attention to a breach of order or rules.

point of order privilege: Statement by a member that his character or motives have been impugned and his refutation of the alleged charges; or a statement that the integrity of the proceedings has been called into question.

political catfish: Those caught right in the middle of the river — not going up and not going down . . . just treading water.

politician: Person who never met a tax he didn't like.

pork barrel: The slang expression for federal appropriations for local improvements which are actually political favors to local politicians or citizens.

privilege of the floor: Permission to view proceedings from the floor of the chamber rather than from the public gallery; also access to the floor granted particular personnel or individuals for specific purposes.

pull a Florio: Common phrase used around legislative halls referring to New Jersey governor who rushed through a mammoth tax bill early in a session . . . which was his political suicide.

pull down your bill: Withdraw your bill.

quick jig: Temporary law to temporarily solve need.

revenue enhancer: What Art Buchwald called a new tax or fee.

rig count: Refers to TV antennas on trailers gathering for a special event.

sand bag: Sucker them in.

Secret Squirrels: Press Corps term for reporters who overhear their fellow reporters, then rush to call in the story themselves on a pay phone.

seniority rule: The custom that provides that the chairman of a committee shall be the person who has the longest record of service on the committee.

sign off: Signing or putting your initials on a document.

sine die: The end; final adjournment. (Last forty-eight hours in Senate.) In the last seventy-two hours of session, neither House nor Senate can consider a bill that has not cleared committee.

smart map: Latest census data listed on a map.

smell test: Something is not right about the piece of legislation.

smoke and mirrors: Unrealistic budgetary planning.

SOP: Standard operating procedure.

stopping the clock: The practice of extending the hour of final adjournment on the last day of a session in order to complete clerical duties of the session; no votes or action may be taken by either house.

stress diet: Diet a filibusterer uses before session.

tag: A representative can "tag" his particular interest legislation, requiring a longer waiting period before committee action.

train wreck: A political catastrophe. More than a difficult problem: a head-on collision.

trash bill: A bill that just does more of what the state is already doing.

the trials: A vote against the trial lawyers would mean that legislators would have opponents with campaign kitties stuffed by business.

turn up the burner: Put the heat on.

wannabes: Office-holders who want to move up the political ladder.

warts: Political scars from lost battles.

Washington Monument Syndrome: In Washington, this refers to when the U.S. Parks Department budget is threatened, they cut the hours visitors can visit the Washington Monument.

"We are making a survey": "We need more time to think of an answer."

wedge issues: Issues used to divide and conquer political opposition.

whip: An official of the majority or minority party in Congress whose task is to have members of his party present for votes on important measures.

"Yes, we heard your bill in committee, and it has been sent to subcommittee for further work": "Turn out the lights, the party's over."

Senator Don Kinnard buttonholes Rep. Tim Von Dolen.

— Senate Media Services

Quotes/Sayings/Slogans

"A big shot is a little shot that keeps on firing."

Baggett, Dennis: "Guiding a bill through mark-up is remarkably similar to participating in a hog butchering."

Barnes, Ben: "Let's have a level playing field." (Re: speed train hearings.)

Barrientos, Gonzalo, on final passage of his bill requiring arenas to build 1.5 women's toilets for every one built for men: "The House watered it down." *(Dallas Morning News)*

Berka, Paul: "The House regards the Senate as being paid for by the plaintiff's lawyers, while the Senate regards the House as being paid for by the business lobby." *(Texas Monthly)*

"Big business is every kind of business except the kind from which the person who's complaining about big business draws his pay." (O'Rourke)

Bubba, best definition: "The guys who drive pickup trucks with shotguns across the back window while listening to country music and throwing beer cans out the window. Some people think of them as the average Texan." *(Dallas Times-Herald* columnist Molly Ivins, quoted in *USA Today)*

Bullock, Bob: "Talk doesn't cook rice, and they haven't cooked any rice yet."

Bully pulpit: The governor's office.

Carpenter, Liz, on fear of flying: "I know in my heart the Wright Brothers were wrong." (Chariton, *Texas Wisdom)*

Cavazos, Eddie: "You sound like a lawyer . . . . I was trying to think of the worst thing I could call you and that was it."

Clements, Bill: "Nothing is ever so bad that it can't be worse. Or better." (Chariton, *Texas Wisdom)*

Connally, John: "In short, if you are not willing to be quoted by name, you should not be speaking." (Chariton, *Texas Wisdom)*

Cousins, Norman: "The lottery is a tax on morons."

Crowley, Mary, originator of home interiors, said, "Be somebody. God doesn't take time to make a nobody." (Chariton, *Texas Wisdom)*

Delco, Wilhelmina: "You send up a trial balloon and see how high it goes and who shoots it down." (On education funding proposals.)

Democracy: "The only thing more depressing than democracy at work is democracy not allowed to." (O'Rourke)

"Education is hanging around until you catch on!"

"Never before in Texas history have redistricting maps been drawn with so many squiggly lines, fingers, and claws than this year's version. Lines look like four spiders having an orgy." (Sam Attlesey, *Dallas Morning News*)

"Spectacular feats are being performed in the game of Texas politics today. Never in Texas history have so few done so much to so many in the interests of so few." (Kinch/Proctor)

Ferguson, Jim: "Politics is like a game of billiards — when you put up your cue, the game's over." (Dewitt Bowmer book)

"Giving money and power to government is like giving whiskey and car keys to teenage boys." (O'Rourke)

Glasgow, Bob: "We are more interested in libations than legislations, so we quit." (Senator Bob Glasgow, formally notifying the House that the Senate had completed its work.)

"We're talking about vague numbers because everybody's got a number."

"Good laws derive from evil habits — macrobius." (O'Rourke)

"Gramm-Rudman-Hollings was like trying to stop smoking by hiding cigarettes from yourself and then leaving a note in your pocket telling you where they are." (O'Rourke)

Gramm-standing: "The tendency of Texas Senator Phil Gramm to seek the spotlight for himself." (*Dallas Morning News*)

Granoff, Al: "Our duty is to exaggerate but not totally mislead our fellow members." (*Dallas Morning News*)

Hale, Seldon (chairman of the Texas Department of Criminal Justice Board): "This is Texas, where politics is a blood sport." (*Amarillo Daily News*)

"He has shot himself in the foot so many times, he doesn't have any toes left."

"To keep the budget axe from swinging their way how come when something upsets the left, you see immediate marches and parades and rallies with signs already printed and rhyming slogans already composed, whereas whenever something upsets the right, you see two members of the young Americans for freedom waving a six inch American flag? Answer: Because they have jobs." (O'Rourke)

"I haven't felt this bad since I found out George Washington had slaves!"

"I am so tired, I am lefthanded!"

"I was already nine years old when I was born."

"If men were angels, no government would be necesary." — James Madison

Incumbents in Washington: "The longer they serve, the more effective they become in discharging their duties in the Capitol while the less they become responsive to political demands at home." (*Two-Party Texas*, John Knaggs)

"It is widely speculated that all Texans eventually go to heaven because hot air rises." (Chariton, *Texas Wisdom*)

Johnson, Lyndon: "All things are possible when God lets loose a thinker and a doer in the world." (Chariton, *Texas Wisdom*)

"We don't all see everything alike. If we did, we would all want the same wife." (Chariton, *Texas Wisdom*)

"LBJ thinks an extremist is anybody who believes Austin ought to have two TV stations." (Knaggs)

Junell, Rob: "Competition in the legislature is nothing new, even in the necktie category. But Tuesday, Rep. Robert Junell, D-San Angelo, won handily. His red, white and blue tie with the design of the U.S. Flag caused quite a stir. The lawmaker's favorite response came from a colleague: "I don't know whether to salute you or burn you." (*Dallas Morning News*)

Kuempel, Edmund: "I don't make it a habit in any way, shape or form of going around and stepping on people's toes, or pulling on somebody's britches or popping somebody's bra strap."

Leedom, John: After a huge ruckus over a minor amendment, John Leedom likened support of the amendment to "defending Bunker Hill against Red Square."

"The Legislature avoids obligations like a mutt fleeing a soapy tub."

Lewis, Gib: "I don't have a dog in this fight." (His reply to fellow legislator who asked him to enter into a debate.)

"To some people listening to a speech like that might be like going to watch a guy get a haircut."

Informed that Tuesday was the thirtieth birthday for Rep. Curtis Soileau, the fifty-four-year-old Lewis replied, "You know, some of us have ties that are older than that." (*Dallas Morning News*)

"Let me get my tongue out of my mouth here."

"I want this ethics issue dissolved." (*Dallas Morning News*)

"Got run over by the University fund in 1986. First case of road kill."

"Look cool and confident on the surface while running as hard as a scared jackrabbit." (Knaggs)

"The man on the street does not live by the standards that he expects his politician to live by." (Kinch/Proctor)

"Many lawyers know as much about the law as a $2 hooker does about love, an old philosopher in Texas once observed." (Chariton, *Texas Wisdom*)

Marchant, Ken: "We are the do-nothing, are-nothing, know-nothing committee."

Munificence: Means "lavish giving" as in lobby gifts.

"Nothing Congress hates more than to have to make a decision."

"One belief about the American political system: God is a Republican and Santa Claus is a Democrat." (O'Rourke)

"Ordinary folks spend money. The government makes appropriations!"

Parker, Carl: "The thing that a politician can least afford to do in the face of a crisis is nothing."

"Experience has taught us that letting members read the bill only causes problems."

The caliber of arguments prompted Sen. Carl Parker to exclaim, "This is the day you pray for a bomb threat." But one aide ascribed the thin skins to more than just an ornery Monday: "Can you tell redistricting started last week?" (*Dallas Morning News*)

"We have an alien plastic creature out there."

"I don't wish to establish any kind of precedent in voting against fat ugly guys from Port Arthur."

Politics: "The aim of practical politics is to keep the populace alarmed (and hence clamorous to be led to safety) by menacing it with an endless series of hobgoblins, all of them imaginary." — H. L. Mencken (O'Rourke)

"Power tends to corrupt. Absolute power corrupts absolutely."

"Practicing law may not be the oldest profession, but the results to the client are the same." (Chariton, *Texas Wisdom*)

"Pull a Florio": Refers to New Jersey Governor Florio, who rushed through a mammoth tax bill early in session.

Rayburn, Sam: (Re: living a long life) "My prescription would be to keep busy, do not get angered about little things, eat plenty, sleep long, and never feel like you are getting old." (Chariton, *Texas Wisdom*)

"If you want to get along, you've got to go along." (Gus Mutscher was fond of quoting this.) (Kinch/Proctor)

"The size of a man has nothing to do with his height." (Chariton, *Texas Wisdom*)

Richards, Ann: "We've got these fancy pens. I think they're good for one letter before they run out of ink."

"Brylcream agenda — A little dab'll do ya."

"Cowboys bite the mare's ear to settle her, and lawmakers are biting the ear of government long enough to get a saddle on it and turn it into a workhorse."

"Focus on the horse, not the rider."

"Scrubbing down" — Bullock on government agencies.

Sharp report: "Like most strong medicine, it is best swallowed in one gulp. Savored sip by sip it might not go down so well." (A&M Economist Jarred Hazelton)

Sharp, John: "Riding on a merry-go-round that's spinning out of control, after a while nobody knows where they are."

"The only difference between conservatives and liberals is that both spend all they have, but every once in a while the conservatives feel bad about it."

Simms, Bill: "I just wanted to say that the cabrito is getting cold down there at Scholz's beer garten."

Smith, Preston: "Let him who is without stock throw the first rock." (Kinch/Proctor)

Stevenson, Coke: "I'm wondering what it would feel like to shoot a man." (Caro)

Stiles, Mark: "This thing is going to be stinking around here for a long time and we're all going to be smelling bad again." (*Austin American-Statesman*)

Tandy, Charles, founder of Tandy Corporation: "To catch a mouse you've got to make noise like a cheese." (Chariton, *Texas Wisdom*)

Tax, regressive: A regressive tax is one in which not everyone pays a fair share. A regressive tax hits the lower income citizens harder since they pay more proportionally than higher income citizens, at least in Texas because Texas relies on property and sales tax.

"Texas state capitol is the largest state capitol in the U.S., even larger than the National Capitol. It had to be built that big to keep the politicians and lawyers from stealing it." (Chariton, *Texas Wisdom*)

"There's a little Bubba in all of us." — From the menu of the Lone Star Cafe.

Trevino, Lee: "The older I get, the better I used to be."

Truan, Carlos: "I talked twenty hours about shrimp, and I think children are much more important."

Whitmire, John: "I carried a bill to ban pay toilets (while) in the House in the 1970s, and I'm still trying to get over it."

"Why do people take an instant dislike of Sununu? Answer: because it saves time!"

Williamson, Mary Beth: "You don't have to move people around. You can move information around because of technology."

Wilson, Ron: "I'm like the ugly guy at the dance; I get better looking around 2 o'clock in the morning."

"You can talk to a fade, but a hook won't listen." (Chariton, *Texas Wisdom*)

Zaffirini, Judith: "Half the population of Texas are women. And cumulatively, we are mothers of the other half."

Hide and Seek:
Maneuvers on the Hill

"Let us defend the status quo, but only if the quo still has some status."
One-liner prayer by the Senate Chaplain, Dr. Gerald Mann

Part of the problem with the legislature is getting record votes on controversial issues. Many members avoid conflict by asking the legislative leadership to keep issues off the floor.

☆ ☆ ☆

Texas legislators displayed their ability to use the system to their own advantage in reworking their retirement benefits. Legislators in Texas have a relatively low salary but very large retirement benefits. This is because they need voter approval to amend the former but not to change the latter. Also, legislators tied their retirement benefits to bills affecting health and retirement plans of state employees and, if that weren't enough, they proposed it quietly and at the last possible moment; therefore it received little scrutiny. They have also attached their benefits to the salaries of state district judges, greatly increasing their amounts. Benefits requirements were relaxed to include younger legislators who have served for less time: now fifty-year-olds who have served twelve years can receive full benefits — down from age fifty-five and thirty years of service.

☆ ☆ ☆

One of the persistent myths about members of the legislature is that their $600 per month salary is inadequate. Consider the total compensation package under the new retirement bill: A fifty-year-old legislator who has served for twelve years will be able to retire and start receiving $1,606.50 per month for life plus state medical insurance for himself or herself and his or her family.

☆ ☆ ☆

The National Conservative Action Committee claimed credit for defeating several prominent liberal senators in 1980. Since the group did not formally align with campaigns, it qualified to make unlimited "independent expenditures," meaning it could pour hundreds of thousands of dollars into slashing negative advertising to tear down a liberal incumbent while the conservative challenger could devote more time and resources to selling his or her positive virtues.

☆ ☆ ☆

Holding a bill in committee is another tactic, forcing the bill to die a slow death without ever getting a hearing.

☆ ☆ ☆

While campaigning, Matt Davis said he'd promised his mother on her deathbed that he'd get to some office. Every time he ran for office, he just substituted the new position into his story. Davis eventually made it to the Court of Appeals. In my mind's eye, I can picture his mother smiling down from heaven . . . .

☆ ☆ ☆

Byron Tunnell told Sam Rayburn that a fellow who called him a communist had applied for a national bank charter. Mr. Sam said, "Is that a fact?" That was the entire conversation on the subject, but the bank charter was denied. Notice that nobody asked anybody to do anything.

☆ ☆ ☆

Strategy for "important" legislation: Lay out the things you *know* you must have, such as a budget issue or water rights for your constituents. Then sit down and think of one tough issue to get the troublemakers scrapping. Propose the controversial issue first, so those members will get all excited and waste their energy fighting. When they wear themselves out, give in on that issue and get around to the other things that *really* matter. A well-known strategy of labor.

☆ ☆ ☆

Customarily at Sine Die time, the House places a paper sack over the clock to "hold time" until business is completed. If no one actually *sees* that final minute tick away, House is still in session, right?

☆ ☆ ☆

When Emmett Morse was Speaker, members would punch the vote buttons of colleagues who weren't at their desks. These enterprising members would get twenty votes before anyone could stop them!

☆ ☆ ☆

Waggoner Carr recalls an aborted maneuver: "One of the most colorful characters of my time was Jerry Sadler. I was having this very close, heavily contested race with Joe Burkett for Speaker and it was a gimmee. Joe didn't trust me — he tried to prove I was buying votes or something. Jerry told me that he had pledged his vote to Joe, but that he wanted to help me. Jerry said, 'Waggoner, when I come in to talk to you and I pull my coat off, that's a signal that I'm not wired. But if I don't pull my coat off, I'm recording everything you say.' I finally won by 4 votes out of 150, and there were never any tapes of me buying votes."

☆ ☆ ☆

Jim Bowmer remembers how legislators would pull the wool over constituents' eyes. "The ballot for prohibition was simply marked "for" or "against." Ms. Bowmer, being against alcohol, marked "against," thinking she was voting against liquor. When she got home she realized she'd voted against prohibition instead of against drinking. Jim said this demonstrated the unfairness of the double negative.

☆ ☆ ☆

Gib Lewis became Speaker of the House under odd circumstances, and with no small amount of luck. In 1980 he asked Bill Clayton for permission to take "seconds," pledged support from House members that if Clayton didn't run for Speaker, they'd vote for Lewis. Clayton, anticipating no obstacle to his election as Speaker, said yes. A few days later, however, Clayton was indicted on a bribery charge. Lewis had the race in his pocket.

☆ ☆ ☆

Ed Wendler of Austin, an attorney who was lobbying for the Texas Vending Association, finagled an amendment to a vending licensing bill in the Senate. During the hectic final hours of the 1969 legislative session, when it appeared that either Wendler's bill or *no* bill would pass, the measure was approved by Clark, Mauzy, and the legislature. Clark and Mauzy said later they were not aware that Wendler, the vending industry's lobbyist, had amended the bill in such a way that it produced the *direct opposite result* from what Clark originally intended. The bill, as it finally passed under the guiding hand of the very industry it was supposed to reform, tended to strengthen the power of the vending machine owners; although it prohibited vending operators from owning tavern licenses, it permitted them to own the real estate on which taverns were located; and it prohibited tavern operators from owning their own vending machines, but rather forced them to lease machines from vending firms — at a lower tavern operator "take" from the machines, too. A separate licensing provision also effectively forced restaurant owners to lease vending machines from vending firms.

☆ ☆ ☆

Two members got into a shoving match over a podium on the House floor. The fracas occurred when Rep. Ron Wilson (D-Houston) went to object a bill. Anticipating the move, Houston Republicans John Culberson and Mike Jackson stood in front of the podium, hoping to block Wilson for the few seconds it takes the Speaker, hearing no objections, to bang the bill passed. Wilson got to the podium, but only after a short scuffle. After watching the display, Rep. Robert Earley (D-Portland) was moved to comment, "They've been watching the (Detroit) Pistons playing for too long."

☆ ☆ ☆

Senator Eddie Lucio tried to stop a filibuster against his bill by raising a point of order. He contended that Mr. Truan, the filibusterer, was wearing blue jeans — outlawed apparel in the Senate Chamber. A parliamentary ruling was made: The pants were blue twill.

☆ ☆ ☆

Whenever times get tough for Texas, the legislative budget board proposes dramatic cuts in some state agencies to show lawmakers a way to balance the state's budget without raising taxes. Such recommendations raise a question: Should the budget board's proposals be taken seriously, or does it merely employ "scare tactics" to convince the public and lawmakers of the need to raise taxes?

☆ ☆ ☆

Most candidates campaign for Congress the hard way: They learn a lot about the issues, shake a lot of hands, raise a lot of money. Then there's State Senator Frank Tejeda (D-San Antonio), who will win a seat in Congress because the political lines were drawn just for him. Tejeda is the only candidate — Democrat or Republican — on the ballot in the 28th congressional district, and no write-in candidate has emerged. Thus, Tejeda gets a free ride into a job that pays $125,120 a year. "Not having opposition certainly does reduce the stress," Tejeda told reporters.

☆ ☆ ☆

The LBJ bill allowing LBJ to run for two offices at the same time is probably one of the best known maneuvers.

Or, Allan Shivers getting the Democratic Convention to nominate a Republican has got to be near the top!

The Unwritten Code

Get your senator's permission before you are appointed by the governor.

Always applaud when a senator recognizes constituents in the balcony.

Never launch a filibuster without informing the lieutenant governor and sponsor.

"I reluctantly rise" . . . "Does the gentleman yield?" . . . "Ask unanimous consent" — these things serve as a constant reminder that things are never supposed to get too personal.

Don't knock bills off the uncontested calendar without first informing the author.

One must follow etiquette, explained Rep. Al Granoff. "The first month is devoted to relationship development." That's where members go from desk to desk shaking hands, complimenting each other's attire, making jokes and generally not paying attention to what's happening in the Speaker's podium.

It is rude to discuss specifics of business while on the floor socializing — that's what offices are for. Besides, Representative Granoff said, experienced lawmakers use the relationship-development period "to line up support for your bills without talking business."

Never act as though you know more than another senator.

Never waste the Senate's time — this particularly applies to freshmen.

Never resort to ideology unless it is the issue.

If you don't have anything to say, don't say it.

If you don't know what you're doing, don't do it.

The tradition of having a "Doctor of the Day" in attendance for legislators while they are in session is twenty years old.

The bolo, or string tie, has been outlawed on the Senate floor. A TV cameraman was recently asked to leave because of the bolo-attire flap — even though his expensive new bolo featured the State of Texas in its design.

The custom in the House has been for the Speaker to pass out pledge cards to lawmakers, on which members can say whether they will support the Speaker in advance of the actual vote. Lawmakers then cast their recorded vote on the floor.

A secret ballot, say some lawmakers, removes the coercion that some of them say exists in the public recorded-vote method the House now uses. Voting in secret — just as voters do when they elect public officials — allows lawmakers to vote their conscience.

There has been an unwritten rule that lobbyists stay with "friendly incumbents," those legislators who have voted more or less along the lines of what their clients wanted.

John Lemon couldn't seem to decipher the Senate Code. He contested uncontested bills in committee looking for hidden meanings that weren't there, implying that he knew bills better than their sponsors.

Lemon caused one senator to lose his patience to the point where he raised a parliamentary objection, something senators never invoke against full-fledged members of their club.

When lobbyists went to talk to Lemon about a bill to change the way harbor pilots were appointed and regulated, all Lemon wanted to talk about was why the state shouldn't regulate pilots at all.

When he opposed funding of centers for battered women with the argument that it would speed the breakup of families, the bill's sponsor told him he was living in a fantasy world.

In an effort to squirm out of a redistricting plan that would force him to run against another senator, Lemon proposed a plan that resembled the Caribbean Islands: noncontiguous parts of districts floated free, a clear violation of law. When it was plotted on the map, the audience broke into laughter.

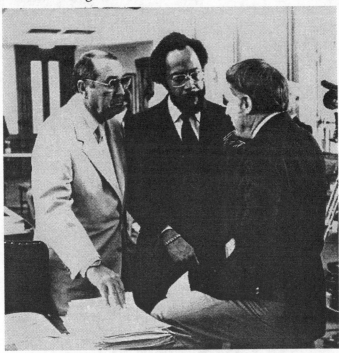

Senators Peyton McKnight, Craig Washington, and Jack Ogg.
— Senate Media Services

Dean Robert Jeffrey, UT School of Communications; Tom Granger, president, Headliners Club; Walter Cronkite; Kathy Cronkite; and H. C. Pittman, chairman, Headliners Club Board of Trustees.

Lieutenant Governor Ben Barnes and floor advisers.

— Senate Media Services

ERWIN
ROAST

"Legislation is damned serious business . . ."
— Courtesy State Representative Neil Caldwell

Headliners Roast of Frank Erwin

September 9, 1978

Jabbers

J. J. Pickle	Allan Shivers	Don Walker
John Henry Faulk	Peyton McKnight	Babe Schwartz
Bob Bullock	Ben Barnes	Jeff Friedman
Roy Butler		Barbara Jordan

Master of Ceremonies Extraordinaire: Neal Spelce

Intro: H. C. Pittman, Chairman, Headliners Club Board of Trustees

Pittman: The "Wick Fowler First or Last Annual Roast" carries on a sacred tradition of roasting Texas colorful characters. Following this tradition, this roast could not have a more deserving person than our roastee. Wick Fowler was one of the most colorful characters in our great state. In his will, he provided for free drinks at the Headliners bar for his many friends who had known and loved him.

He said, "I know that someday you all will have a tribute to me. You'll have a head table, the program will be long, and I want to take money out of my estate to buy water from Mexico for the Dais. That ought to keep the program short."

He has provided ample amounts of Two-Alarm Chili (bugs and all) for this roast.

Now, let's raise a glass to Wick and let Spelce get things moving.

Neal Spelce: Our first roaster is a man who has been in Congress for fifteen years — a record that would not have been possible without a great deal of sacrifice, mostly on the part of his constituents. Here's your congressman, Tong Sun Pickle.

Congressman J. J. "Tong Sun" Pickle: Mr. Chairman, Frank "Often-wrong-but-never-in-doubt" Erwin, distinguished guests and friends. Last night when I left the Sheraton Crest after attending an Urban League function, I went outside and found my car had been broken into and they stole a TV and a briefcase. It made me mad. What really made me mad was that my speech was in my briefcase. They read it and threw it on the ground, so I'm having to kind of reconstruct it today.

It's not easy to think of funny things to say about Frank Erwin. He's not a very funny person. In fact, when most people talk about

Frank, they are deadly serious. Now, I just returned from Washington where two days ago, we sustained a present veto on the $2 billion nuclear carrier. Now we've got to decide how we're going to spend the $2 billion. Chairman George Mahon said that we need to develop some new destructive weapon systems. I suggested that a new weapon that is potentially more awesome than the nuclear carrier would be Frank Erwin in a Cadillac. It could be worse than the neutron bomb.

Now, Frank is well-respected in Washington. During the time that President Johnson was in the White House, Frank had a key — a University of Texas key — to the Federal Treasury and no questions were asked just as long as he promised to build a geriatric center and the LBJ Library, and it turned out to be a good deal for all of us. Now, I've always felt that whenever Frank and the president were dealing, and there was a lot of dealing going on, when they left each other and went outside, I think they both felt like drying off their legs.

President Carter called me the other day and asked if I thought Frank would come to the White House as an adviser, and I said, "Mr. President, are things really that bad?" The president replied, "Well, better that than my brother Billy, or Bob Strauss, or John White, or Ray Marshall, or J. J. Pickle."

I understand that Frank really was being considered for a top-level job at the White House, but they finally decided that the Federal Treasury couldn't afford Roy Minton's legal fees. But they did go ahead and run an FBI background check on Frank. When Frank filed a Freedom of Information Request to get a copy of the FBI report, they told him that there was a law against sending pornography through the mail.

Well, when President Johnson was in the White House, Frank used to come to the White House quite often and was almost a regular there. He even had a special place there. Now, we had the blue room and the green room and the red room and they thought about adding a pink elephant room, but instead, Frank just went to Sam Houston Johnson's room and felt very much at home. I think that's where the Quorum Club really started.

Well, I'm sorry that Frank doesn't like to come to Washington anymore now that the policemen don't know him, the parking attendants don't know him, and especially because the White House does know him. Perhaps there's been too much talk about Frank and we ought to let up on him. Frank, on that basis I think you ought to come back to Washington because you'd be surprised how little they do talk about you up there now.

It was interesting dealing with Frank on the last-minute reorganization of the Austin Geriatric Center . . . Until Frank began to admit that Senator John Williams of Delaware was trying to put him in jail. There are a lot of people who still think that was a good idea.

Now, in closing, I'd like to read a telegram that came in this morning from Washington for this tribute to Frank. It says, "Peace on you," signed Jimmy Carter and Bob Strauss and John White and Ray Marshall, but not J. J. Pickle. Frank, we love you.

Neal Spelce: Thank you, Congressman. You have a phone call here from Washington that says to call Elizabeth Ray at the usual number.

Our next roaster is the chairman of the Board of Regents of the University of Texas System — a man who in his lifetime can point with justifiable pride to many, many incredible accomplishments. Unfortunately, none of them were his . . . Former Governor of Texas, Allan Shivers.

Allan Shivers: Thank you, Mister Chairman, Ladies and Gentlemen. I think it is a really nice thing for so many people to turn out here tonight in an effort to make Frank feel at home. Of course, they all have one thing in common with him . . . . They all hate to eat on an empty stomach.

Frank gets more publicity accidentally than most people do intentionally, but he's basically a shy, retiring sort of person who does a lot of things that he does not receive proper credit for. He has been, for example, an aid and comfort to women's lib. Just the other day he was bragging about the great progress the Headliners Club had made since it began admitting women to membership last year. I had not really thought of it until he summed it up this way: "We've already abolished the annual fiesta party; we've abolished the annual stag luncheon; we've increased the monthly dues; we've increased the food prices; we've increased the drink prices; we've redecorated the club twice; and now we've started rearranging the furniture every month."

We all know that Frank has done a lot for the University of Texas, but some of us do not realize what a hard act it was to follow him as chairman of the Board of Regents. You had to admire his style. When he wanted something approved, he would take a vote by simply saying, "All those in favor say, 'aye'; all those opposed say, 'I resign.' " Frank got a lot of credit or blame for all the money that was spent on bar bills, but you also have to admire his logic. He explained that if the good Lord had wanted people to save money, he never would have invented the Texas legislature.

Frank is unique in Texas history. He's the only man ever to serve as Speaker of the House, lieutenant governor, and governor without having ever run for any office. He is truly a brilliant political strategist. A lot of people owe their present position to Frank's help. Ben Barnes, for instance. And then there's Price Daniel, Jr. And of course Connally. And now strong rumor has it that the friends of Bill Clements are trying to get him to endorse John Hill. Some people never forget a friend. Frank never forgets an enemy. Serving on the Board of Regents with Frank is something like having arthritis . . . You just have to live with it.

I'd like to close by giving Frank this little reminder: Frank, if this program winds up by your getting a standing ovation, just believe it's some guy getting up in a hurry to get to the parking lot first.

Neal Spelce: Thank you, Governor. We have a phone call for you also from Florida. Anita Bryant is calling . . . Something about three members of the Alpha Tau Omega fraternity out at the University.

I guess I should have referred that call to our next roaster, the man who heads up the University of Texas System. He's big enough to handle any problem. As he walks to the podium, notice his excellent posture: he doesn't slouch, he doesn't slump, he stands tall and straight. All of that from years of having his back to the wall. The president of the University System, Don Walker.

Don Walker: Frank, I'm really quite disappointed in you. You know we've been friends for a long time, through thick and thin, through the Bauer House, campus riots, a considerable number of UT presidents, and even through a few afternoons at Forty Acres Club. But, for better or worse, I always thought you had good taste. Now I find out how wrong I was. I've seen you in some bad company before, but nothing compared to the likes of this head table. I believe this is the worst bunch of characters I've ever seen assembled at any table. Of course, that doesn't include the chairman of the Board of Regents, you understand.

I guess I should be careful because there's some very high government officials here today. Do you know what a high government official is? Well, I didn't either until I read about some of those Washington parties that Dr. Peter Borne went to. Speaking of characters, there's Bob Hardesty sitting back there like the cat that swallowed the canary. You know, he's a person we all have to be thankful to for giving us the fifteen-cent postage stamp. And if you wonder why you didn't get your tickets mailed to you after you sent your check in, the club couldn't afford it.

But to get back to my colleague Frank Erwin . . . Most people don't know this, but recently Frank went on a secret mission to the White House a few weeks ago. The president called him and asked him if he would come up and confer with him and Frank replied, "I don't know why I'd want to do that, Mr. President. I'm not even going to vote for you." And the president said, "Well, if that were any criterion, I wouldn't be conferring with anybody." Well, Frank went on up anyway and the president said, "Mr. Erwin, you're a man who's been in just about as much trouble as I'm in right now. I'd like to know what you did to survive." Frank said, "Well, Mr. President, I had some friends in high places who I could count on to support me — friends like Dolph Briscoe and John Silber, Page Keeton, Steve Spur and Billie Carr." The president looked visibly relieved and he said, "Well, if that's all there is to it, I guess I'm in good shape. I have friends like Bert Lance, Midge Costanza, Jerry Brown, Teddy Kennedy, and, of course, my brother Billy." Of course, this wasn't the first time that Frank had advised presidents. He's advised President Johnson on the war, President Nixon on the tapes, and President Ford on the pardon.

As Governor Shivers said, his track record is pretty good locally. He was Ben Barnes' closest campaign adviser, and I told him and told him and told him not to get involved with the Bauer House.

But I'd like to close this statement with this last comment about my friend Frank. A friend of mine was driving down Ninth Street late one afternoon when Frank went roaring by him in his car. My friend caught up with him at the next stop light and he rolled down his window and asked Frank, "Where are you going in such a hurry?" Frank said, "Well, I'm going down to the Quorum to get drunk and Lord, do I dread it." And that's just about the way I felt about coming here today. Thank you.

Neal Spelce: Well, as everyone knows, there's no substitute for a good speech. So, hell, let's try again here. Our next roaster is the only person here whose courageous fight for his principles has been featured on television, in books, and in countless articles around the world. He's a humorist who approaches vast subjects with half-vast ideas, that farmer from Madisonville, John Henry Faulk.

John Henry Faulk: Thank you. I want to say that this is one of the most intelligent, perceptive, and brilliant audiences that I have ever stood before. That's a damn lie, but John Connally says it's a hell of a good way to start a speech.

John's not here today, as y'all have noticed, and I'm very sad about it. But he asked me to kind of fill in for him because he loves Frank Erwin. John always wants me filling in for him. He knew I'd be to the right of Allan Shivers today. A lot of you think, "Well, John's off cavorting around with those rich Republicans in Dallas," or, "John's off with those Arab sheiks somewhere where the money is instead of here at the Headliners with his friend Frank Erwin where he should be." That ain't so. John's for the little man. He just come out for John Tower.

I didn't come here to roast Frank Erwin. I came here to toast him. One of the most misunderstood, mistreated, abused, denigrated citizens of this state, Frank Erwin . . . A man I've learned to love and respect . . . This gentle, self-effacing; this, in action, an angel, in apprehension, a God; this beauty of the world; this paragon of animals, Frank Erwin shan't be roasted by me. In the first place, let's settle it: Frank's been stewed too damn often for us to start roasting him today. But actually, it's my function here today to clear up some of the canards and abuses that have been heaped on the shoulders of this distinguished and great Texan, the lies that have been set afloat and that have become common belief through our society.

For instance, take the thing that the faculty of the University, certain narrow-minded little people, put out against Frank when he was chairman of the Board of Regents that Frank Erwin was arbitrary, had a contempt for the faculty, and was indifferent to them. I asked Frank about that myself and he said it breaks his heart to hear people talk that way. He said, "Johnny, I always loved them and I respect them even if they were the most overpaid incompetent bunch of nincompoops. They all ought to be fired, I admit."

This other canard, and I think the one that hurts the most with Frank, is this thing they put out about the stadium (the Longhorn Stadium) — that he and John Connally connived to build that second deck on it so that they'd have a launching pad when they came to leave this earth, and could ascend from there directly into heaven. Without any foundation, it was put out by that law school crowd, if you want the truth of it. I asked Frank about it and he said, "Johnny, you know for a long time I've said that I don't care where I ascend from as long as I don't have to change planes at the Dallas/Fort Worth Airport." And John Connally, as is well known, is going to ascend directly from Floresville. He's already made arrangements with Billy Graham for that.

It's this kind of thing that has hurt Frank very deeply, and I hope today to heal some of those scars. For instance, this thing that Frank Erwin is a secret Republican. That was put out . . . I don't know who put that out, but somebody put that out and it got wide vintage over this country, and it just shocked the daylights out of Frank when he heard about it. He said, "Johnny, there couldn't be an uglier lie than that. I've never been a closet Republican." There are such in Texas, I'll admit. Maybe it's because the dearest friend I've got in the world, John Connally, was . . . You know, he saw the light and got the gospel here awhile back and became a born-again Republican. They put that off on me, but I love John, and let me tell you, it wasn't politics with John that made him a Republican. John Connally is a great humanitarian and a great nature-lover and he became very interested in the endangered species list, so much so that he joined it. In other words, my loves, whatever we might say of Frank . . . About Frank Erwin, let's give him the benefit of the doubt. Sure, we're going to get a hell of a lot of doubt and very little benefit, but it's worth it. Thank you.

Neal Spelce: Now, excuse me, on the phone, Mr. Chairman (and I always refer to Frank Erwin as chairman), we had planned this as a surprise for you with a telephone call, and we planned to have it at the end of the program, but as I understand, we now have on the telephone live, direct from Washington, the president of the United States.

Neal Spelce: Hello?

Mister President: Well, I'm really glad that I can be a part of someone who has been such a stalwart of the Democratic Party like
   Frank Erwin for many, many years. But I understand this is a
   roast and I've always thought of Frank Erwin as the Andrew
   Young of Texas. No, actually I consider the two men in Texas
   that have the greatest vision as Lowell Leberman and Frank
   Erwin. How am I doing, Neal?

Neal Spelce: Real good, Mr. President. I understand the call is coming through the White House patched through the switchboard
   there through Camp David. How are your talks going there now?

Mister President: You know, I can't comment on the talks, but I can
   say I've really enjoyed being the Star of David. Incidentally, Ham
   Jordan sends Ben Barnes' best. Actually, he's keeping the best for
   himself.

Neal Spelce: Mr. President, there's a lot of talk down here in Texas about the election and everything. How are you viewing the election?

Mister President: Oh, I'm not doing anything on the election front, but I do have an idea for Frank Erwin for the 1980 presidential election. I understand Ted Kennedy needs a driver.

Neal Spelce: Mr. President, you know we've got a number of distinguished visitors here and guests. We've got a couple of members of Congress, Jordan and Pickle, former Governor Allan Shivers. John Connally couldn't make it, though.

Mister President: You know, we really miss John Connally up here in Washington. Ever since he left, our milk is delivered late. Is Jeff Friedman there?

Neal Spelce: Yes, sir, Mr. President. Jeff Friedman is here.

Mister President: I've got a message for him: "Don't call us; we'll call you." Incidentally, can you tell Jeff Friedman this message: "Tell John Hill, 'Don't call us; we'll call you.' "

Neal Spelce: Mr. President, we thank you very much for calling, and we appreciate you.

Mister President: Frank Erwin is a great man and I thank you. I've got to go now, Neal, but thank you very much.

Neal Spelce: Well, thank you for calling. Direct from the White House, President Carter. President Jimmy Carter, thank you very much.

Moving right along . . . The roasting of Frank Erwin would not be complete without hearing from some members of the legislature. Here now is one of the best politicians that money can buy, State Senator Peyton McKnight.

Peyton McKnight: Thank you, Neal. Ladies and Gentlemen, Mr. Chairman, I'll be damned if I'm going to start off by saying I'm glad to be here today. In fact, I've asked myself this question many times in the past few hours: Why are we honoring this man? Have we run out of human beings? Roasting Frank Erwin is like Connally running for president. It's no-win and never-ending.

But seriously, Frank, I was tickled to death when you called me and invited me to be here. I'm pleased to be here and I'm pleased to participate; but for the life of me, ladies and gentlemen, I don't know what in the hell we're awarding him for. Jimmy Phillips, who, several years ago after checking a pat hand to Preston Smith, said, "How in the hell did I know you was going to be governor?" And Bill Moore, the new dean of the Senate who wrote the current best-seller *Serving in the Senate for Fun and Profit,* he never got an award. And John Connally, who once said to President Nixon, "For God's sake, Dick, hold on to those tapes!" never got an award like this. And even Will Rogers, who never met Howard Cossell, he never got this kind of a deal either. And Janey Briscoe, who said, "Dolph, you need a third term to complete your program," she never got a deal like this. Earl Campbell, the great Heisman trophy winner from the University of Texas, the current Houston Oiler, when asked by a television announcer why he had selected communications as his major in college said, "Uh . . . Uh," he never got an award like this. And Babe Schwartz — tapes of his features are used to make Russian spies confess, he never got this kind of deal. And Billy Carter, who once said to his brother, "You lusted where?" Nobody ever gave him this kind of deal. And even Lady Churchill, Mrs. Winston Churchill, who said to her husband, "How do you expect to accomplish so much with so little a thing?" never got an award. And even Ben Barnes, who, after the tears had cleared his eyes, called Preston Smith and said, "I beat you! I beat you!" He never got this kind of deal. So I think you can understand my confusion.

Here we have Frank Erwin, who may never have killed two birds with one stone, but he did cripple six hippies by felling one tree. Hell, he gets an award. Frank Erwin, whose lawyer once told him as he left the courtroom, "I don't care what the problem is, Frank; you've got to get off that medication." Hell, he gets an award. Frank told me one time, he said, "I want to tell you one thing. Be damned sure you don't get arrested in Mexico." He said, "I had to pay a $5,000 fine for overparking." Of course, he was parking over a Mexican at the time he got fined. I'll tell you what . . . All this proves to me is that no matter how deserving you are, if you want to get the recognition that you know you're entitled to, you got to get out and organize just like Frank did on this deal here. And Frank, you've done one hell of a job. So as soon as all this is over, all of us here on the dais are going to go out and do something in your honor. We're all going to go out and uproot a tree in your name. Thank you.

Neal Spelce: As Peyton McKnight said, our next roaster is one of the most eloquent and most loquacious members of the State Senate. In fact, Senator Schwartz prompted this poem by a reporter: "I've covered many a legislative session and have heard Schwartz's speeches, which were for the birds. What Texans really need now is a proposition 13 for words." You can see what that reporter meant now as we welcome State Senator Babe Schwartz. Five minutes only, Senator.

Babe Schwartz: It's really great that President Carter gave us a bit of advice here this morning because I recognize that his advice is a whole lot like Frank Erwin's advice politically. It was President Carter who opened the Camp David Summit Meeting with Begin and Sadat by saying that they all ought to get together because it was the Christian thing to do. Frank Erwin is a lot like that. He's been known to try to get into a fellow's good side occasionally when he needed him.

I remember the first time I met Frank Erwin. It was the first time he ever needed me for anything. He came into my office with a brief-case and had a sticker on the side that said "Israel must live." He's a joy to be around. The reason he hadn't been active in the Briscoe administration is because Governor Briscoe brought him in and said, "I need your help with this screwworm program." Old Frank looked at him and said, "Hell, we're not screwing worms. I know how to get at the big shots." He says the legislature's not going to be no problem.

So anyhow, Frank dedicated the last four years — six years (God it's been a long time) — to a restful period so he can come back into prominence. You know he thought he ran the government when John Connally was governor and Barnes was Speaker of the House and then lieutenant governor. Barnes thought . . . Well, I mean not Barnes, but at least Frank Erwin thought he was running the government. But unfortunately for some of us in the legislature, Connally and Barnes thought so too, and they let him do it. I wish Governor Connally could be here today. I wish Billie Carr would have been here. I don't know why they're all together. We got a message that they were engaged. I don't even know that they go to the same hairdresser, but I'm delighted. Well, at least, I'm delighted that they were both invited to participate.

I remember Billie Carr through Frank Erwin's messages to her at various state conventions. It was usually, "Get that redheaded broad out of the hall. Throw her out." And he said that occasionally to members of the legislature. Told Barnes that a couple of times. "Throw him out."

I do have a message from one of your friends, though, Frank, and I knew you'd want to hear it. This one is from a very good friend of yours: "I very much appreciate your generous offer to submit my name to the search committee who are meeting to elect a new president for the University of Texas at Austin. Unfortunately, John Schwartz (that's my son) and I are revising my latest book, *The Invaded University,* and it will be impossible for me to accept your kind offer." Signed

Ronnie Dugger. If you all haven't gone out to read that book, and obviously you haven't because you didn't laugh, you must read Ronnie's book.

It is fun to joust a little bit with Frank when he's on the receiving end, although he is going to get the last word, as I understand it. It's not often you get the last word on Frank Erwin, and I'm glad that I got at least to get a word in.

You know, once during a Senate debate, Kennard, who is here today, was trying to break the world's record, and he did. Kennard had proposed the "University of Texas at Dallas amendment" to one of Frank Erwin's favorite pet bills to create the major University of the Universe at Dallas (a part of it, at any rate) and Kennard was in this filibuster and we came up with an idea that we would make a hall of fame to the great dignitaries of this state. In calling the names, the roll call, during the evening we got up to 280. Frank Sharp and Frank Erwin came to mind and what we were going to do, we were going to dedicate this hall of fame to great people and name university schools in their name. It was going to be the Frank Erwin School of Diplomacy, college presidents, and students.

And we lived through Kennard and we lived through that filibuster and the University of Texas at Dallas and all other good things, and we're here today to honor this great man and to do it in the best way we know how and to be certain that his day would not be marred in any way or shape or fashion.

In closing I want to assure you, Frank, that we came here with all good graces for you and congratulations and warm wishes, and I brought your favorite expert medical witness to testify to your sobriety, Dr. Bill Levin. Thank you very much.

Neal Spelce: Our next roaster is only one of many state officials who gained fame in the past few years as the driving instructor for Frank Erwin. The Headliners Club is deeply indebted to Police Chief Frank Dyson for allowing him to be with us. State Comptroller Bob Bullock.

Bob Bullock: Thank you very much, Mr. Chairman, and Ladies and Gentlemen. I'm delighted to be here today. You know, most of you that are here paid $25 to get through the door, but in my case I paid a heck of a lot more than that to be with my good friend Frank Erwin today. I paid a year's probation, a $500 fine, a $500 lawyer fee, a $500 car repair, and a $600 bar bill. That's right, Frank. You probably got it right. I've been given the little chore tonight to do some discussion about your driving and drinking. We're going to talk about that a little bit.

When Bob Hardesty asked me to come, I told him, I said, "Look, I've never seen Frank take one drink." And I can honestly say that. But I've seen him take one hundred. The problem is, Frank, you and I neither one are sophisticated enough. We ought to have a little bit of this stuff that Hobby's got. For example, he can get by with a jug of Gallo, an old family friend that no one heard of, a creek bank at a picnic.

But honestly, the Headliners Club is indebted to Chief Dyson and the Austin Police Department for letting Frank and myself and some of his other good friends come here today. Of course, there was a condition to it. We couldn't drive; we had to come in Bob Armstrong's canoe and he had to paddle it.

Actually, I have no complaints against the Austin Police Department, and I shouldn't have. They were extremely polite to me, Wade, when they picked me up but I think that was because, in contrast to Frank, I didn't keep trying to run into their patrol cars. As a matter of fact, they were so polite they kept calling the lady who was in the front seat with me Mrs. Bullock. And, as anyone who knows me very well knows, on any given day you better check the county courthouse before you call somebody Mrs. Bullock. As a matter of fact, that particular one at the time was in Dallas. She's a Republican and will not leave the city limits of Dallas. But, frankly, I don't know how we can thank the Austin Police enough, Frank, for providing the politicians and those who associate with politicians here in Austin with escort services.

By the way, I bet some of you didn't even know that Agriculture Commissioner Reagan Brown has been the recipient of one of those escort services. Yep, he sure was; but Frank, he was honest and fearless. He didn't try that old medication route. No siree. Not Reagan. He stood right up there. Reagan's tough. He's tough. He's really the only one of us that had the courage to stand up and tell the police that the only thing he knew was somebody must have slipped whiskey in his Coca-Cola. He really did it.

Frank, I appreciate you sending me and old Roy Minton sitting over there, too, by the way. Roy is one of the greatest lawyers I've ever known. He can absolutely create miracles. But in my case, he couldn't do it, Frank. Couldn't do it at all. He didn't understand my case. When I first went with him and went to him and talked to him about it, all he could say was, "How many times did you hit that curb?" And, "What did you call the police?" Actually there was good reason that I was hitting that curb because on that particular night in question, I could have sworn I saw John Hill standing right on the edge of it. And you know, Frank, I really believe this: I think you would have done the same thing. Just imagine if a student had been standing there. Now you know there's a lot of people who've been going around telling some malicious lies — that I don't like John Hill and that I have a feud with him. Well, nothing could be further from the truth. It's not correct at all. Also I imagine some of you may think I have some dislike for the name "John." For example, John Hill and John Connally and John Tower and John Barnes, but there's really nothing to that at all.

Frank, I want you to have fun today. They told us backstage before we came out, to old Peyton and I, that there would be three parties later on backstage — a Republican, a Democratic, and a cocktail party. I have no doubt that you'll feel at home at all three, which we will all attend with you.

But seriously, Frank, you and I and Reagan Brown and Hobby and some other of our friends, we take a little bit of ribbing about our drinking. We probably should from time to time, but I just want you to remember, and I paraphrase, those immortal words of our leader Wilbur Mills as he was chasing Fanny down the tidal basin in which he said, "Let him who is without drink raise the first stink." Thank you very much.

Neal Spelce: We move now from a current state office-holder to a person who wanted — God, how he wanted — to be a current state office-holder. No matter how much you may feel about this dynamic young leader, I'm confident the history books of Texas will indicate that this politician has risen dramatically out of obscurity and faded right into anonymity . . . The Lieutenant Governor, Ben Barnes.

Former Lieutenant Governor Ben Barnes: Thank you very much, Neal. Brownwood doesn't get Austin television. As a matter of fact, Brownwood doesn't get very much television but I understand that Neal Spelce is the strongest thing on Austin television since Big O, God rest his soul, is gone today.

I'm delighted to be here. I'm delighted to be back in Austin. It's brought back a lot of memories. However, Senator McKnight and Senator Schwartz's remarks reminded me how glad I am that I don't have to listen to the State Senate any longer. Frank, it was great. For one brief shining moment, there was a Camelot. Preston never did learn how to spell it, but it was here. And just think, 350,000 more votes and there'd have been three terms on the Board of Regents.

Frank is back in Austin practicing law now. He's spending a great deal more time here since the May primaries and since General Hill is now the Democratic nominee. The past six years, he's spent most of his time in Galveston, still going through those medical records. Frank is my friend without prefix or suffix and there's no way that I could ever publicly or privately thank him enough for his friendship and his counsel and advice. I can't keep from recalling on this very important occasion in his life some of the real true moments in our relationship, truly great moments, and some of the great advice that Frank gave me.

I'll never forget that bright shiny Saturday morning when he told me that, "Ben, the thing for you to do is to go down to El Rancho and get some food to go, and to go down to New Braunfels and meet those marchers on the highway and have lunch with them." Nor will I forget that 1971 tax session when he said, "Barnes, it's going to be a lot easier to put a tax on food and drugs than it is to increase the tax on whiskey." And I suppose at that time it didn't seem very important to Frank or me, either one, that very candid piece of advice he gave me during the special session in 1969 when he said, "Barnes, it's just a little banking bill," and he said, "something Preston just wants and it doesn't mean a damn. You go ahead and pass it."

But Frank is my friend. We've been through a lot of good times, a lot of hard times, and a lot of very memorable occasions. I'll never forget the night that the students burned, or were attempting to burn, down one of the ROTC buildings on the campus and Frank called and said, "I suggest you put on your khakis" — I still had a pair of khakis — "and let's go out on the campus and see what we can do to stop those dirty nothings." So I got on my khakis and we went out on the campus, and I don't know why that Frank and I didn't think we'd be recognized and immediately we were recognized by about fifteen students, and I think it was probably one of the most frightening experiences of my life because one of the students looked at us and said, "Let's don't take them alive."

But Frank's friendship will always mean a lot. His advice and counsel are priceless. I used to think that probably the most significant thing Frank had ever said was to that patrolman — or to one of those patrolmen he's had an opportunity to visit with in the past few years — when he told that patrolman, "But, Officer, you know that you can drive a lot longer than you can walk," was perhaps one of his most famous ones. But I think truly probably one of the best pieces of advice that he's ever given me is, "Barnes, just remember we don't want justice. We just want to get even." Frank, we're getting even today. Thank you.

Neal Spelce: I've known our next roast master as a man, as an adolescent, as a child, often on the same day . . . The former hippie mayor of Austin, Jeff Friedman.

Jeff Friedman: It's a pleasure being here — not so much for Frank because I don't think I've ever met you before tonight. I've heard a lot of tales about you. The interesting thing . . . I don't know how many of you out there can see this, but I am wearing the last remnant of the "dirty nothing" days. Frank had the opportunity back when I was in law school here to refer to some of those other students, the troublemakers and a few of the faculty like Dean Silber and Dean Keaton and a few of the others, as troublemakers, and then used the words "dirty nothings." Well, I am wearing the last living remnant of the buttons that were created then, and the reason why I mention it is because it helps my ego because I'm the only one on the dais who can read it without having to come up four inches away from it. So, those of you out there who want to try and see how young you are can get about two feet away from it and see if you can read it later on.

But, Frank, it's a pleasure to be here. There are a lot of things that we have in common, and I know everybody knows I was kidding when I said we'd never met before because I'm sure all of you are familiar with the father/son relationship that Frank and I have developed over the last few years. I mean, what else could it be? Every time I turn around he's calling me a son-of-a-something or other, but it doesn't really matter. What does matter is that we're giving up a long afternoon, Frank, and I've been with Roy Butler out on his ranch drinking Schlitz. It's a lot funnier to Roy, folks. I'm not going to say too much about Roy; after all, he was my predecessor, he is my elder . . . Not my better but my elder.

But Frank has done a tremendous amount for all of us. It is Frank, believe it or not, in 1970, prior to my entry into politics here, who took me aside one night before drinking, so I knew he was deathly serious, and told me that if you're going to do something for the people in your community, you should do it honestly and above board. "Don't try and cheat, and, above all, pick yourself an idol in history, and there are plenty of good examples, to set your goals towards and try and live up to that ideal so that if that person were ever to come back, that person would look at you and say, 'You've lived your life like I would.' " But Frank — Attila the Hun? Just a little strong.

You know, it's been interesting when Dean Silber, who couldn't be here (he had to still be in Boston apparently to open schools, which never used to bother him; he'll close them here), when he was fired, a gentleman true to his word, never said anything bad about Frank. And we always thought that was interesting since Frank banned all Lone Ranger movies from the university campus thereafter because he kept referring to the Lone Ranger being a friend of Hi-Ho Silver's. Frank doesn't hear too well when he's out partying.

The interesting thing, the other thing that we have to remember, is Frank's political advice. There is no one on this dais, there is no one in this audience, and perhaps no one in the state of Texas who has been able to benefit more from his wise political advice than John Connally. John isn't here. That's probably the wisest advice he's ever taken from Frank. But several weeks ago, it was Frank, unurged, unapproached by anyone, but taking it upon himself to stand by his friend John Connally, that just prior to the election of the new Pope, Frank himself filed the papers changing John's name to Canneloni and asked Nellie to join a convent. It didn't work then, of course. It didn't work for Ben or anybody else either, but it doesn't really matter. Frank is always in there plugging away.

Before I sit down and give way to some of Frank's friends . . . I think there may be one here . . . Let me just say that those of you who are enjoying the afternoon here and the drinks and the beer and what-have-you, you have Frank to thank for that, because it was Frank who approached the City Council here in Austin after being stopped by a few of our safety patrol boys, as Frank used to refer to them, and said, "Listen, we've got to allow drinks on campus. You've got to change the city ordinances. Those kids out there have a right to enjoy themselves. And I have every right to be there with them." And, Frank, you have that right and I'm sure every ATO member is grateful to you, and I just hope that as time goes on, we'll be able to continue our relationship.

And again, let me say for the years of advice that you've given me, both private and public, it's been a great honor to know and work with you and I know your affection is unfounded. As I was stepping up to the microphone here, I heard you lean over to Jake Pickle, my future opponent, perhaps, and listen to him calmly as you described to Jake the words that I have always heard you mention whenever I appeared before you, Frank . . . "Damn Jew."

Neal Spelce: Congressman, you'll get equal time next week. Our

next roaster is a man who set the example for Jeff Friedman: Former
Mayor Roy Butler.

Mayor Roy Butler: Thank you, Ladies and Gentlemen. I'm reminded that any man who would bring a lady here ain't no gentleman,
and also any woman who would come here today ain't no lady . . . In
this group especially. Folks, in this surrounding and in this country —
where else could it happen? A boy is born into a poor family. He fights
desperately to earn a living and to work his way through the University
of Texas; he gets his education; and then he decides to devote his life
back to service, to the benefit of other people, to those individuals who
have been less fortunate. And then, finally, he achieves the love, the
admiration, and the respect of all. But enough about me.

I came here today to talk about my friend Frank Erwin. But first,
on behalf of the committee, I'd like to thank Congressman Jake Pickle
for making the arrangements for the General Services Administration
to provide all of the drinks, food, and other materials for this fine
event. I notice the congressman eating several bowls of Three-Alarm
Chili. It looks like Congress is finally going to pass something. We're
all proud of Jake. We're proud of the way that he has remained un-
tainted while many congressmen were involved in sex scandals. You
know, now days, Beryl will even tell Jake to go upstairs and take a hot
shower. But Jake has many distinctions and many honors in his life.
One in particular he shares with many other Texas women: when in the
University of Texas, he roomed with John Connally. Sorry the governor is not here. He's in Africa at the moment.

I can't tell you how delighted I am to see my old cohort Jeff
Friedman here. Jaws, Jr. My successor when I traded Mopac for a six-
pack. I remember when I was mayor of this great city . . . Boy, those
were the good old days — "B.F." (Before Friedman). And I don't think
Jeff has ever really forgiven me for an accident that occurred when the
council attended a council ribbon-cutting. I gave Councilman Lowell
Leberman the scissors to cut the ribbon, and that was the day that Jeff
Friedman had his second bar mitzvah. But I've got to admit that Jeff
gave me some real good ideas when we served together. I didn't accept
them all. Some of them were good, but some of the ones I rejected
were: "Let's sponsor the first annual Cinco de Mayo boat race on Town
Lake." He also proposed Hugh Yantes for chief of police. But basically
I'm grateful to Jeff because if it were not for him, I probably wouldn't
be in the beer business today. After four years of Friedman, I was
drinking so much that I figured I might as well get in the business and
buy it wholesale.

It's good to see our friend Ben Barnes here today . . . Texas' most famous flared nostrils. He's a whole lot like Will Rogers, who once said, "I never met a man I didn't like." Ben said something like that. I don't know if Ben's planning on getting back into politics or not, but I do know that he's studying the obituary list every day.

I'm pleased to follow Comptroller Bob Bullock. I'm glad to see that he's here. He's the only man ever to flunk the breath test while blowing out the candles on his birthday cake. After the luncheon, he, Erwin, and Bill Hobby are going to hold a lodge meeting. Seriously, though, I think Bob Bullock is the greatest athlete in the state government. Any man who can walk a tightrope with one arm around Dolph Briscoe, patting Preston Smith on the back with the other, and kicking John Hill in the ass at the same time is a great athlete.

And, Frank, what an honor it is to be here today with you. And I'm sure that all of you know that Frank is now a member of Teetotalers Anonymous. That is the organization where if you're about to quit drinking and go on the wagon, you call in and they send over two drunks to talk you out of it. The latest temptation that Frank had, he called and they sent over Bullock and Hobby. You know something, it worked!

The last time Frank took the driver's test, they tell me he got three tickets on the written part. And the other rumor, and I don't think this is true, is that last week, Frank drove through three red lights. The only problem was that two of them were on the back of a Trailways bus.

But in spite of all the fun and respect that we have for Frank, a lot of fun we're having with him today, he is really Mr. Couth of the twentieth century. A man of diplomacy, a man of delicacy, a man of poetry who, confronted some time ago by some angry students who were offended when he ordered the destruction of some oak trees outside the Memorial Stadium, he responded with the following point: "I refuse to offer an apology for getting involved with ecology. I'll cut down the trees whenever I please, so stick that up your physiology." A real defender of women's rights who said the woman who jogs topless in Memorial Stadium has a perfect right . . . And a perfect left to match. And so, Frank Erwin, a man who has done more for the University of Texas than the TCU defensive line, I lift my glass of my favorite beverage to you. You are unique and for that we are all grateful.

Neal Spelce: Sometimes I get the feeling that the two biggest problems in America are making ends meet and making meetings end, but we're making progress because I would like for you to welcome now the distinguished congresswoman who is resigning her post and coming to Austin (rumor has it) to run against Sheriff Raymond Frank. The Honorable Barbara Jordan.

Barbara Jordan: I'm coming to Austin, but I'm not going to run for anything. I assure you that I'm glad to be here for a number of reasons today. I understand that this is the first, the first time women have been invited to this kind of an event. Well, I'm . . . That's nice, but now women having been here today, you know we haven't missed a thing.

Do you remember 1966? Nineteen sixty-six was a banner year for Texas. It was November of that year that I was elected the first everything to ever come to the Texas Senate. And it was in December of that year that Frank Erwin was named chairman of the University of Texas Board of Regents, so 1966 was a very good year for the state, and the state has not quite gotten over it. But I want you to think back with me for just a little bit about that 1966, and here I am getting ready to come to Austin and be a member of the Senate. I did not know anything about Frank C. Erwin, Jr. But it seems to me that as I knew that I was coming to Washington, the name of Frank C. Erwin, Jr., and the University of Texas were almost synonymous. So, in my naivete, I thought Frank C. Erwin, Jr., must be the head cheerleader of the university, and if he were not that he must be a UT quarterback, and then I got to Austin and found out he's both.

That, however, was a part of my tentative beginning. I knew so little about what went on in the whole University of Texas that I thought "hook 'em horns" was some kind of cattle disease. Well, I got into the office and one day, Frank made a courtesy call, one of those obligatory calls, and I heard these people trying to detract from him. But I got one look at that angelic face, that lovable disposition, and I could not believe that Frank C. Erwin, Jr., could have detractors. That made no sense. But Frank and I started to give attention to how the two of us could do business together. How could we best represent the people of the State of Texas? Now Frank has taken a lot of ribbing here this afternoon about his drinking, but I'll tell you Frank knows how to put his drinking to constructive purposes. As we sort of searched around for the best way that the two of us could communicate with each other, we found a common bond and that common bond was scotch. And it held us together. Frank and I decided that the place we would do our talking would be in the lieutenant governor's apartment, just there behind the Senate Chamber. So Frank would go out and get the biggest bottle of scotch the lobbyists would give us and we'd go back there to Barnes' apartment and while the colleagues, Babe Schwartz and all of them, were out there debating those weighty and not-so-weighty issues, Frank and I were trying to kill the bottle. Once the bottle was dead, the issues were solved, whatever they were. We had it all together and we've kept it all together.

Now, in early 1969, there were eleven people elected to the Senate called liberals. I was one of those, and some of them got a little bit excited about the prospect of refusing to confirm the real appointment of Frank to the Board of Regents. And the liberals thought they had it all locked in until I told them about the angelic disposition of this man, and that there was no way I could vote against him. Who could vote to bust Frank Erwin? I said, "Babe, you and Oscar, you all can go on and do that little number if you want to, but I know what I'm supposed to be about and I'm not voting against Frank." Well, my disposition caused a little bit of surprise and some consternation among that faction of people called liberals, and I have been surprising them and throwing them into consternation and constipation ever since. But that doesn't bother me. I'm coming back home and I'm glad I am.

You know, I wanted to tell you a serious true thing about Frank Erwin. When I was in the Senate, my father died. Frank came to the funeral and about six years after that death, I overheard Frank talking to someone and he was telling them about having attended my father's funeral and he didn't only talk about having attended it, Frank recalled the minister's name, the sermon, the text, and proceeded to preach it to this person he was talking to. Well, I can't forget that and for a person who has that kind of attention to detail, I'm not going to roast him. I'm going to toast him, and I'll do that.

And finally, Frank, you are the only one who could have provided me with sufficient reason to leave Jimmy Carter, the natural gas pricing bill, Washington, D.C., and all of that to come here. Now, I apologize that I couldn't get Jimmy to leave. But all I have to say to you, Buddy, is you're tough, you're resilient, you're lovable, you're acid-tongued, and, as far as I'm concerned, you're a point in the Lone Star.

Neal Spelce: Well, Headliners, would you welcome the Honorable Frank C. Erwin, Jr.

Frank C. Erwin, Jr.: When my good friend Bob Hardesty, this year's president of the Headliners Club, first asked me to serve as the so-called honoree of this affair, my initial instinct was to decline since the invitation quickly reminded me of the man who, while being ridden out of town on a rail, commented that if it weren't for the honor of the thing, you'd just as soon have walked. However, when Hardesty insisted that the club was trying to start this as a tradition and that I was the most "roastable" man he knew, a somewhat dubious compliment in itself, I decided to cooperate because I comforted myself with the thought that every bad thing that I've ever done has already been fully published in every daily newspaper in Texas.

But having sat through this little lynching today, I feel constrained to state for the record that I have never been involved in a drinking-related auto accident and that thanks to my good judgement in hiring Roy Minton — who as you know is the world's legal authority on the change of venue in misdemeanor cases. Thanks to him, I've not been convicted of driving while intoxicated either. So much for statements for the record.

I am truly grateful to Congresswoman Barbara Jordan for flying down from Washington to be here today because while I have never been involved in a drinking-related automobile accident, I have been involved in one or two drinking-related accidents. I well remember that a few years ago, the leading citizens of Houston had an elegant reception in a downtown hotel ballroom in honor of Ms. Jordan, and I went there with hundreds of others to pay my homage to this great lady. The receiving line was long, and when I finally reached her position on the receiving line, she threw her arms wide to greet me, and we engaged in a great big embrace in the course of which I accidentally poured my entire glass of scotch and soda down the back of her beautiful, long white evening gown. Thank God, it was scotch and soda instead of bloody mary. But even so, it's a wonder she's ever spoken to me again, let alone come here today. But my sincere thanks to her for being here.

And my good friend, Babe Schwartz from Galveston. When, in 1969, Governor Connally reappointed me to the Board of Regents for the second six-year term, Schwartz took the lead in trying to get the Senate to reject my appointment. He asked me all the ugly questions he could think of in the Nominations Committee hearing and spoke against me on the floor of the Senate, and the Senate finally approved my appointment. But about a year after my confirmation, a Jewish professor from out at UT-Austin called Senator Schwartz to complain about something I had done that the professor thought was outrageous, and the senator told him, he said, "Professor, last year when I was trying to bust Erwin's reappointment, neither you nor any of your colleagues had guts enough to come down to the Capitol to help me although I urged you all to do so." And he added, "In fact, the only help I got from the campus was from an Arab student named Kavusi who came down to testify against Erwin." He said, "Now, your complaint comes either one year too late or five years too early." Since that time, Schwartz and I have decided that we can work together far better than we can work against each other, and today I count him and his lovely wife, Marilee, among my best friends.

I regret that Governor Connally could not be here today because I treasure the opportunities that I have had to be associated with him. However, one such opportunity sticks out in my memory because some government professors at UT–Austin have included me in their textbook as a classic example of how government should not be run. In 1963, during Governor Connally's first year of office and shortly after he had appointed me to my first term on the board, the regents were going to award an architectural contract for a major building on the UT–El Paso campus to an El Paso architect who was a recognized Republican leader in that area and who had opposed Governor Connally's election a few months earlier. Well, I objected to the selection of the Republican architect and after I reminded the board that the General Appropriations Bill at that time required the governor's prior approval for the award of any architect's contract with a state agency, they passed the matter to a later meeting. After that meeting — and at that time I had a good deal more vigor than judgement — I wrote a letter to the chairman of the regents building grounds committee in which I said that since architects refused to bid competitively for state contracts, the award of a contract to one of several equally competent and equally qualified architects was simply the award of a financially valuable gift, and that in such a case, Governor Connally preferred that such a gift be made to one of his friends rather than one of his enemies. The regent to whom I wrote that letter was no friend of Governor Connally and, as it proved, no friend of mine, and he released the letter to the press. Now, I don't know how the governor's new Republican friends view that affair today, but it endeared me to the governor forever and immortalized both him and me as the guys with the black hats in the government textbooks at UT–Austin.

It also secured for me a valuable piece of advice from a politician of long experience who later became thirty-sixth president of the United States. Shortly after that incident, and speaking about it, then

Vice-president Lyndon Johnson told me, he said, "Frank, don't ever write a letter when a phone call will do, and don't telephone if you can talk to the man in person," and for the last eleven years of my service on the Board of Regents, I used very little stationery, but I had a lot of long distance telephone calls.

Congressman Pickle seemed to have such a good time participating in this roast awhile ago. I remember sharing so many incidents with him and I love him, even though he's still the greatest con artist around. Now come to the end of this program and somewhat like Congressman Pickle on the occasion I told you about, I've asked a friend of mine to explain my position and to make a final statement on my behalf. He will be far more articulate and pleasant to listen to than I could ever be. I give you Mr. Troy Dale.

Troy Dale:
("I Did It My Way")

And now the end is near,
and so I face the final curtain.
My friend, I'll say it clear,
I'll state my case, of which I'm certain.
I've lived a life that's full,
I've traveled each and every highway.
And more, much more than this, I did it my way.
Regrets, I've had a few,
but then again, too few to mention.
I did what I had to do
and saw it through without exemption.
I planned each chartered course,
each careful step along the byway.
And more, much more than this, I did it my way.
Yes, there were times, I'm sure you knew,
when I bit off more than I could chew,
but through it all when there was doubt,
I ate it up and spit it out.
I faced it all and I stood tall and did it my way.
I've loved, I've laughed and cried.
I've had my fill, my share of losing.
But now as tears subside, I find it all so amusing.
To think I did all that and may I say, not in a shy way,
oh no, oh no not me, I did it my way.

For what is a man, what has he got?
If not himself, then he has naught.
To say the things he truly feels,
and not the words of one who kneels.
The record shows I took the blows, and did it my way.
The record shows I took the blows, and did it my way.

3:30 P.M. — *Adios!*

Twenty-fifth Headliners' Celebrity Party.

H. C. Pittman with Neal Spelce, Frank Erwin, and Punkin Pittman.

Longtime Dallas newswriter and author Richard Morehead presides at Headliners Club, sharing the stage with Gen. Jim Taylor, Governors Price Daniel, John Connally, Preston Smith, Bill Clements, and Dolph Briscoe. Emcee H. C. Pittman checks his notes.

HASTA
LA VISTA

"Fish gotta swim, birds gotta fly, lobbyist gotta . . ."
— Courtesy State Representative Neil Caldwell

Hasta la Vista

"If men were angels no government would be necessary."

It may be that many of the cat-calls have been aimed at public officials in general instead of at one particular person. But individuals who are members of a group inevitably are going to be blamed for the actions of the group, regardless of its size and composition. Politicians suffer to some extent in this regard but most of them have a tendency to blame, unfairly, all members of "the press" for the actions of a few who may be irresponsible.

The truth of the matter, as usual, lies somewhere between the two extremes. Most people, whether they be legislators or newsmen or voters, are not all good or all bad — and neither are their actions. And it may well be that forty-nine percent of any group hates to be judged by the acts of the majority.

Garth Jones, chief of the Associated Press Austin Bureau, took note of this in a column a few days after the 61st Legislature's second special session ended:

> When the sound and fury of a legislative session subsides, it is interesting to note that the noise-makers usually are not among those credited with the real accomplishments of the session.
>
> In both House and Senate a small group of quiet, efficient businessmen and lawyers take their law-making seriously and respect the responsibility handed them by voters.
>
> These legislators are not the ones who leap up on tables to attract the photographers' attention; who lose their tempers in public debate and cuss and rant and even try to settle legislative matters with their fists.
>
> These are not the ones who read long flowery speeches, which later are reprinted in political campaign literature, trying to blame everyone but themselves for legislative failures. These are not the leather-lunged filibusterers who roar like a lion when the spectators gallery is crowded but lapse into a hoarse whisper when the pep squad disappears.
>
> No matter whether the Speaker or the Lieutenant Governor or the Governor or the House or the Senate dominates or sabotages an issue, it is the nucleus of good legislators that keeps state government operating in the best manner possible.

O'Daniel said, "We have four divisions of government and the

288

fourth division (overlapping bureaus) in many instances performs all three functions of government . . . legislative, executive and judicial. In fact, most of the business of the state, established through the influence of the state, is established through the influence of a relatively small group of selfish individuals, operating through a cunning central of powerful lobbyists, generally referred to by some as 'the Third House.' "

Some consider this combination of the Third House and the Fourth Division as the basic cause of most of our state government ills.

Well, we have been inside our "Third House" for quite a spell now and, as they say down at the feed store, "Time to make good or make room." As Winston Churchill said, "Democracy is the worst form of government, except for all others."

We plain sure were lucky to have been borned here instead of somewhere with those who haven't had our luck.

Aren't we glad that at creation we were cut out of the herd to enjoy what we have in "our house" and that we have the right to be funny, lucky, and to maneuver plumb loose like that, knowing most all we have to do is keep the would-be "termites" from destroying our house!

To all of you, from Dime Box to our back porch, who have helped in this project, we'll list you later but thank you right now.

A backyard philosopher once pointed out: "If you don't do nothing, you don't get blamed for doing something!" Let's do something to keep what we got!

For now, don't forget to latch the screen door!

Senator Chet Brooks presides at Senate hearing.

— Senate Media

Kay Bailey Hutchinson, treasurer for the State of Texas since January 1991 and leader of the Texas Republicans. Former Texas legislator.

Senator Ray Farabee explains.

— Senate Media

290

Justices Ruel Walker, Zollie Steakley, Joe Greenhill, Jack Pope, Chief Justice Bob Calvert, and the author.

— Johnny Jenkins Photography

te Representative Lena Guerrero was ted in 1984 to represent Travis unty. Formerly president of the Texas men's Political Caucus. Appointed Ann Richards to head Texas Rail- d Commission.

Governor Preston Smith with DeWitt Greer, Texas Highway Department chief.

Muchas Gracias

The author gratefully acknowledges the use of selected anecdotes and quotes from the following publications:

Deadly Blessing, Steve Salerno
The Influence of Frank Erwin on Texas Higher Education, Deborah Bay, Ph.D.
Straight From the Heart, Ann Richards
Cactus Pryor Inside Texas, Cactus Pryor
Two-Party Texas, John R. Knaggs
Here Comes the Judge, Robert W. Calvert
Molly Ivins Can't Say That, Can She?, Molly Ivins
Richard Morehead's Texas, Richard Morehead
Money, Marbles, and Chalk, Jimmy Banks
Race and Class in Texas Politics, Chandler Davis
Kingmakers, John R. Knaggs
50 Years In Texas Politics, Richard Morehead
This Dog'll Hunt, Wallace O. Chariton
Connally, The Adventures of Big Bad John, Richard Morehead
Texas Monthly
Texas Under a Cloud, Sam Kinch, Jr., Ben Procter
Allan Shivers: The Pied Piper of Texas Politics, Sam Kinch, Stuart Long
Connally, The Lone Star of Texas, J. Preston, Jr.
Preston Smith, The Making of a Texas Governor, Jerry Douglas Conn
Our Sacred Monkeys or 20 Years of Jim and Other Jams (Mostly Jims), Don H. Beggers
Ferguson, The Impeachment of Jim Ferguson, Bruce Rutherford
Daddy's Story, Dewitt Bowmer, Jim D. Bowmer
The Miracle of the Killer Bees, Robert Heard
Dewitt C. Greer, Richard Morehead
The Texas Almanac's Political History of Texas, Mike Kingston, Sam Attlesey
Congressional Anecdotes, Paul Boller
Texas Wit & Wisdom, Wallace O. Chariton

Index

293